The Rich Spoils of Time

The
RICH SPOILS
OF TIME

Frances Campbell-Preston

Edited by Hugo Vickers

THE DOVECOTE PRESS

To the memory of Patrick and Laura

First published in 2006 by The Dovecote Press Ltd
Stanbridge, Wimborne Minster, Dorset BH21 4JD

ISBN 1 904349 47 1

Designed by The Dovecote Press
Printed and bound by Biddles Ltd, King's Lynn, Norfolk

All papers used by The Dovecote Press are natural, recyclable products
made from wood grown in sustainable, well-managed forests

A CIP catalogue record for this book is available
from the British Library

5 7 9 8 6 4

Contents

The Illustrations

(Between pages 96 – 97)
Frances as a little girl.
Laura and Frances in Kitzbühl 1922.
Hilda Grenfell (Frances's mother) with her older daughters,
Katie and Mary.
Arthur Grenfell (Frances's father).
Sir Robert Baden-Powell, HRH The Duke of Connaught, Arthur Grenfell
and his uncle, Field Marshal Lord Grenfell.
Harry, Vera and Reggie (all three in 1911).
The dining room at Roehampton in 1912, with the Titian.
Joyce photographed by Sasha shortly before her wedding, 1929.
Patrick as ADC to the Governor-General of Canada, 1938.
Lord Tweedsmuir (John Buchan), Governor-General of Canada.
Lady Tweedsmuir.
Patrick and Frances's wedding in 1938.
Patrick with Mary Ann just before he returned to the war.
Patrick with Mary Ann and Robert in 1949, after he came home.
The War Office telegram announcing Patrick as missing.
An eyewitness sketch of the Warburg escape over the wire.
Patrick with Martin Gilliat and Mike Grissell in Colditz Castle.
A group at Colditz.
Colin Mackenzie, and Douglas Bader.
The 'Immobile' Wrens – Frances at the back, on the right.
Frances fishing on the River Awe in 1941.
Princess Elizabeth greeting Hilda Grenfell.

(Between pages 192 – 193)
Bobby and Angela's wedding group at Blair Castle, 1950.
Patrick with Brigadier Russell in Berlin in 1950.
Laura before her dance in 1946. A portrait by Lenare.
Hilda Grenfell during the war, 1943.

A family group – Robert, Patrick, Frances with Colin,
Helen and Mary Ann.
Ardchattan Priory.
Patrick and Frances.
Bernard and Laura, when Bernard was
Governor General of New Zealand.
Prince Charles's visit in 1967.
Sir Martin Gilliat, the Queen Mother's Private Secretary, in the 1980s.
Joyce, Frances and Robert in Scotland.
The Queen Mother with those members of her Household and staff who
had been in the services, photographed at Clarence House after the D-Day
anniversary celebrations in 1994.
The Queen Mother and Frances in an open landau
outside Clarence House.
Frances and Laura on the Royal Yacht *Britannia,* New Zealand, in 1967.
A royal duty. Frances following the Queen Mother on a visit to the
Princess Alice Hospital in Esher, 25 March 1996.

Acknowledgements

I would like to thank my nephew, Geordie Fergusson for permission in allowing me access to the Fergusson family papers, now held in the National Library of Scotland, in Edinburgh, and for permission to quote from the letters of his mother, my sister Laura.

My cousin, Sir Edward Ford, kindly read the proofs as did Nigel Jaques, both of them were as eagle-eyed as I could hope.

For help with typing and the complicated business of word-processing, I am grateful to my granddaughter-in-law, Caroline Campbell, who started the typing (not easy as she lives in Fife and I in London), and to Lucy Clayton, who between them typed the manuscript with skill and accuracy. To my editor, Hugo Vickers, my debt is immeasurable, and I owe so much to my family, immediate and extended, for endless support and encouragement, particularly to grandchildren who gave their holidays and free time to nursing me through ever-recurring computer problems with patience and forbearance.

FRANCES CAMPBELL-PRESTON
September 2006

Grenfell – Lyttelton

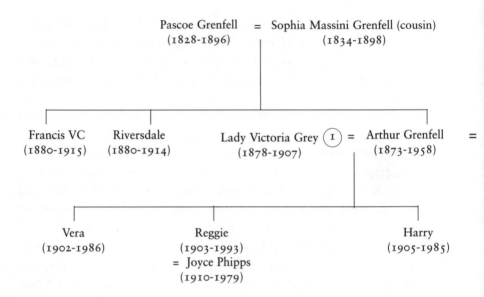

Pascoe Grenfell = Sophia Massini Grenfell (cousin)
(1828-1896)   (1834-1898)

Francis VC   Riversdale   Lady Victoria Grey (I) = Arthur Grenfell   =
(1880-1915)   (1880-1914)   (1878-1907)   (1873-1958)

Vera   Reggie   Harry
(1902-1986)   (1903-1993)   (1905-1985)
               = Joyce Phipps
               (1910-1979)

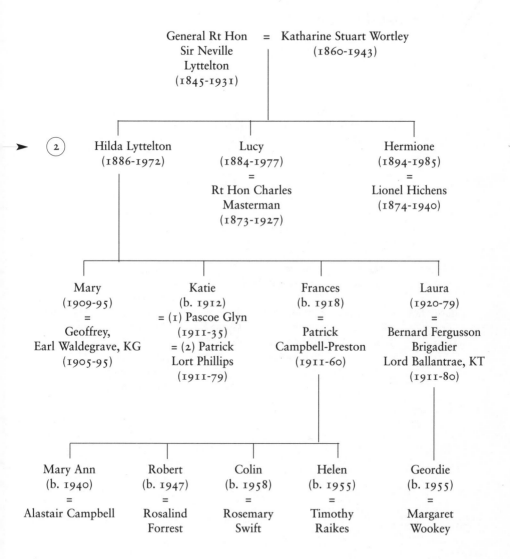

General Rt Hon = Katharine Stuart Wortley
Sir Neville (1860-1943)
Lyttelton
(1845-1931)

2

Hilda Lyttelton   Lucy   Hermione
(1886-1972)   (1884-1977)   (1894-1985)
=   =
Rt Hon Charles   Lionel Hichens
Masterman   (1874-1940)
(1873-1927)

Mary   Katie   Frances   Laura
(1909-95)   (b. 1912)   (b. 1918)   (1920-79)
=   = (1) Pascoe Glyn   =   =
Geoffrey,   (1911-35)   Patrick   Bernard Fergusson
Earl Waldegrave, KG   = (2) Patrick   Campbell-Preston   Brigadier
(1905-95)   Lort Phillips   (1911-60)   Lord Ballantrae, KT
      (1911-79)   (1911-80)

Mary Ann   Robert   Colin   Helen   Geordie
(b. 1940)   (b. 1947)   (b. 1958)   (b. 1955)   (b. 1955)
=   =   =   =   =
Alastair Campbell   Rosalind   Rosemary   Timothy   Margaret
      Forrest   Swift   Raikes   Wookey

Campbell-Preston

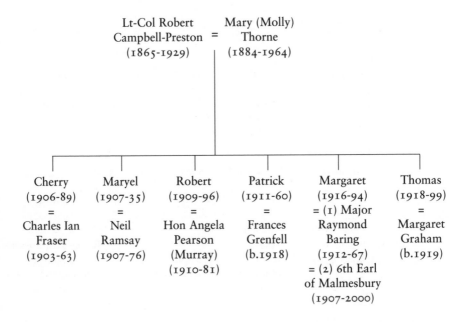

Lt-Col Robert
Campbell-Preston = Mary (Molly)
Thorne
(1865-1929)   (1884-1964)

Cherry	Maryel	Robert	Patrick	Margaret	Thomas
(1906-89)	(1907-35)	(1909-96)	(1911-60)	(1916-94)	(1918-99)
=	=	=	=	= (1) Major	=
Charles Ian	Neil	Hon Angela	Frances	Raymond	Margaret
Fraser	Ramsay	Pearson	Grenfell	Baring	Graham
(1903-63)	(1907-76)	(Murray)	(b.1918)	(1912-67)	(b.1919)
		(1910-81)		= (2) 6th Earl	
				of Malmesbury	
				(1907-2000)	

Introduction

BY HUGO VICKERS

Dame Frances Campbell-Preston has written a fascinating account of her life, which comprises many intriguing strands. First there is her extended family. Her parents were extraordinary and the family is presently joined by an actress of the future, when Joyce Phipps marries her brother Reggie Grenfell.

Most touching of all the sibling relationships is her close friendship with her sister, Laura, later Lady Ballantrae. Of this Laura wrote: 'What different lives you and I are led by fate to live and how satisfactory that they are so mutually satisfying to us?'

For those of us who did not live through the Second World War, the chapters that deal with the war are especially vivid – the long years of separation while her husband, Patrick Campbell-Preston was serving in Europe with the Black Watch, and imprisoned in various prisons, ultimately Colditz.

Latterly she writes of the years when she was Lady-in-Waiting to the Queen Mother. She cannot say it herself, but her husband's fellow prisoner, Sir Martin Gilliat, later the Queen Mother's Private Secretary, often wrote of her stalwart support: 'She, anyhow, goes from strength to strength and has a most splendidly stimulating and down to earth outlook on all our activities – bringing any form of overt pomposity very quickly down to earth.'

Dame Frances has written every word of this book herself, and my only role as editor has been to prepare the typescript for publication, with the occasional cut, or request for more, the kind of help that every writer needs – happily fortified along the way by the occasional 'Clarence House' gin and tonic.

Prologue

ONE DAY IN 1966 I had a dream. I was driving down the Mall towards Clarence House in my daughter Mary Ann's Mini. We had loaded the car with a large trunk of my clothes and I was feeling nervous. Mary Ann kept trying to speak to me and I rounded on her saying that at any other time I would listen to her troubles but just this morning I was concentrating on my arrival at Clarence House. Mary Ann broke in again, saying urgently, 'Mummy I am only trying to tell you, you've forgotten to change. You're still in your gardening clothes.' I looked down to see I had on a large gardening apron and Wellington boots. I woke, laughing nervously.

It was to be my first day as lady-in-waiting to the Queen Mother, to which I had recently been appointed – much to my surprise. Martin Gilliat, the Queen Mother's secretary and an old friend, had asked me to a drinks party in the early summer of 1965. I had never met the Queen Mother before, but that evening she engaged me in conversation and on that brief acquaintance I was offered the post.

I felt totally inadequate on many counts. I had not had a job since the war, and my war work was hardly good training for the high life. I felt ludicrously inexperienced.

Clothes were another worry. I had worn a cast-off dress of my sister-in-law, Joyce Grenfell's, at Martin's drinks party. There were three of the Queen Mother's ladies-in-waiting there, all rather well dressed. Olivia Mulholland explained that she was going on to a dinner engagement. She was wearing a long evening dress of quality, amply supported by jewellery – little of which I possessed; Ruth, Lady Fermoy (whose grand-daughter was the future Princess of Wales), had the same love of clothes and dress sense as Diana and the money to enjoy them, while the third, Lady Jean Rankin, if not quite up to their standard was still considerably above mine.

My mother was renowned for her beauty. She dominated whatever clothes she wore and was not much bothered with them. In the family budget, rich or poor, clothes were a low priority. She never appreciated that her daughters were not blessed with her looks or elegance. We grew up with no self-confidence about clothes. We did not know how to choose them or how to wear them. Mary Waldegrave, my elder sister, was once invited to some prestigious evening party and, wishing to please her husband, splashed out on an expensive evening gown. Her husband was delighted, but Mary's pleasure was somewhat blighted when she discovered that she had worn it inside out.

Any doubts I felt were set aside when the Queen Mother wrote me a kind letter of welcome. After expressing her delight that I was to join her Household, she wrote: 'When we met at Martin Gilliat's house, I felt at once, that if *you* felt able to take on this job, that I would be very happy. I do hope that you will find the life interesting and rewarding, and I look forward *so* much to your arrival . . .'

I almost did not receive this letter. As with all royal letters, it was sent Special Delivery, and the village post office, spotting a reliable school boy who lived near us, consigned it to his care to deliver. But he met a friend on the way and merely dumped the letter on a tree stump in the garden. I only spotted the letter by chance, by which time it was besmirched with West Coast of Scotland drizzle.

So I started my new life as a Woman of the Bedchamber, the official title. This was to last for thirty-five years, and I often wondered how I got there. Two of the Queen Mother's earlier ladies-in-waiting had been friends of my mother's. Lady Helen Graham, daughter of the Duke of Montrose, had struck me as beautiful, elegant and powerful, in as much as her chief role in my mother's life was as Chairwoman of the YWCA. If she backed up my mother's schemes they were likely to succeed. Lady Delia Peel was the other friend, a daughter of Lord Spencer. My predecessor was Lady Caroline Douglas-Home, whose father was Foreign Secretary and later briefly Prime Minister.

During my first year I was 'temporary' but after a year I got a letter from Sir Ralph Anstruther, the Queen Mother's Treasurer, saying: 'This is just a line to warn you that at any moment now you will see in the *London Gazette* that you have ceased to be temporary, and are now a Real Woman.'

I was a widow with four children, one of whom was a married daughter. The younger ones were a post-war family consisting of Robert aged 17 at Eton, Helen aged 9, and Colin 6 – not perhaps the most usual background for a member of the Household of the Queen Mother.

ONE

Grenfells & Lytteltons

THE FORTUNES of my family never ran smoothly. My parents, Arthur and Hilda Grenfell, steered an erratic course. We were rich, we were bankrupt. Arthur was a financier with a soaring imagination. Although never totally dedicated to any political party, he was keen on making money, had Conservative leanings politically and liberal leanings religiously. He was certainly non-dogmatic.

Hilda was a devout Anglican Christian with a deep suspicion of money and riches. Reared in Liberal circles, she was conservative in religion and Liberal in politics. Arthur was profoundly unmusical, while music was a lifeline to Hilda. Despite these paradoxes, which could have caused a divisive family, the opposite was the case. Arthur's first wife, Lady Victoria Grey, had died young leaving him with three small children. His marriage to Hilda Lyttelton three years later added four daughters. Hilda gave all her capacity for love and understanding to her three stepchildren, resulting in a seamless family of seven children who rarely remembered there were any half relationships. The children had great affection for their parents, were often profoundly embarrassed by their eccentric behaviour, but admired their resourcefulness and undoubted courage, and took satisfaction from the family life this apparently ill-assorted couple created for them.

Arthur and Hilda never kept the children segregated from them. Meals were eaten together, not a usual practice among their contemporaries, many of whom lived lives in nurseries or schoolrooms, only meeting their parents briefly for 'children's hour' after afternoon tea. From an early age we learned to communicate with adults and grew up prone to argue and debate.

Arthur and Hilda met through Victoria Grey's family, her younger sister Evy being a friend of Hilda's. They had mutual friends, but stemmed from disparate traditions.

Arthur's father had married his second cousin Sophia, whose Grenfell father served in the Brazilian Navy under the British Admiral Lord Cochrane, and married a Miss Massini, a member of an Italian/Spanish shipowning family, which had fled Italy in the face of Napoleon, taking their ships with them and settling in Montevideo. The Massini line brought in dark Spanish looks, Arthur often being described as having the face of a Spanish grandee. They also had a talent for making money, equalled by one for losing it. As a result of living in South America Arthur's grandfather felt strongly that the colour-bar was wrong. In his letters describing battles against 'negro' rebels he decried the inhuman punishments meted out to them as unjust. In a letter written to his Uruguayan brother-in-law, Ramon, in 1830, he voiced his opposition to slavery:

The greatest blight on America is African slavery. It is a public crime, an offence so atrocious against the human race that all who permit it or defend such barbarism will not escape deserved punishment from God. The magnanimous act of the British Government, an action without equal in the history of the world, giving liberty in all its colonies and paying the owners is the first act in a Drama beginning in the Theatre of the World . . . It is against the miserable short-sighted policy of populating this beautiful country with ignorant negroes.

He had reason to express these forthright views, as his Grenfell relations did business on a world-wide scale, presumably with some influence.

On Trafalgar Day, 21 October 1873, my father, Arthur Morton Grenfell was born into affluence, the 14th child and sixth son of

Pascoe Grenfell and Sophia. His father was a merchant banker in the City, and had amongst his business interests the Argentine and Canada. There was a large country house, Hatchlands, in Surrey, and subsequently Wilton Park, Buckinghamshire, also one in London, and a yacht. His mother, Sophia, had been educated in Montevideo, returning to England when her father retired and became the Brazilian Consul General in Liverpool, but keeping her Spanish connections, and giving her four daughters Spanish names Dolores, Maraquita, Juanita, and Florita. The nine boys conformed to English – Pascoe, Cecil, Reginald (Reggie), John, Harold, Arthur, Robert, and the twins Francis Octavius and Riversdale Nonus. Dolores, the eldest of the family (our Aunt Lola), outlived all her siblings except Arthur, and died aged 96 in 1956.

After the death of their parents within two years of each other, Lola became surrogate mother to the twins then aged 16, and never forgave their deaths in the 1914-18 war, maintaining hatred of the Germans, and illogically, of Lloyd George. The children grew up in a carefree environment and concentrated their talents principally on sport, one of them coming second in the Grand National. The younger twin, Riversdale, won the then prestigious horse riding prize, the Kadar Cup, as a civilian visiting his soldier twin Francis in India. This was an outstanding achievement in military circles. Shooting and games were included in their rituals, particularly cricket. On the death of their parents, when the twins were sixteen, their uncle Francis (Field Marshal Lord Grenfell) became their guardian. He wrote them a letter of advice which ended: 'Read your Bible every day and shoot well ahead of your cock-pheasants.' Francis went on to win the Victoria Cross before his early death in 1915.

All the sons went to Eton. Several of them, including my father, played in the Eton Cricket XI at Lord's. Educational prowess, although thought admirable for some, was not their priority.

This cheerful and secure background may have caused my father to be a naturally happy person and certainly an overly optimistic one. He had to live through many disasters, both national and personal and moments of depression. But even at such times he reached for some sense of the ridiculous, to make some joke against himself.

After school he went to New York to work for J.P. Morgan. He turned down Mr. Morgan's offer of a job in the Morgan branch office in London, thinking this would always remain a small subsidiary of New York. His cousin Edward Grenfell was wiser – the firm became Morgan, Grenfell and made Edward wealthy. On leaving New York my father joined his own father's merchant bank.

From this base he went on to various South African mining enterprises, which in due course brought him into association with Cecil Rhodes and his future father-in-law, Lord Grey. In 1901 he married Lady Victoria Grey, and was well on his way to becoming a millionaire.

When he married his second wife, my mother, in 1909, their married life began in considerable style. They owned Roehampton House (now a hospital and a centre for the fitting of artificial limbs). It would seem to modern eyes a large enough house, but my expansively-minded father commissioned Lutyens to build an extra wing.

In the winter of 1912 my father had a serious hunting accident, knocking him out of his business for months. When he returned to work in 1913 he found the London Stock Exchange depressed. There was intense political tension in both Eastern Europe and Ireland, where civil war was believed to be imminent. The City of London feared a collapse of my father's business and several London finance houses intervened privately to prevent a too drastic liquidation, announcing that his account had been satisfactorily settled.

Although a grave crisis was narrowly averted, my father's personal position was irredeemable. Shortly after this he relinquished all his directorships, and also sent to Christie's for sale all his pictures, including works by Cuyp, Vecello, Reynolds and Gainsborough. The jewel of the collection was his Titian, *The Man with the Glove*, which had been discovered by Sir Hugh Lane, who sold it to my father and then re-bought it in the sale, later selling it to the Frick Museum in New York. My father was declared bankrupt in August 1914 just after the outbreak of war. His personal debt was in excess of £1,000,000.

Predictably, this major disaster affected my parents for the rest of their lives. But first the drama of the First World War took all his attention. He immediately went to France in the Buckinghamshire Yeomanry, his Territorial regiment, and later served as a Major in the 9th Lancers.

The war brought heavy losses to the Grenfell family. By 1915 my father's twin brothers Francis and Rivy had been killed, as had their cousins, Julian and Billy. In letters to his cousin, Willie (Lord) Desborough, Julian and Billy's father, my father described how he went to try and recover Billy's body. It is a chilling and vivid description of battle over what seems to have been a relatively small yardage of ground: '. . . our Regiment has been there so long – Francis was killed just beyond Billy – that they knew every inch of it. I should have liked to bury Billy near Francis, but I am afraid the cursed Germans hold the ground'.

In November 1915 my father also wrote a remarkably frank letter to Henry Frick, who had bought his Titian:

You will be surprised at receiving a letter from me, but I look back so often to the pleasure I had of meeting you and seeing your beautiful pictures that I felt I must write & tell you so. I suppose in times like these one's emotions get stirred up & big things appeal to one – amongst them one's recollection of the really big pictures & so I look back & live through those happy moments again. Poor Newton has been killed; you may remember he was with me; my brother Rivy too. Most of my friends have been killed or wounded & yet one doesn't see any sign of this Armageddon coming to an end. It has been a terrible war – the most savage and cold blooded killing machines versus human nerves & endurance. A big bombardment is a thing no one can imagine. The earth trembles, the air is simply hissing & shrieking – at times one gets almost hypnotized. There is nothing to be done but sit & wait wondering every moment if the next one will hit or miss, but one gets callous & I find myself quite interested in trying to note my feelings & in watching the effects on others, almost as if one was an onlooker.

We have had a terrible amount of leeway to make up. The French weren't as ready as one suspected & the Russians had made no provision. Our fleet did its work splendidly but we were always supposed to send only 160,000 men. Our casualties today amount already to 500,000 men! & I suppose we shall lose another million before we get through, but that we shall get through alright there can be no doubt. Our men have established a superiority over the Germans, their best men have probably been killed, some of our best, all volunteer soldiers, are just getting their first experience & they have fought quite splendidly. Man for man they know they are much the best & therefore start full ofconfidence – but our enemy is a professional soldier, we are mostly amateurs & so our experience costs us heavily. The most dreadful part is the absolute & hopeless destruction. Ypres is simply a mass of bricks & rubbish heaps – all the country round is as though a volcanic eruption had run over & destroyed everything. My other brother won a V.C. only to be killed later on. He [line missing] & others have been invalided home from the Dardanelles where they suffered a good deal. So far I am alright. I am attached to this Regt my two brothers were killed in also. We [nerved?] up for the Loos battle the other day & had various alarms generally about 2 a.m. that the German retreat had begun & we the Cavalry were to be let loose, but it didn't quite come off. I suppose you are in your new house, I hope fit & well . . . Hoping we may meet again. Alas, if I get through this war I will have to pay for my mistakes and start life again, but a good many others will have to do the same, though they were not to blame, so I suppose I must hope to do my best. For the present we have a big enough job on hand. One lives from one day to another – one certainly gets a new perspective of life . . .

After being wounded twice, mentioned in despatches three times, winning the DSO and reputedly having been recommended for the VC, he was invalided from the front line in 1917 and became a Lieutenant-Colonel in the Royal Flying Corps, still a unit of the Army till 1918. A contemporary described him, 'lamed, half deaf, bankrupt and on the brink of middle age with a single-minded resolve to retrieve his fortune and pay his creditors'. His bankruptcy was discharged in 1925.

In an account of my father, one writer concluded: 'Most men would have been broken by his misfortunes in 1914, but Grenfell, with courage, persistence and boldness, constructed for himself a second and honourable career. He was a man of great personal charm with a strong power of persuasion, and a robust good humour; these advantages he used to overcome the suspicion and hostility in the City. Throughout he was indefatigable, ingenious and immune to discouragement. In appearance he was lithe, lean and alert; outside of his business his enthusiasm, courage and laughter made him widely loved.'

Hilda's Lyttelton family was rooted at Hagley in Worcestershire where they had been since the 13th century. They tended to be clergymen, lawyers, civil servants, and scholars. Her grandfather, the 4th Lord Lyttelton was a brother-in-law of Mr Gladstone – they married sisters, the Miss Glynnes. In 1873 he addressed the question of his title in a letter to Gladstone:

Dear W

I am about to ask a question, implying a request about myself which I fear will appear to you preposterous. And it is fair to say, which I do with perfect sincerity, that if I was you I should without hesitation refuse it. It is, whether I might be made an Earl. I have one reason why I wish for this which I also fear will appear a foolish one. But before mentioning it I will fairly say what appears sufficiently strong against the request. I apprehend that since the Reform Bill (though not before) Earldoms have not been given except on the ground of eminent public service or great wealth. The two have often, if not always been separated. To the former of course I can make no pretence, nor to the latter at present. I may however add that I have heard that persons of judgment say that there may be outward circumstances apart from wealth which might justify it: such as possession of an estate of great antiquity and in some respects not without celebrity.

The reason is, that I cannot keep off a certain promotion in this same line which will come to me or my successor without fault or merit of ours, without a shilling of income; and which would be extremely disagreeable to me. Unless the present Duchess of Buckingham dies, and the Duke marries again and has a son (unlikely events) I shall become Viscount Cobham. I greatly dislike the rank of Viscount. The title is ugly and ungainly, the historical avocations not good. The only two Lord Cobhams known in our annals, the one a great Lollard (unconnected with me however), the other through whom I shall inherit, a bad tenth rate politician of the last century now hardly remembered, except as a lying panegyric by Pope.

Of course I do not mean to make much of all this; and you will not suppose that either I look for any sort of personal bias on your part, or should feel anything worth the name of disappointment if you refuse. I need not ask that it be kept a dead secret.

    Yours Affec.
    Lyttelton

Gladstone replied:

My dear George,
I have received and read your letter and I shall show it to my wife which I consider to be entirely within the limits allowed by your injunction to secrecy. I however put down my first impressions. They are to the effect that it would be best for you that the request be not pressed. I am sorry to say that your aversion to Viscount is distinctly a reason against a request for an Earldom. It is our

*business to give as much value as possible to the lower ranks of title
and honour . . . to encourage personal depreciation of Viscountcies
is directly to lower that order of the Peerage...*

*I am afraid that Cobham impends but one can hardly say the
danger is proximate.*

Always affty yours

W.E.G

*P.S Catherine concurs. I translated those few pretty lines of
Aristophanes on the way to town, and will send you my version.*

When he got Mr Gladstone's expected refusal he wrote: 'I do
not doubt you are right . . . finally I ask you pray for the life of
the Duke of Buckingham, that Charles (his son) and not I may be
Cobhamed.'

Hilda's father, General Sir Neville Lyttelton, was Lord
Lyttelton's third son, not an affluent position in a peer's family.
He was a soldier, joining the Rifle Brigade after Eton, and served
in Canada and India, was a General in the Boer War, and the first
Chief of the Imperial General Staff between 1904 and 1908.
Finally, he became the last life Governor of the Royal Hospital
Chelsea, living there from 1912 until his death in 1931. Our
grandfather was tall and straight backed with a large white
moustache, and seemed to us a very old man, a gentle and lovable
person. When in South Africa he was described as 'having a gruff
voice, which makes an excellent foil to the refinement of his mind
and words.' We would climb onto his lap when he played us tunes
on his penny whistle. He shared a love of cricket with Arthur.

Our grandmother was Katharine Stuart Wortley. Through her
we can claim direct descent from Lady Mary Wortley Montagu,
who was responsible for introducing Dr Jenner and his smallpox
vaccine into Britain. Katharine was a formidable and aloof
grandmother, much preferring boys to girls. She was an
impressive intellectual, her Liberal friends including John Morley,
Augustine Birrell, Edward Grey, and among writers Henry James,
George Meredith, and Sir Alfred Lyall.

THE RICH SPOILS OF TIME

Our Lyttelton grandparents were prominent figures in our lives and we were frequently at the Royal Hospital, where they established a centre for a close cousinhood of relations, Katharine being extremely hospitable. In my childhood I naturally presumed that my grandparents owned the place.

Hilda Margaret, our mother, was their second daughter, born in India in 1886. She had been brought up to a life where church and religion were central. You observed, with discipline, the rites of the church. You talked about and discussed every nuance of church politics, in which she felt deeply involved all her life. She read religious books of every description, she imbided all the religious feelings from her inheritance. The tension between religion and science particularly exercised her, and she never doubted there was a resolution to the problem. This added scientific books to her reading. At the end of her life, she felt she had found her Holy Grail when she came upon the writings of the French Jesuit priest, Teilhard de Chardin. This became something of an obsession in her late seventies. It also became a conversion, because included in her Anglican Church life was aversion, suspicion, distrust and prejudice against Roman Catholicism. Liberals they might be, but here was the limit to tolerance.

When I was launched into 'coming out' at 17 I advanced to meet a possible future husband knowing two vetoes: if I wanted to marry a Roman Catholic, my grandmother would be appalled, my mother distressed. If I fell for an old Harrovian, my grandfather and father would feel much the same. Later when I did become, respectably, engaged to an Old Etonian/Anglican, I met a Lyttelton great-uncle while we were staying with Patrick's Roman Catholic relations. In spite of my assurances that neither of us was contaminated, the uncle appeared at our wedding and insisted on coming into the vestry to view the Register 'just to make sure' – as he told my mother.

My mother had an older sister, Lucy, always called 'Meesee', the name given to her by her Indian ayah. She married Charles Masterman, a Liberal politician, friend and colleague of Lloyd

George. Ten years younger was Hermione, who married Lionel Hichens in 1919; he had known the family since South African days when he was a member of Lord Milner's 'Kindergarten'.

My mother spent her early years in India. When she fell seriously ill, aged about 6, the family had to be brought back to England by my grandmother. It was a time when the mortality rate was high among British families, and must have created an atmosphere of dread. Certainly she remembered her extreme fear of the dark to which no concession was made in the strict 'stiff upper lip' ethos of the time. An early photograph of her, aged five or six, shows a frail little girl with scared eyes. She grew into a considerable beauty, tall and slim with a long neck and perfectly proportioned face, blue-eyed with shading lids, a small straight nose and a bowed mouth, with a profile admired by painters and photographers.

Her late teens were spent in South Africa, where her father was commanding in the Boer War. The families of many of the officers went out to Cape Town and set up a social life, the interlinking of soldiers, government officials and business making it interesting and hardly an exile. On coming home my mother found herself going through the rite of passage which existed into my generation of 'coming out'. She was launched into balls and house-parties. She was widely courted. Painters wanted to paint her, another attention she found irksome. As a result, only one later portrait exists of her, by Sir Gerald Kelly, and that is unfinished as she frequently failed to turn up for sittings and Kelly abandoned the painting.

She had enormous energy and more than her fair share of determination and courage, but she could be cripplingly shy and lacked self-assurance at unexpected moments. When she was a debutante, heartiness frightened her. Staying in a house party for a hunt ball, the young guests were all to be taken to the ball in a bus. As she was dressing for dinner her hostess put her head round the door and said pleadingly to my mother 'You *will* try and be jolly in the bus, won't you?'

Hilda was passionately musical and after surviving coming out went thankfully to Paris to study piano at the Conservatoire. She might have become a concert pianist if she hadn't married Arthur. (My mother used to find him standing to attention for *Auld Lang Syne*, in case it was 'God Save the King'). In spite of the many 'suitable' suitors, my mother, to her own mother's sadness, chose my father, a widower of thirty with three small children, with questionable church affiliations, and Conservative leanings. Her childhood had not been spent in affluence, yet she suddenly married into riches.

While Arthur's temperament led to an overdose of optimism, it was mitigated in their marriage by my mother's tendency to pessimism. She had to cope with the loss of friends who deserted when bankruptcy happened. She always had to pick up the bits – concertinaing from big houses to small, coping with a large family and frequently trying to pay the bills. Every time her sense of insecurity increased. She felt considerable malaise about the wealth into which she had married.

War was also a constant theme – her close connection with the Boer War, fourteen years later the 1914-18 war, and then, barely twenty years later, the 1939-45 war. Even post-war the Cold War with its menace of nuclear war, the Korean War and the encounters in Malaysia and Cyprus, all affecting younger members of her family who were in the army, hung over her. She was not one to take any of this lightly.

My father always supported my mother and came to church with us. When we jibbed at the inexorable rule of church on Sunday, he was apt to appeal to our sporting instincts saying, 'Oh, come on, you must support the padre.'

TWO

Childhood

MY PARENTS had married in Dublin, where my Lyttelton grandfather was stationed. Before the First World War they had two daughters, the eldest, Mary, born in 1909 and Katie (Katherine) in 1912.

Pre-war photographs show the life at Roehampton. Against the background of a lovely house, there are large spacious elegant rooms – library, dining room, drawing room – hung with old master paintings, later sold at Christie's in 1914. Accompanied by grooms, there are Vera, Reggie and Harry riding on ponies in Richmond Park, Mary and Katie in the arms of smartly dressed nannies, wearing bonnets, sitting in huge prams; pictures of garden parties at Roehampton with eminent members of the contemporary Establishment from the Duke of Connaught to Baden-Powell, the ladies in large Edwardian hats, with sweeping long dresses and stylish parasols.

Then in 1914 everything crashed, their whole way of life disappeared, a casualty of the Great War which consumed them for the next four years.

The world into which I was born was very different. The war still had a little more than two months to run when I was born on 2 September 1918 at St Leonards-on-Sea, where my father was serving at an RAF Training Camp at nearby Hove.

The deaths of my father's twin brothers still left their grief raw at the time of my birth in 1918. They had hoped for a male child, partly to replace them. I was to be called Francis Oliver. As a female I became Frances Olivia.

By the time of the armistice, on November 11, so much had changed. The car had superseded the carriage but Vera, Reggie and Harry still played tennis in the garden of Dorchester House in Park Lane, then a private house owned by their uncle George Holford. Roehampton had been replaced by a small terraced house in Gloucester Terrace, London W2.

Laura completed the family when she was born in 1920, so was eighteen months younger than me. We were the afterthoughts of the family, divided from the rest not only by years but by being post-war babies. This made us a unit within an entity always known as 'The Babies'. We were physical opposites. Laura inherited our mother's long neck and her elegant figure. She was blonde, with arching eyebrows, a long Grenfell nose and a smaller version of her mother's mouth. Her temperament was quite different. She had an optimistic streak, took life with equanimity, could get indignant about a cause and was fearless and funny, shrewd and intelligent. She was a premature baby born at seven months, which had left her with a cleft palate and affected her voice, so that strangers were startled. In the family it went quite unnoticed and affected Laura herself very little. It never inhibited her when in later life she found she had to make public speeches. To me she was almost faultless and her memory is a bulwalk.

In 1920 my father took his whole family to Vienna where he organised the formation of the Danube Navigation Co. This business expanded to negotiating loans to Austria, Czechoslovakia and Hungary to create an international railway freight company. Because of his 1914 bankruptcy he was not a director, but despite this he was able to attract businessmen of importance. Among those that backed him were the future Lord Cowdray and the bankers Hambro, Cox, and Robert Fleming.

After his bankruptcy was discharged he became director of a more ambitious, but successful Continental freight scheme, and through this became associated with bankers from Germany and numerous other European states. He also acquired chrome mines in Albania. Much later Hitler's war destroyed his work in Central European transport and mining, and led to their loss.

Life in Vienna was turbulent in the 1920s. Inflation was

rampant in Germany and Austria; the pound was a currency that went a long way.

Curious incidents occurred. Waiting to travel to London, my father was approached by a stranger, an Austrian lady, who thrust her jewellery into his hands, begging him to take it to London to bank it for her. In astonishment he asked why she trusted him? She said because she had to – it was her last and only chance to save something. He did bank it for her, but never saw her again.

We spent the Austrian summers in various rented schlosses outside Vienna, eventually finding a permanent one, which we rented on a long lease. Although we returned to live in London after two years, Schloss Tollet was the place we went to stay every summer holiday and sometimes more often, until 1928. All the summer friends and relations poured in to stay. Amongst these were Alan Lennox-Boyd, then at Oxford with Harry, and later Colonial Secretary, Roger Makins, later a diplomat and eventually Lord Sherfield, and Phyllis and Rachel Spender Clay. In 1929 Rachel married David Bowes Lyon, the Queen Mother's brother, and Laura and I were taken to their wedding and I saw the Queen Mother, then Duchess of York, for the first time.

Schloss Tollet was in Upper Austria just outside the village of Greiskirchen, near Linz and Wels. It became a beloved place to us all. It was perched on the top of a hill, surrounded by a dry moat: a rambling house built round a courtyard with a terrace where meals were eaten and where everyone lounged. In my memory the days were all sunny. The domestic staff were Austrians except for Minnie, our nanny, and Blundell, our butler. Toni, the cook, had been a kitchen maid in some Austrian Royal Family and her food was never matched; Janko was the gardener, always ready to build tree houses for us, or carts or whatever took our fancy, and a gamekeeper called Putzendeöbelu was our avowed enemy.

Although it was only a few years after the war, children were able to play freely at Tollet. Katie, in her early teens, knew most of the children in the village and played with them all day.

When we came back from Vienna we moved to Gloucester

Terrace – in circumstances which were still somewhat straitened as it was not a large house for a family with seven children and the statutory number of domestics – butler, cook, and beloved Minnie, who on my arrival had moved over from being my mother's lady's maid to be nanny to Laura and me. All operations were performed at home for fear of germs in hospitals. At Gloucester Terrace Laura and I had our tonsils out on the nursery table, being chloroformed with a large mask over our faces. Later Katie had her appendix out, and Reggie his varicose veins.

From this house, Laura and I went to our first school. It was a small PNEU (Parents National Educational Union) school run by two ladies, Miss Burney and Miss Fluky, with two assistant mistresses called Miss Hart and Miss Hind. They also had a friend said to be called Miss Mouse who was a missionary in China. We had to take one penny every Friday towards Miss Mouse's work, when we all sang the hymn 'God is working his purpose out' and felt we and Miss Mouse were definitely helping. Fierce religion ruled at this small but 'fashionable' school. We made many friends with the offspring of our parents' friends. After this, we split from this group of friends who, if they were boys, went on to prep schools and public schools, while the girls returned to governesses.

Our elder sisters, Mary and Katie, went to St Paul's Girls School. There was soon a change of fortune on the financial front, which moved us from Gloucester Terrace to a large establishment in Connaught Place, a house with a view across the Bayswater Road to Hyde Park. It had a marbled front hall – large rooms and a lift (said to cost ½d every time you used it). There was plenty of room and guests flowed through it constantly.

During this phase, which lasted until 1929, we still holidayed at Tollet. My father's eldest sister, Lola, spent most of the summer holidays with us. As my mother mustered her troops for church, she asked Lola if she wished to go. Lola declared that she had been to church twice every Sunday for the last six weeks and so was six weeks in credit before she needed to go again.

My father's change of fortunes allowed him to once again attend the auctions at Christie's and buy pictures. My mother suffered terrible pangs of conscience about being 'well off' so dived into her voluntary work with the YWCA. Shortly after we moved to Connaught Place the General Strike happened and the whole family was galvanised into action – Vera manning canteens, Harry and Reggie helping out Southern Railway. To this day there are a few silver ashtrays in my children's houses donated then by the grateful SR. A cousin was briefly a bus conductor. A large collection of these workers came round to share experiences and the house was always full of excitement. From our balcony we watched the Hunger Strikers from the coalfields march down the Bayswater Road.

We were aware of the terrible conditions in the Durham coalfields and the massive unemployment. Vera had gone to work for the MP for Durham, Sir Cuthbert Headlam. He had started an agency to get employment for people in London; we had one or two working in the house, mere children of fourteen. Vera had had a rude awakening visiting some of the affluent houses in London's West End, persuading people to give jobs to these boys and girls.

She was appalled by the conditions that these children were asked to work in, and the long hours, and frequently came home relaying terrible stories. There was a firm segregation between upstairs and downstairs, and between 'upper' and 'lower' servants. Laura and I spent quite a lot of time below stairs. The kitchen was always rather a fascinating place, as was the butler's pantry; there was often teasing and laughter, but I fear we were much too spoilt and insensitive to be interested in anyone else's life.

Vera was unremitting in her efforts and sold the idea to our mother that my father needed a secretary. This was unlikely since he went to his City office every day where, apparently, he had an ample supply of secretaries. But my mother was persuaded. Vera was sure that she had found a paragon who would fill every requirement, a tactful, skilful and hard-working young man. The problem was that he was so low in funds that he needed clothes before he could even think of coming to London. So Reggie and Harry's wardrobe was raided and he was sent a selection. Laura and I waited for a Mr Baxter such as P.G. Wodehouse's Lord Emsworth had, and our mother broke the news to Minnie and Blundell that this rather superior addition was joining the household. On the day of his arrival my mother had her sitting room door opened by Blundell, who announced gravely 'the new secretary'.

Into the room came a white-faced, terrified boy, trailing over his arm the far too large trousers he had been sent. Later my father asked how his wonderful new secretary was turning out and admitted it was proving rather expensive as he was sending him to school.

For some reason, during what must have been turbulent social times, my father prospered. Mary left St Paul's with an Exhibition to Somerville College Oxford. Mary was the clever one of the family. She inherited our mother's intellect, but was grounded by inheriting Arthur's pragmatism. She never soared to the unreal realms to which my mother often took off and she had an ordered mind. She would undertake meticulous historical research, and, later, would sit up all night mending some intricate toy, which one of her seven children had broken. As an elder sister she was the source of wisdom. She was a little aloof but witty and tender-hearted and patient. She read history at Oxford, but left to marry before getting her degree. Her contemporaries at school included Monica Dickens, the author, and Celia Johnson, the actress.

Katie was a different pupil, her prowess being games and sport.

THREE

Joyce Grenfell

BEFORE THE end of the Connaught Place era, my half-brother, Reggie, got engaged to Joyce Phipps, the first in-law to break the family circle. It was a good break and Joyce opened so many windows. There was no indication that as Joyce Grenfell her future would be as a famous star in America, Australia and New Zealand – as much as in Britain. To us she was a typical grown-up debutante. She went to parties, often went to 'the flicks' in the afternoon with her girlfriends, had tea at Lyons Corner House, and occasionally read books or played jazz to the current songs on the drawing-room piano. She used make-up, had lots of friends, liked and talked of clothes, her picture appeared in the *Tatler*, she and Reggie won a dancing competition at the Kit Cat nightclub – in fact she made no bones about going to nightclubs. It was not normal to my parent's generation, who viewed such places with horror. It wasn't that any of these things were banned, it was just that none of us had done them. She had a fascinating but unreliable mother, and also had a very rich and frightening aunt, Lady Astor.

Joyce and Reggie were married in December 1929 at St. Margaret's, Westminster. It was billed in the tabloids as 'the Society Wedding' and was accorded Lady Astor's full treatment, including a wedding reception at the Astors' London house in St. James's Square. One of the strange wedding rituals was to lay out all the wedding presents as an exhibition for the reception. This was quite a labour and we all turned up to help lay out the array.

At the end of the day, our labours completed, everyone was standing around idly. Harry had returned from New York where he had been working, and there was a certain gloom as Reggie had lost his job the week before because of the stock market crash. My parents had a reserved view of Lady Astor and were wary of Joyce's mother Norah. Paul Phipps, Joyce's father, had been a friend of Rivy, and Francis and my parents were fond of him, but knew that Norah had been a wayward wife. As we stood round, Lady Astor took centre stage and rounded on Joyce saying there was still time and it was obvious she was marrying the wrong brother, it being plain that Harry was preferable in every way – he even had a job.

My parents froze and an ominous silence prevailed. Laura was standing beside a Lyttelton aunt, DD, widow of my mother's uncle Alfred. Aunt DD was also a friend of Lady Astor's. Laura tugged on DD's hand and said: 'Who is that mad old woman who thinks Harry is nicer than Reggie?' DD broke the silence: 'Nancy, out of the mouths of babes and sucklings. I've got a young lady here who wants to know who the mad old lady is?'

After Christmas we left Connaught Place for a considerably smaller and much less grand house on Hyde Park Square. The number of bathrooms shrank, as did the domestic staff, but Minnie and Blundell the butler were still there. Laura and I followed our sisters and started our St. Paul's career. Mary was by now courting Geoffrey Waldegrave. After Joyce he was the next in-law and they married in October 1930 in the Chapel at the Royal Hospital – about the last party before my grandfather's death. Geoffrey's arrival in the family was more gradual than Joyce's. He had been a friend of Harry's, was a relation and protégé of the Greys at Howick. He was the only son of a clergyman and heir to the title of his uncle, Lord Waldegrave, and to his estate in Somerset. He was absorbed into the family and became part of the scene at Connaught Place. He was a good-looking, dark-haired young man with considerable zest for life, amusing and good company. He was musical and knowledgeable about theology and church politics, and thus in sympathy on both subjects with his future mother-in-law. We grew very fond of him.

His mercurial nature we found enjoyable, admittedly irritating at times, but he entered into, and instigated the debates and arguments that comprised our conversations. Geoffrey was a dedicated arguer. His and Mary's home at Chewton in Somerset became a frequent haven.

We did not live in Hyde Park Square for long as by 1933 we were on the move again, my father's chrome mines in Albania apparently succeeding and gold mines in East Africa adding to his wealth. First came a large maisonette on the top three floors of a house in Chesham Place, and then a country house in North Wales was rented on a long lease. Life became expansive.

We all had ponies and there were stables and a groom. None of us made the grade that our Grenfell uncles had achieved. We used to go out for family rides but seldom came home without having been in some sort of incident, usually one of us falling off.

In this period we also acquired a Rolls Royce. It was unplanned. My father and I were walking round Berkeley Square and stopped to look in the windows of the smart Rolls Royce shop. To my astonishment my father said, 'I think I'll just go in and get one.' In we went to find there was an almost new second-hand one. My father told me to get in the back and see if I liked it and when I did, he ordered it, signed the necessary contract and arranged for it to be delivered. Going home on the bus he got a bit twitchy, having suddenly remembered that he had to tell my mother. It wasn't the sort of thing she liked at all. There was already a perfectly adequate car, with a nice young chauffeur. Reluctantly she acquiesced. When the car arrived, it turned out it needed a specially trained driver. As the driver was married he required a home, so a house in a nearby mews was bought and several happy motoring years were enjoyed. The mews house came in handy a few years later when the Rolls, the chauffeur, the top floors of Chesham Place and the gold mine went. The family moved into the mews flat and the basement and we all battened down again. Later this proved useful in wartime.

Nannau Hall, near Dolgellau in North Wales, became a place to which we could ask our friends and family to stay. Thus we saw a lot of our relations and certain characters stand out. Joyce was one. Both Mary and Katie had married. Katie had married Pascoe Glyn (in the Grenadier Guards) in the early days at Chesham Place, and soon afterwards, Pascoe had been posted to Cairo. Mary was regularly pregnant, so Joyce, who was frequently at Nannau, filled the gap left by elder sisters. She had become integrated into the family. We were aware that she was different. She brought a whiff of American culture – a good thing – but she was never a person apart. She loved Nannau and joined in our lives and interests, even trying, with a certain amount of heroism, to ride, although she complained that trotting made her bottom red hot. She and her great friend, Virginia Graham, rode out bravely together one day, arriving home late, trudging wearily and leading their ponies. They had found it impossible to remount once they'd got down to open a gate.

Joyce even took a fleeting interest in the grouse and pheasant shooting which Reggie enjoyed. But she drew the line at duck shooting in the gloaming, as the ducks flew home to roost. When she was taken to watch this she burst into tears, and I share her same horror and loathe duck shooting to this day. Joyce did not appear to either disapprove or be surprised when Laura and I began to have boyfriends. She even made them sound rather glamorous by referring to them as 'beaux'. She taught us practical things which were apt to escape the mind of our mother or Minnie, like using deodorants, and introduced us to powder and lipstick.

Over the years Joyce and my mother forged a warm friendship but it had to be worked at. The sad irony was that they were by far the most devout and religious amongst us, but were wholly divided by the strength of their respective beliefs. My mother looked on Christian Science as a somewhat balmy American sect, while Joyce felt that all the ritual of the Anglican Church made direct communication with God impossible. The only angle these two opinions found on which to agree was profound disapproval of the Roman Catholics. Later my mother eased her position on this. Joyce never did.

When Joyce and Reggie's childlessness began to be tragic, Joyce said she had the best and most comforting letter from my mother – in fact, I think, the only communication she ever had from any of us on that difficult subject. As usual there was a 'gap' between the generations, but she bestrode both sides. My parents were teetotal, my father by persuading himself that alcohol caused deafness, and my mother by choice. Joyce joined them in this because of her religion. Vera in the 'flapper' era of the 1920's had learnt to drink cocktails and gin – viewed with deep parental suspicion. Although my father provided drink for his friends, he never quite came round to including gin.

Neither of my parents drove a car. My mother had tried once soon after our return from Vienna, but she was quite unable to remember that she was not driving a horse, and in a crisis trod on the accelerator, and pulled on the steering wheel. We were the generation who all clamoured to drive, and did. It came as naturally to us as computers do to our grandchildren.

The telephone was used sparingly. Immediate communication was by telegram. The telephones were upright with a removable receiver which you held to your ear. When talking, my father bellowed into it as if to raise the dead. It was almost unknown to ring long-distance, or make a 'trunk' call before six o'clock in the evening, except in a death-threatening emergency. It became unpatriotic to use the telephone during the war and we were restricted to calls of three minutes.

Joyce was the first in the family to pioneer radio use. She was an enthusiast for the new medium and explained that it could be used for entertainment as well as the news, even in lieu of reading and for listening to music. There were some fierce arguments between her and my mother, who maintained that the quality of the sound distorted the music, especially the piano. Joyce dismissed this as rubbish.

Joyce became Radio Critic to the *Observer*, her first job, and the radio – or the wireless – became part of life. She was one of the first to have a portable wireless. The sole wireless at Nannau was a large oval piece of furniture neatly decorated and camouflaged so that it fitted in. It stood on a table and enabled my father to listen to 'the News'.

On the whole my father took up gadgets and innovations more easily and enthusiastically than his wife. Ever since the 1914 war he had become progressively deafer, but as soon as hearing aids came in he tried them with varying success but great persistence. He was convinced that they would improve over the years. At the inception of the NHS in 1946, he was shocked to find that hearing aids were not considered a necessity, and thus he joined a consortium of deaf people to get an amendment to the Bill. This consisted of galvanising the House of Lords to put the amendment, resulting in a debate, headed by the deaf Duke of Montrose and argued by bawling deaf peers accompanied by squeaking voice boxes – the hearing aids of that time. They won, and succeeding generations owe them a debt.

All through our childhood books were the chief source of entertainment and imagination. As we grew to understanding, the theatre was added – first in the form of pantomimes, such as *Peter Pan*, and later Shakespeare, with John Gielgud as hero and interpreter. The cinema began with the 'silents', which for us were Charlie Chaplin, Harold Lloyd and Laurel and Hardy. Then it seemed suddenly the 'talkies' arrived, to huge excitement by us and enormous bewilderment to our poor parents. Charlie Chaplin, talking, they could master, but musicals with Fred Astaire they found baffling. How did someone in a hotel room suddenly have an entire orchestra accompanying them to dance or sing? How did the actor get from the sitting room, balcony or doorstep to somewhere else when he had not opened a door or walked down a passage? My mother went for a dream sequence – this led to complicated unravelling.

Joyce made the 'flicks' as they were called, a must. Most of the culture in those years between the wars veered towards stories with happy endings. Perhaps the horrors of the 1914-18 war and the subliminal fears of the next war made people long for 'happy ever after' solutions? Joyce's Christian Science beliefs coloured her view and certainly affected ours. A guest who came every year to see our parents was Ruth Draper, the American monologist of great genius who had a one-woman season at the Haymarket Theatre. She often took Laura and me to sit in the wings of the stage during her acts, totally entranced and absorbed. Ruth Draper was a cousin of Joyce's, and was her inspiration. Sadly Ruth rather resented Joyce's subsequent successes.

In the 1930's, my mother was thinking of other issues. After Hitler came to power, she began to pick up on the persecution of church leaders and the hounding of the Jews through her contacts on the International YWCA. After working in Austria and throughout Europe both my parents had a number of friends and associates, many of them Jews. She began to be seriously alarmed at the little amount of knowledge that was getting through to people in leading roles in this country and the 'head in the sand' attitude adopted by most people.

Although she refused to give way to her fears, she felt in her bones that we could be heading for another war. My father was still in a mood of high optimism. His mining interests now included a gold mine in Tanganyika, and his plans for improving Nannau knew no bounds – a sunken Dutch garden on the lines of one he had had at Roehampton was among structural plans – and Clough Williams-Ellis, the Welsh architect who had created Portmeirion, was consulted and was often a guest.

My mother was trying hard to square the circle of these different moods. In order to try and gain attention to her concerns, one of her ploys was to sit in the lobby at the House of Commons. She would nobble a policeman, who knew the names of all the MPs, to stand close to her and alert her when an MP she wanted to confront came by. She would then pounce and engage him in a long discussion.

Over the years, through her sister Lucy Masterman, as well as through the YWCA, she got to know Mrs Churchill and once went to see the Churchills in their flat in Morpeth Mansions. She found Mr Churchill profoundly depressed, saying there was nothing he could do or say, he was finished and no one listened to him, although he agreed with her. His son Randolph was there and tried to cheer him up saying, 'You know, father, you will be Prime Minister one day.' Mr Churchill rounded on him replying that if that were true it would not be until Great Britain was on her knees.

My mother came straight home with this chilling story. It was hard to believe their forebodings against the background of youth and fun, so we tended to hope and try to forget these grim warnings. There were plenty more cheerful prophets about.

Another meeting with Mr Churchill was stage-managed by Alan Lennox-Boyd. Mr Churchill was writing the life of his ancestor, the Duke of Marlborough. Geoffrey and Mary Waldegrave had moved into Chewton Priory in Somerset and on going through the archives Mary had found a diary believed to have belonged to Sarah, Duchess of Marlborough, which described the great Duke's deathbed at Cumberland Lodge. The Churchills came to dinner and a memorably magical evening developed as Mr Churchill read out the diary, commentating richly on it, and added other descriptions. Sadly Mary's diary turned out to be a copy. After this Mr. Churchill began to describe the Battle of Blenheim to us.

Laura and I loved St Paul's. Our parents were remarkably liberal, giving us independence and letting us go about London unaccompanied. Frequently in the summer, if there was a cricket match to enjoy, we would rush from school for the close of play, even going by ourselves if necessary. We came and went to school by bus alone. Soon after we had moved into the sumptuous quarters in Chesham Place, our mother, worried that riches might corrupt us, dispatched us to school as weekly boarders.

In those days, St Paul's had a boarding house for about fifty pupils, run by a Miss Cunningham, an understanding Irish lady whose chief pastime was riding to hounds in Ireland. She had an excellent sense of humour and an eminently reasonable approach to life. We were devoted to her.

I found myself in a dormitory with several other girls, allotted two baths a week, which was cold and uncosy. I thought this an unreasonable plan considering that I had a comfortable bedroom with my own bath tended by Minnie at home, so I decided to leave. After a fortnight I returned home. On the other hand Laura loved it and stayed there till the end of her school career.

When I was sixteen I sat the 'Matric' exam. This was the last exam to be taken, and if you went on to university you had to pass the individual university exam. This meant that for Matric you sat about ten subjects at one go; you had to pass every paper or you failed the whole exam, and if you sat it again, you had to retake the whole exam. In my defence I did get honours in seven subjects, but failed all the compulsory maths papers spectacularly. It was accepted that however often I took the exam I would always fail maths, so I left school in the spring of 1935.

It was the first time Laura and I had separated to go our own ways. Laura noted in her diary: 'Frances has left school, it feels odd'.

A year after Katie's marriage to Pascoe Glyn, and but three weeks after her baby daughter was born in Cairo, Pascoe was killed in a riding accident there. This was a sad shock for all of us. Laura described in her diary how Katie spent an unhappy time being homeless, although she lived with Reggie for a time when Joyce went to America. Finally she settled in a small London house. Two years later she married Patrick Lort Phillips, a fellow officer of Pascoe's in the Grenadiers. As Laura's diary remarked: 'so it has all ended happily.'

In our liberal education one ingredient was missing. Any form of sex education was taboo. No inkling was given of the facts of life, no hints as to the relationship of the sexes, while any questions were adroitly sidestepped. My mother soon diverted these into a complicated religious homily. When she read the Bible to us she jumped all words such as fornication or adultery, which made the story difficult to follow. As we had no idea there was anything to be curious about, it didn't worry us. My aunt Hermione had once said to her mother: 'What *does* adultery mean? You keep telling me, and I keep forgetting.'

When I left for school in France, the sum of my knowledge, gleaned from my sisters' marriages, was that married couples had babies because for some reason they slept together. The actual process of birth was known to us – we knew better than storks and gooseberry bushes. But when I left for Fontainebleau that was all I knew, except that I had heard rumours that the French had their own rules – lovers and mistresses came into the historical novels I read.

The school carefully selected by both my mother and the mother of my friend, Pat Napier, was presumed to have no more than five pupils and concentrated teaching. When we arrived we found twenty other pupils, no curriculum and nothing organised. Pat and I, both teenaged and greedy, took to the delicious cafés and ate our way through the day on cream gateau. The only entertainment laid on by our Madame was a weekly *thé dansant* with officers from the local garrison. These were stilted affairs, difficult conversationally, with dancing at arm's length. Owing to the gateau, I put on a great deal of weight and my periods stopped. I knew this happened when one got pregnant, and so, adding this to the suspicion there was something 'funny' about Frenchmen, I presumed the *thés dansants* had somehow infected me. I wrote to explain these obvious facts to my mother and tell her I was pregnant and got a cabled reply: 'Very unlikely often due to weather'. She then sent Harry and Laura out to see me, and, having been told the facts by me, they returned home with the report that I certainly looked pregnant. This brought my mother out. She removed me from Fontainebleau, put me into a Paris family (not having found out they were French Fascists) and took me to a specialist who recommended a slimming diet of boiled fish and milk pudding. She went back to London.

The only restaurant I knew in Paris was Prunier, a haunt of my father's, and a top fish restaurant. So I lunched there daily on boiled fish (lobster) and crème brulée. The specialist soon rumbled this life style and sent me back to London.

After a term at this disastrous French finishing school, it was agreed I could 'come out' at 17, said to be a young age. This was not welcomed by my mother. It was not a ritual of which she much approved. She had chaperoned Vera, Mary and Katie and found it a tedious exercise, and, in view of her interests and work in the YWCA, she thought it irrelevant on many counts.

My mother occasionally made efforts to slim me. In the 1930s there had appeared in London a Professor John Plesch, a distinguished scientist, an associate and friend of Einstein. He set himself up in a penthouse in Park Lane as a doctor, although he refused to go through the accepted British training process. In spite of this he took a certain section of society by storm and chronic invalids flocked to him with real or imaginary illnesses. One was my mother. She enjoyed his company as he was an extremely intelligent man, even if his English was quaint and his diagnoses quainter.

His verdict on my figure was a little strange. He explained to my mother that he had observed that statues, such as ancient ones in Italy, on being exposed to the elements, often had their contours worn away. On this principle he foresaw that a jet of water administered to my contours plus a sharp rubbing by such as a horse brush could reduce me quite a bit. It was never certain whether the professor's English was rightly interpreted or not. Anyway my mother took him literally, got Cripps, our butler, to fix a powerful hose to the cold tap in the bath and bought a horse brush. For a week I was hosed down and brushed, but remained rounded. Then I rebelled.

A bit frustrated, the dear professor then suggested an alternative – that I should run round Hyde Park 'in a little vest'. Fortunately my father vetoed this on the grounds of decency.

FOUR

Coming Out

LAURA stayed on at school, but even there she was not safe from external events – one entry in her diary telling of a lecturer who had worked in German schools and brought leaflets to show the girls those being given to German pupils: 'It was horrid slogans – to hell with the Jews – all intercourse with Jews are criminal, mean, foul etc'. Laura was distressed that a Jewish friend at school should have to see this. 'I am sure Ruth's mother wouldn't have liked her to read it'.

At St Paul's both Laura and I found ourselves with a new spectrum of friends, amongst them several left-wing families. The children of Victor Gollancz (the pre-eminent left-wing publisher) were our contemporaries. Books passed from hand to hand among the students, a popular writer being Beverley Nichols who wrote *Cry Havoc*, an anti-war book. I read this when Laura and I were at the boarding house, and I wrote home enthusiastically about it. By return, my father wrote to me, I now see, something of an anguished letter, in fear that I would reject all the sacrifices of his generation.

It left me not wholly convinced, but not entirely won over by Beverley Nichols either. I did join the 'Peace Pledge' movement and marched down Whitehall in protest or support – I wasn't sure which. It was more a case of joining a new idea than quite understanding how the ideal could be realised. But I think I can claim to have been the only lady-in-waiting who ever marched down Whitehall with a placard.

The anti-Semitism that prevailed in many circles was not something I was brought up to support. Reading my father's letters today, his references to Jews would be deemed anti-Semitic. We were aware that Jews were ethnically different. My father admired and envied their financial skills, my mother and our experience at St Paul's taught us of their contribution to the arts and science. We all loved the musical culture, almost entirely Jewish, that came out of America. One of my Lyttelton grandmother's closest friends was Lady Rothschild, who lived in a large house in Piccadilly next to the Duke and Duchess of York. Lady Rothschild, who was known affectionately as Lady Wash (a child's rendering) was fond of our mother.

Every Christmas a message came, asking what we wanted *most* for Christmas? As a result to this day in our children's houses are the desks that Laura and I were given, our first travelling clocks from Asprey's, a bookcase each, and one of the earliest home cine cameras with projector.

But the most loved present, our first memory of these years of generosity, was given when we were in Vienna – two wax dolls of enormous beauty, the most sought after toy then. We loved them but one terrible day, fearing that our beloved dolls might feel the cold we put them by the nursery fire. We returned to find them melted. It was my first experience of bereavement.

In spite of the fact that almost all our peers at school were aiming at university or training for some profession, we were still directed towards 'Coming Out'.

This 'Coming Out' was, crudely, an upper-class marriage market. The structure and mores of it were comic. Someone somewhere made a list of the year's debutantes. (In 1936 we all had to wear black for Court Mourning owing to the death of King George V. This gave us intense pleasure as otherwise we would never have been allowed to wear it). Hermione thought that in order to cheer the scene up, she would gave a dance, no doubt daringly, during the mourning period.

During February and March the ritual was to give and go to deb luncheon parties, so as to get to know your fellow participants. Cocktail or sherry parties, as they were known, were also on tap where you began tentatively to meet your male counterparts. The list of young men who were available was yet more mysterious but it was said that if you were having difficulty in squaring off a dinner party, you either rang the adjutant at Wellington Barracks and he sent along a Guards officer – or you asked the garrison commander at the Tower of London, who did the same.

The dinner parties for a dance were always in private houses – the hostess for the dance selecting a hostess to give a dinner, and providing her with the names she should invite.

One rule could not be broken. You had to be presented at Court. Unless you had been presented, many of the so-called delights of the season were denied you. You could not get into the Royal Enclosure at Ascot, go to a State Ball, nor could you present anyone else unless you yourself had been presented. You risked 'Outer Darkness' for any future daughters you might have (or daughters-in-law for that matter – for after I was married, my mother-in-law presented me again – as a newly married woman).

I was finally presented at court in the Coronation summer of 1937. In a letter to Laura who was abroad I wrote about this arrangement. We set out in the family car driven by Cripps, the butler, who had been coerced into doubling as occasional chauffeur:

Well, we went to Court last night. Great fun, but a terribly silly performance really. Mummy had a lovely silver sort of tinsel dress, patterned like moiré with a low V neck, little frills over the tops of her arms, and a bright blue moiré train. She had Mary's tiara, Katie's tiara as a necklace (I had forgotten how lovely it was, diamonds and pearls), Vera's big diamond and pearl bow brooch at her V neck. She looked quite startlingly lovely. I had a silver and white frock, with a square neck and little high standing sleeves just over the tops of my arms. I wore Vera's two little diamond brooches at the corners of my neck and Mummies pearls round my neck and Vera's round my wrist. Long gloves really are lovely, they feel so nice.

We meant to arrive very early, because a man called Sir Hill Child had promised to get us in to the throne room. Cripps is the funniest driver in the world, didn't even know the way to Buck Pal, and of course got so flurried when we got into the queue that he went to the wrong side of all the policemen (Daddy yelling from the back 'Don't go there, O damn we're being shot out!' meaning of the queue.) and so we got to the end of the queue instead of the front and were among the last 50 people. So we had to wait hours in the forecourt and then hours in an anteroom to the throne room.

Of course everyone looks so silly in feathers and veils, like a sort of super confirmation, and the trains are of course rather ridiculous, and nothing but females, with a smattering of male escorts in lovely uniforms I must admit. But court dress, which Daddy was in, is very ridiculous and Froggy-would-a-wooing-go-ish. Eventually we filed into the throne room (leaving Daddy outside), with very much the feeling of confirmation candidates. The throne room is exactly like a very secular church. It is a huge high cavernous room.

The King and Queen, she looked delicious in a very lovely high tiara, which was obviously very uncomfy so she had to keep easing it, and he looking very sunburnt and handsome in Air Force uniform, sat looking very small and young at the end of the room, in two enormous thrones. Somehow the whole procedure seemed out of date, impersonal and very ridiculous. I should have thought it would obviously be one of the first Court ceremonials to die out.

Courts did not take place during the war, but were resumed until the Duke of Edinburgh caused them to be dropped in 1958. The rest of the summer was spent dancing most nights and sleeping all morning – before the habitual lunch date.

Dances varied; some were agony and some fun. If you were not dancing, then, rather than be a wallflower, you took refuge in the ladies' cloakroom and sat praying for your mother to come and take you home. At one dance there began a rumour that an extraordinary lady had climbed into the bed in the lady's cloakroom and was sitting under all the mink coats and wraps with her letters spread around her. My heart sank – I knew immediately who it was. When I went to see, my mother greeted me merrily: 'It's all right darling, I'm here, go and enjoy yourself. I've got lots to do'.

Everyone else's mother was sitting sedately on 'the bench' watching to see that their little darlings weren't dancing too often with the same man.

My mother was determined that my time was not entirely wasted and, having apparently spotted that I seemed to have some latent interest in art, fixed that I should be coached by a nice young man of the Byam-Shaw family – as an art critic. Poor fellow, he had a dismal task, as my head was full of young men and parties and had no room for much else.

Before that, the most absorbing event of the period had been the Abdication in December 1936. This was a great shock and was treated with enormous seriousness. Stories had circulated for some time about the King and Mrs Simpson, but only in certain circles, not in the press. There had been a fierce argument at Nannau during the summer, when Sir Dougal Malcolm[1], who was a friend of Cosmo Gordon Lang, the Archbishop of Canterbury, had said that the Archbishop was quite ready to accept the situation if she remained the King's mistress but that marriage was out of the question. The young Grenfells were outraged at such hypocrisy. Their more Edwardian elders were less dogmatic.

When the news broke, every paper was read, everyone consulted, and Geoffrey Dawson, editor of *The Times*, who had married my mother's cousin Cecilia Lawley, came to dinner whenever he was free. My father felt a sense of betrayal. The Prince of Wales had been at the Front in the 1914-18 war, and although not allowed in the front line, the fighting men thought that it was where he wanted to be. My father felt that his

---

1. Sir Dougal Malcolm (1877-1955), President of the British South Africa company, a close friend of Cecil Rhodes, and Sir Leander Jameson, of the Jameson Raid. He had been Private Secretary to Lord Selborne in South Africa from 1905 to 1910.

generation had sacrificed everything for their country, and now suddenly the Prince was 'ducking out'. This was the line that Queen Mary took. My mother realised that it was a great personal tragedy for Queen Mary and the rest of the Royal Family, and it just added to her general feeling of malaise.

At the height of the crisis I was due to go to a dance, escorted by a young man called 'Tim' Egerton. My parents had quite a fierce argument about whether it was appropriate for us to go. My mother took the line that to appear to be celebrating at such a moment was wrong. My father thought exactly the opposite – that it was a moment to celebrate as we would probably get a splendid young King. 'Tim' and I were determined to go and so we went.

Years later, when I found myself sitting next to Sir Seymour Egerton, Chairman of Coutts' Bank, at a lunch party at Clarence House, we found that we both remembered the occasion vividly, particularly the evening paper posters flapping in the wind in a totally deserted Belgrave Square with the one word 'Abdication', which made us feel strange and apprehensive.

In the summer of 1937, Laura left school to go to Germany and then on to Oxford. Cricket always had a central place in our lives. We absorbed the Church of England from our mother, and cricket from our father. In my letters to Laura, sadly exiled to a cricket-free world, I wrote of matches I had gone to on my own, and how New Zealanders were defeated after making a sporting declaration and other highlights.

Ever since we were both small, one of the high spots of our social year was the Eton and Harrow cricket match at Lord's each July. We were allowed new outfits for it – dress *and* hat, sometimes even a long dress. My father hired a coach from Bertram Mills's circus, which was towed to Lord's the day before the match started and placed on a mound to the right of the pavilion. By climbing a small ladder up to the top, we were able to see over the heads in the stand.

The site for the coach was inherited by my father from his

father. Aunt Lola always put in a highly partisan appearance. The men wore top hats, tail coats and suitable button-holes, Etonians sporting carnations dyed light blue, and Harrovians genuine cornflowers. I wrote Laura a long description of the match.

Besides the family, the party on the coach were Bob Palmer, a Wykehamist and younger son of Lord and Lady Selborne, our cousins, Lewis Dawnay and Cynthia Shaw-Stewart, Charles Fletcher, a young doctor who was to become an eminent professor and an expert among other skills on lung disease in miners, and Dougal Malcolm, an old friend of both our parents, who had spoken of the Abdication and the Archbishop.

At seventeen it was irreverent of me to refer to him as 'little Dougy', but he crossed the generations, and we looked on him as much as our friend as theirs. He and his wife were childless, but they had had Laura and me to stay weekends with them in their country cottage since we were quite young. He was short and plump, with a mane of white hair, a large white moustache, with a straight gaze from amused but somewhat mournful eyes. He was later to help Harry's career in Africa. He frequently stayed at Nannau, and was also a patient of Plesch's and narrowly survived his ministrations during the war. Later in life he had links with my in-laws as he came of the family of the Malcolms of Portalloch, who lived in Argyll. He liked accuracy. On a Sunday evening, I wrote to Laura:

I am seething.

We had a wonderful Eton and Harrow. Raining and depressing Friday and rainy beginning to Saturday, and then phew! Harrow made a very sporting declaration after tea, left the Etonians about 150 to make in 1½ hrs. We, of course didn't think they'd try, typically, but they went for it. It meant over 1½ runs a minute. Good pace, with a very bad first innings score behind them. In the first over an Etonian was missed.

Daddy and I were meant to be dining with the Dawnays at 7.30 in white ties. Did we ever look like being in time? It would have taken the Golden Arrow or Queen Mary to move Pop an inch. Luckily the Dawnays couldn't leave either. We had on our coach Reg and Harry, Bob Palmer and Charles Fletcher, Lewis, Cynthia, Dougie, Vera and me. At the most exciting moments when Etonians were hitting 4's round the place the whole coach swayed and I turned round to see Harry and Reg dancing madly in the back half of the coach, arms waving, in a complete Ginger Rogers/Astaire style.

Lewis's face was the colour of a healthy red begonia. He sat beside me on the front seat, absolutely silent, his arms clasped round him. All he said was, 'Don't talk to me or I shall be sick. I think Uncle Arthur is having a fit.' His mouth was shut in the firm tho' windy line of a man determined to keep his dinner down. He said later his heart moved at least 2 inches.

Nothing can describe Daddy. He sat like a very small boy on the edge of his seat, his overcoat wrapped round him, shivering with excitement and yelling like a six-monther. I never knew he had such lungs. 'Well played Ee-eton' – 'Eeton' – 'Well hit Sir' – 'Hit it' – 'Play up Eee-ton'.

Little Dougy was purple with excitement dancing on his behind, covering his match cards with calculations. He was so excited he kept forgetting how many runs they had to make in how many minutes, so every second he had to work it out again. I was so excited I felt as if I had no diaphragm at all. I was also laughing so and clutching the side of the coach as Reg and Harry swayed it wildly about with their native dances.

All the old Salisburys were on the next coach. Lady Salisbury, as Lavinia would no doubt express it, laying eggs violently, with all the appropriate noises. Lord Salisbury waving his hat wildly. Lords was echoing with cries and counter cries. The stands at the nursery end opposite us kept shouting 'How's that?' every time an Etonian touched the ball. R and H always answered 'Not out', you know like they do. It was a wonderful hour. They only did it with ten minutes to spare. If it hadn't been for one over when Mann hit the Harrovian Captain for 17, we mightn't have done it. Harrow really deserve the credit for a very sporting declaration. Dad has written Watson, the

Harrovian Captain, a tremendous letter all about saving schoolboy cricket for the Empire v Turkey etc etc . . .

When it was over and we got off the coach, Daddy and Lady Salisbury nearly kissed each other in their excitement. O how I longed for you. It was the best party of the whole summer. I think I was wrong. I couldn't marry a Wykehamist, they don't get excited enough. I think I'll marry Mann, he hit jolly well yesterday.

Isolated in Baden-Baden, Laura reacted strongly to this:

Your letter about the Eton and Harrow upset me more than words can say. I should have completely dissolved into tears, and may do so any moment now. But I roared with laughter at the same time. Gosh what fun it must have been – how I wish I'd been there. I can imagine you all – oh you lucky things – I don't feel this year at all right, its now got an awful hole and everything's funny. But please don't you stop writing about anything because you think it'll make me homesick or anything, as I love hearing it all.

The Eton and Harrow match continued as a social occasion into the 1970s, Harry inheriting the coach entitlement from our father. But as times changed, new stands were built at Lord's and there was no more room for coaches. Now, although the match is still played at Lord's, it has lost its special flavour.

During my year as a deb, I went to a party at Ditchley, in Oxfordshire, given by Mr and Mrs Ronnie Tree. This was the house later famous as a wartime retreat for Winston Churchill, 'when the moon was high' and Chequers too visible a target for German bombers. At the time I recorded that 'the flowers were magical, jewellery and diamonds everywhere . . . Crinolines in fashion again, one of the Paget girls in a white crinoline with wire petticoats and all. Lovely, of course, but quite impractical in these days with small houses.' I certainly got caught up in this way of life, as I told Laura:

The more I see it the more the glamour of life as lived by Reg and Joyce among high-spirited young people and old people who have achieved something – vast fortunes and lovely houses – fascinates me. The awful danger of marrying young seems to me to be premature middle-agedness and lack of progress. Having got all you want in the way of husband and children, you just sit with your hands on your stomach and don't stir except when the fifth housemaid gives notice; then you have fits for a month. For heavens sake let's avoid it.

I wrote to Laura to describe a splendid day when Reggie and I and various of Joyce's relations went to Ascot thanks to the kindness of Lord Astor. We had expected to go on the wrong side with the gypsies, but Lord Astor got us into the paddock:

He also said he would give us a lift in the Cliveden car, to Ascot. Then a butler brought in a tray of race cards. We rather sheepishly took one each, feeling a little guilty. Then Lord Astor came in. He said 'Have you got Race Cards, if not take some, I'm getting your Paddock tickets and lunch tickets. O Frances you'd like a buttonhole, Bill give her one (a tray was brought in with orchids, carnations etc, all made up). Have you got field glasses, here are some.' Never in two minutes have I been given so much. We then discovered a whole car had been ordered just for us. Cost about £5 to park. When we arrived Lord A gave us our Paddock tickets at £1.10 each, gave us our lunch tickets, probably 10/- each. He really is charming.

Laura was leading a more serious life in Baden-Baden, working hard and attending concerts and opera and complaining that the other English girls in the pension weren't trying, but merely filling in time. Even so the prospect of endless academic work sometimes got her down and at one moment she said that she would not go to Oxford, whatever arguments in favour. In July 1937 she wrote:

If I don't go to Oxford, I shouldn't educate myself ever any more. And every female of our class does that, and obviously the men don't find them interesting at all – and talk down to females all the time. Honestly when I think of people like Vyvyan, who will be coming out next year – just 17. Looking at it as a complete job – an eternal round of fork lunches – hairdressers tea and cinema – dance – dressmaker – its enough to make one feel really sorry for every male she meets – yet I suppose every single debutante is just the same and equally brainless. The silly thing is – that girls could be quite sensible and intelligent if only they didn't always live up to talking-down of the men. This is very complicated.

The family's fortunes began to slip during 1937. The assays from the goldfields were proving controversial, and my father's financial backers began to be wary of further investments. My father's optimism and belief in the enterprise remained undimmed, but in the meantime the profits from the Albanian chrome mines were diverted to pay the workforce on the goldfields. By the autumn we had moved into the mews flat, and the Rolls Royce became an early casualty.

While we had lived in the luxurious maisonette on the top three floors of No. 36 Chesham Place, the ground floor of the next-door house, No. 37, had been acquired as my father's office. This consisted of three large reception rooms, with a passage leading to a couple of rooms for secretaries and the basement, where there were one or two bedrooms, a bathroom and a kitchen, as well as a bedroom and bathroom in an annexe, looking into a small basement garden. From this garden was the back entrance to the mews flat, the erstwhile quarters of the Rolls Royce chauffeur. It had a few rooms and a bathroom, the water heated by a gas geezer which not infrequently blew up.

Extraordinarily, as children, we had never been given a specific account of the details or trauma our parents suffered in 1913-14. They never whined or complained, nor expressed bitterness. As we grew up in the 20's and 30's we appreciated that pre-war life and post-war life were totally different. Pre-war it had been a golden age in which, apparently, almost everyone was rich and prosperous. This excellent way of life was shattered by the war. The loss that had struck our parents was subsumed in the loss suffered by everyone, loss of money being considered not so dire in comparison with so many devastated lives. We never knew that Arthur had been declared bankrupt.

This meant that we never understood the agony Hilda must have gone through facing a re-run of events. I tried to sum this up to Laura at the time:

Whoopee we're up the spout.

Mummy is having minor nervous breakdown at Chewton. Daddy and I are here with lots of bills and no money. Anyhow we're either broke or not broke within the next 10 days.

Actually life has been very very funny. Mum and Dad went to Chew for the weekend. Ma started with a cold and by the time she got to Chew her voice had gone. So Mary firmly kept her there in bed and rang up Plesch, who said: 'Give Ma such a hot bath she would go nearly crazy. Put her to bed without drying her. Put all available blankets etc on the bed, leave for 2 hours. Take her out (Mary thought still wet) then wash her in vinegar'.

All Mary wanted to find out was whether it actually did Ma any harm to have no voice, if not why not keep voice away as long as poss. Plesch won't listen. He probably sweated his own ears off without drying them.

Darling, guess what I have been chored into. St John's YWCA Hostel damn it. I thought it would be better than nothing, but alas I was wrong once more. Ma put me on the Finance (don't laugh) committee. And having failed, conspicuously, to add up the budget I was given all the donkey work to do. Lists for 3 days. O God. Whoopee, let's be cheerful. The words of the latest jazz tune are 'What do I care if it rains and snows, I can weather the storm, because I've got my love to keep me warm.' Ha ha to you old girl. No more news.

Soon afterwards I wrote again to Laura:

Life does seem to be so all over the shop. But I am at that stage, which comes in every season, when I am sick of all my clothes, all my friends, all my conversation and all my effort. I am really very happy, only just now it does seem rather difficult to know how to plan things. I know you feel the same about your plans. One seems to be torn between what one knows one is, and what other people, eg Mummie, thinks one is. I wrote in joke about Mum's plans for you and me the other day, but the aggravating point is that although they are jokes to us, they are absolutely serious to her. Once she sees a picture of us as Lady Mayoresses of Paddington, she sees no obstacles, not even the fact that we are us, if you get me. One knows oneself an ordinary person, with moderate brains and no ambitions, except family ones (!) who with any luck, will amble through life as someone's wife. Ma seems to view marriage as a crime! But damn it, what can one do? Ma is mad about the dowdy interesting life for us. With the result we fall between two stools, no one asks us to their parties, and we aren't yet dowdy and interesting, thank God.

Honestly you know I should go to Oxford. If you only want to get in, no scholarship, everyone I know who really knows eg Mary says it is potty. Once you are in you can do any subject you like. Term is only six months of the year. And as you are absolutely sure of wanting to do something after your season, it would be much more pleasant than any form of London University, or hanging around home wondering how to fill the next six months, like me. No one expects you to be brilliant, and as it is practically impossible to fail any exam at Oxford, you'd always get through.

I went shopping with Joyce the other day. We bought nothing, but marched up and down the streets and round and round the shops having a heated religious argument, which was rather fun. She explained Christian Scientism to me, and as she explains it, it is much more interesting and less footling than it appears. The real answer is that one must never despise or jeer at any religion really beloved by anyone, because if they really believe in any religion, it is the only thing in the world which isn't of immediate material advantage to themselves, so they are almost certainly quite sincere. And sincerity is always worth listening to. Pardon me, what a letter. Please remember when you read this that I am writing at midnight, having had a late night last night.

The greatest difference between Joyce and us was the religious one, which we equated with the American culture she brought. We were not a deeply religious family, apart from Hilda, but the Church of England was a part of us. It represented a normal way of life. We went to church on Sunday, as there was not much else to do. One of the mysterious hypocrisies which caused us but occasional thought was that while we went to church our beds were made, our rooms were cleaned (it was not encouraged to lie in bed in the mornings), and a full lunch including roast beef was cooked, usually for a number of people including the vicar. No one seemed to worry if the 'servants' wanted to go to church; Joyce went to church on Wednesday evenings.

Christian Science flourished in the 1930's. Lady Astor proselytized vigorously and many 'society' families were converted. Although Reggie's devotion to Joyce was total it was the one path down which he could not travel. Jokes were banded about, and Reggie told of a healing service he had attended where a witness gave evidence of having whooping cough, chicken pox and mumps at the same time. When asked his verdict on the remarkable cure that ensued, Reggie said he understood that in the Church of England we usually had these diseases at spaced intervals. Joyce herself was not past some self-mocking when she and Virginia Graham wrote a (private) poem.

We are two Christian Scientists with colds in our noses,
We can't taste the onions, we can't sniff the roses,
Though everyone's kind and says dears 'what a shame',
They're terribly, terribly bucked all the same!

Tho' we've muffled our coughs with considerable stealth,
We're not very good adverts for Science and Health,
But although we are glum that our faith we've betrayed
We refuse to drink whiskey in hot lemonade
We refuse to take Aspros or go to our bed
We're just going to stay here and see that it spreads.
And we offer you now on most generous terms
Our very erroneous mythical germs.
Just to show you you've really made one crack to meddy
Here's a whopping big cold from our dear Mrs Eddy.

Preferring peace to confrontation, and finding himself between his much loved stepmother and much loved wife, Reggie presently gave up church going altogether and never divulged any religious views.

My letters went on describing a different favourite young man constantly, against a background of family financial disaster. I wailed: 'My whole life is spent listening to Mum on Bishops and Life, and Daddy on Mandates.' At that time Tanganyika, a mandate of Great Britain, where the gold mines were, was in danger of being handed back to Germany with disastrous financial results for us. I also complained that our mother was all over the place: 'One can't make plans without her, yet she is never there to make them with'. But I did strike a cheerful, if surprising note in one letter from North Wales:

As to your question, are we living poorly, anybody might think we were millionaires. We have a footman in livery, thousands of housemaids, kitchen maids, cars. Maria and all her children are here, the weather the last fortnight has been glorious, and all our spirits are, I think rising. Mum is being quite good and resting a certain amount. Not writing too many letters and coming on expeditions and things with all of us and the children. With business as it is she only gets the hump sitting in bed alone.

I am probably going to Canada this autumn.

We have been having the Eisteddfod all this week. We went to lovely concert the other night with Harriet Cohen, and conducted by Adrian Boult. V and I went to the chairing of the Bard which was quite fun. Lloyd George made a long speech in Welsh. The Nationalists are trying to wreck it all. The power station with all the electric light for the main Pavilion and the town was burnt out the other night. It is said by the Nat's. They made a scene during God Save the King last night. They are damn fools.

By now we were inhabiting 36 Lyall Mews, previously the chauffeur's flat:

I am feeling a little hysterical, as I am meant to be procuring Produce of every nature for an Xmas Food Market in aid of the club. I have written round the various people with large gardens and they all answer and say they would love to send rabbits. I have now got about 6 doz rabbits – 72 rabbits. I ask you. Who wants 72 rabbits?

We drove to Gregynog and enjoyed an evening of music from a choir conducted by Adrian Boult, and Walford Davies, the organist of St George's Chapel, Windsor. Walford Davies told us that as she walked up the aisle of Westminster Abbey in the Coronation procession, Princess Margaret asked Princess Elizabeth: 'Shall we see Uncle David today?' The reply came: 'Shsh. Of course not, he's married Mrs Baldwin!'

FIVE

Patrick

EARLY IN 1938 it was finally decided that I should go to Canada. Fortunately I was not to be consigned to the care of strangers.

Susie Tweedsmuir was the closest person to my mother after her own sisters, possibly closer. When she realised that my parents were concerned about my future, she immediately invited me to Canada to alleviate some of my mother's strain. The Tweedsmuirs' youngest son, Alastair, was only a week younger than me. Elsfield, where they lived in Oxfordshire, was a house where we often made a day trip from London, playing with the Buchan boys, while our parents talked. Their only sister Alice was a contemporary of our eldest sister Mary.

John, Lord Tweedsmuir, was a more distant figure than Susie. Better known as the author John Buchan, he was a distinguished man with an aquiline face and a wiry frame. He was Scottish and therefore, to us, mysterious and romantic. He wore plus fours in the country, and was a walker who strode across the Border hills of his native Scotland and the Oxfordshire countryside. We knew that the *Thirty-Nine Steps*, his most famous novel, was named after the steps down to the beach where he and his children holidayed at a seaside resort. We also knew he suffered very bad health due to his war service, and that he had been a patient of Plesch who had pronounced a strange diagnosis for him. He maintained that John's false teeth did not fit and therefore caused him to filter air through his teeth. This in turn was responsible for ulcers due to air locks. He prescribed insulin with near fatal results.

John's friendship with our parents went back into the pre-war past when he had been a friend of my twin uncles Francis and Rivy, and in 1920 wrote a memoir of them, a bestseller at the time. He had been a Conservative MP, entertaining many Oxford undergraduates. John kept an eye on those he saw emerging with talent. One he spotted was Jo Grimond. Then, in 1935 he went to Canada as Governor-General and was given a peerage as Lord Tweedsmuir.

I had reason to look forward to this trip with excitement. When seeing me off, Geoffrey Waldegrave said, a trifle wearily: 'I hope this investment will pay.'

The Buchans asked me to stay, with the idea that later I might go to work in the Grenfell Mission in Labrador, founded by our cousin, Wilfrid Grenfell, to succour Eskimos. At much the same stage in her life, Katie had gone there and had had a rough time, acting as a crew member on a boat sailing to remote Eskimo settlements up the Labrador coast in extremely rough weather.

In February 1938 I set out in the Canadian Pacific liner, *Duchess of Bedford*. My father had written to everyone involved on the Canadian Pacific Railway, and so I was afforded a splendid send-off and almost photographed for the Press. When the manager took his hat off to me, one of the pressmen asked who I was, only to be told: 'I don't know. But she's only third class.'

The ten day voyage opened my eyes considerably. After some days of being unremittingly sick, I managed to recover and take my place at the purser's table, which I thought very smart. Here I was regaled with many hair-raising stories about people breaking legs from being hurled about or crushed by moving pianos in rough weather. The purser's stories invariably ended with women fainting and not reviving for days. A Canadian airman invited me for a drink, and surprised me by the quantities he consumed. I shocked the deck waiter by asking for water.

Amongst my fellow voyagers was a lady who asked me to tea and entranced me with the gripping saga of her husband being murdered, and how her sister was in the power of a Scotch lawyer married to a black lady. In a letter to Laura I wrote:

There was a lot about a will and Attorney Generals, the King and Queen and dear Princess Beatrice and a lot about the evilness of life and wickedness of Jews etc. I found she was a violent partisan of the Arabs in Palestine. She informed me we had no more right to talk of our country as 'free' than the Germans. Everything from our newspapers to our farms were run by Jews, that there were more German Jew refugees in London than Londoners etc.

The trip continued with a mad Scotchwoman, Burmese and Norwegian sailors, Canadian mothers, hard-headed airmen, and Admiral's daughters:

I must say I nearly died of giggles when Mrs Brooks started quoting me long extracts from her husband's love letters and finally cried on my shoulder. I consider I stood up to it like a Trojan and carried it all off as though it was quite normal.

Presently I arrived in Halifax, where I was met by a Colonel Oland, who swept me through customs, bundled me into a large car and took me to his house. After showing me round Halifax, he put me on a train with all my luggage and I was reunited with my fellow voyagers, including the Canadian airman who took me under his wing, explained all the tipping difficulties, and gave me fatherly and useful advice about managing my sleeping quarters, and told me what food to eat. He also explained the countryside, through which the train took us, and generally educated me about Canada. Nevertheless, when I arrived in Ottawa, I was in quite a dither of fright.

This soon vanished as I was welcomed to Government House. It was a world of warm fires, deep carpets and cosiness, perhaps not the best environment for an impecunious girl, though good training for my eventual life as a lady-in-waiting.

Susie Tweedsmuir was entertaining some women curlers to tea, so I was looked after by the wife of Shuldham Redfern, the Governor-General's Secretary, and the Governor-General himself:

He is quite the nicest man in the world and made me feel at home at once. In a short three quarters of an hour we covered every subject from Laura's height to the state of the United States (from which incidentally he said he'd had very disturbing reports and he thought they were in a bad way). He has a fascinating way of suddenly breaking into strong Scotch dialect, which makes conversation a little hard to follow at moments. When he starts telling a story, however trivial, you find yourself spellbound.

After tea I was shown my room. It is next door to Susie's and large, cosy and comfortable with a cheerful blazing fire. Opposite is my own bathroom! Soon after this Susie appeared and took me into her room where we had a family gossip. She is a darling too, and obviously very popular here. Dinner was at 7.30 as they had to go off to a lecture, which Susie advised me to miss, so I am lying now on the sofa in my room writing this. There was only the ADC, Patrick Campbell-Preston, who appears to be a red faced bouncing cheerful young Scotchman – and a doctor and the Ex's to dinner.

So far there has been no curtseying, but I rather fear this may be my mistake. Dinner went alright, except that when offered port I naturally said no, saw Susie shoot me an agonized glance – too late – and realized I had bungled the toast. Luckily John drank it in water, so I thought I wasn't in bad company and took a good swig at my water. Also slightly awkward owing to the fact my trunk didn't arrive before dinner, so I had to wear my bedroom slippers and pretend they were my smartest evening shoes. This wasn't made easy by the fact that not so long ago one of Katie's dogs had a good go at their toe with its teeth. I am delighted to hear all women are expected to have breakfast in bed, a really civilized idea I think.

At last I have seen an up to date paper which I haven't done for 10 days. It all seems very remote, but looks as though you must be having a hair raising time in London. Out here no one seems to think it matters much what happens to Austria. The distances are so enormous. Austria must seem to them like a flea, it's so small . . .

Apparently the sister of one of the ADC's Peggy Campbell-Preston, is staying here too. She is away skiing this week-end. Everyone says she is charming, so it will be rather fun having some one to ask advice of. They talk of nothing but skiing and skating, so obviously I shall have to swallow my dignity and cope. Susie says she skates with a chair which helps. So I'll skate with two. One to hold onto and one to sit on.

Soon after my arrival Susie wrote to my mother, with different ideas from mine:

Frances arrived safely bearing a letter from you and one from Arthur. She and I are already friends, and I am hoping she is going to enjoy herself here. I am very glad she is interested in people, as at this time of the year it is not possible to get about much. But there are a great many people to see, and a lot of parties going on. So that is just as it should be.

As regards her food; she may find it a little difficult here, as we are supposed to have the best cook in North America, and I must say I think the food is on the fattening side; but she never need eat bread as we always have Rye-vita, for it suits John better than anything else. I will have a chat with her to see what we can do to give her the right diet . . .

Susie was intending to sail home on 22 April and asked my mother if she wanted me to stay until then and sail back with her, exhorting my mother not to change her plans too often.

As each day passed my stage fright diminished. I began to enjoy myself enormously, largely due to the kindness and charm of everyone at Government House, including the ADCs and one in particular:

The military one is called Patrick Campbell Preston and is fat and very kind and with a giggle. He is in the Black Watch and was at

Eton and Sandhurst with Pat. He is very Scotch and so adored his
Ex, and both Susie and the Ex say he is like a second son. The first
day I was here we were both awfully polite about how jolly skiing
was and skating and how we loved out of door exercise etc etc. After
about an hour of this we both discovered actually we thought skiing
couldn't be more uncomfy, that when everyone was out of sight we
took our skis off and walked home, and that skating hurt from the
head down to the knees and from the ankles up to the nose. But that
anyhow it was all very funny and great fun. He has got a most
awfully nice sister staying here who is returning unfortunately
tomorrow. She has initiated me into Ottawa social life and has been
quite charming.

For the next few months my letters were filled with my attempts
to ski, and descriptions of parties where guests got drunk, and the
adventure of acquiring my first permanent wave. But above all,
Patrick took centre stage. One day the Tweedsmuirs, he and I
took a stroll together:

I was quite at home and exchanging outrageous statements about
mutual friends with John (Tweedsmuir!). He is a fascinating person
with little reserve, a slight Scotch accent and lisp and a power of
making you think he really is desperately interested in you and what
you are saying – Susie is also a darling, very cosy and with a big bit
of Mummy in her, and a faint trace of Mary. She is frightfully
popular and works very hard. The ADC is charming too. He is
rather Scotch, plump and cosy and nice with a good giggle, and
Susie adores him. Yesterday evening we were bundled off for a tête-
à-tête and never drew breath for two hours!

Government House was run like a cosy house-party. The
Tweedsmuirs were perfect hosts, perhaps a little distant. They
combined dignity with friendliness and left nothing to wish for.
John Tweedsmuir never forgot a name or face and was most
popular. He remembered people's pet subjects and his Scotch side

went down well with the Scottish people in Canada. His outlook had become Canadian.

He was more than ably supported by Susie, who was adored by the Canadians. She had real sympathy for their problems and undertook her role with quiet dignity. It was said that the French Canadians adored her even more. Robin Scott, the Naval ADC, and Patrick, relished all the compliments paid to the Governor-General and his wife. Personally I was relieved to find it all less pompous than had been suggested in England. There was only curtseying because the Canadians liked it, and even so, this only happened for a first greeting in the morning and last thing at night, unless guests were present.

While I was at Rideau Hall, giving cheerful accounts of my life there, Laura was having a less happy time. She left Germany to stay with a family in Geneva and attended the International School with the hope of learning French quickly. Her diary recorded the worsening political situation: 'Scare in Austria, German troops entering – Schussnig' – 'Polish ultimatum to Lithuania. Rumour Hitler in Hungary' and 'Killing telegram from Reg "Regarding your letter there's no need to worry as there's nothing to worry about".'

Far away from all that in Canada, John Tweedsmuir would analyse the political situation by leaning back and placing wine glasses round his table, mimicking my father and saying: 'Here is Germany!' I was amused that people I met outside Government House used to think it must be very intellectual and stimulating, little realising that the reality might find Susie giggling over the *New Yorker* and John eagerly awaiting his *Tatler*. One night at dinner, caught for conversation, I volunteered: 'Have you heard there's a peacock's nest in the garden?' to which the Governor-General replied: 'But my dear Frances there aren't any peacocks in Canada.'

John Tweedsmuir could be stern about making conversation. He was nearly always in pain from bad duodenal ulcers from the 1914-18 war and was on a strict diet which made long drawn out dinner parties trying. Once, noticing I was sitting silent by a dinner guest, he said loudly all the way down the table: 'Frances – talk!'

In March we set off in the Royal Train, which, the next year, would carry the King and Queen across Canada:

I have just returned from Winnipeg, and living for very nearly a week on the train. Gee boy what a train too. Never have you known such comfort in your life. We had a special carriage built ten years ago for the Governor-General. The 'cars' as they are called out here are twice the size they are in the Old Country. One carriage consisted of the ADCs' office, bedroom and bathroom (!) and kitchens etc. – also a dining room, and a staff drawing room. The next carriage consisted of both their Exs' and Her Ex's, rooms and the comic English maid, Annie's room, and their Exs' sitting room. Did you ever? As the big white chief himself didn't come, I slept in his room, in comfort unimaginable, with a private bathroom, a vast bed, an enormous cupboard, colossal chest-o'drawers and oceans of room. Travelling was blissful. The trains out here are said to roll and shake horribly, Joan [Pape – Susie's lady-in-waiting] is sick all the time, Annie is very funny about how they shake her bones, and Her Ex just groans. But I rendered myself very unpopular by revelling in all the comforts and just sleeping the clock round.

There is really very little to see in Winnipeg. You never saw anything so flat as the prairies in your life, not even a mole hill. You get the feeling the world is all sky. I went to the grain exchange and saw them buying and selling grain in what is called the 'pit', which is the grain stock exchange. They were all yelling like a thousand bulls and looked quite mad.

But I liked coming back to Ottawa a whole lot. I feel it's just like home and I have quite as many friends here as in the whole of London. You can't think how nice they are. I have made great friends with Patrick (you dare say out of the frying pan into the fire, because it isn't true so there) who is one of the world's nicest people. He took me the other night to hear a debate in the House of

Commons. It was all about Social Credit, and neither of us heard or understood one word, and we both got the most awful giggles. We did hear Mr [Richard Bedford] Bennett, the leader of the opposition, who is a very good speaker, but he spoke about the finances of the bank of Canada, which was more Greek to both of us.

By this time I was being assiduously courted by Patrick, but unable to admit to it openly in my letters home. A crisis arose when time came for the Tweedsmuirs to return home on their mid-term leave. My mother began pressing for some decision on my future. I had no intention of leaving Canada or my close proximity to Patrick. I was thrilled when my mother said I could stay on.

To this aim, I conjured up a catalogue of plans. I could join the Grenfell mission in Newfoundland or I might drive a lorry across the prairies distributing bibles – said to have been done by a cousin Jean McDonell. This plan was vetoed by Joan Pape on the rounds that no kid should do such a thing. I then thought Susie might negotiate a railway pass so that I could go west. At that point Joan Pape went home, and I was called on to act as Susie's lady-in-waiting in her place. I was in my element:

I have actually been quite busy doing mild L-in-W'ing. To-night there is an enormous dinner party and as far as I can see I shall have to do the L-in-W after dinner when the ladies retire. This consists of bringing people up to speak to Her Ex. and giving everyone cigarettes and seeing the right people talk to each other. I shall be terrified. But rather fun really. I am always given all the deaf people to talk to after dinner as I shout at them. It is a most comic performance these dinner parties. You are all sat down in different corners of the room, and people are brought up to you to talk to, and after about ten minutes they are whisked away and someone else brought. The boys spend their time running round moving people. I have become a professional conversationalist now and am really hot stuff.

Last night I sat next the Prime Minister Mr Mackenzie King when he came for dinner, rather smart, what? I had a raging success with him. He was rather a good friend of Daddie's, and so he rather liked me. He is a very cosy looking little man, and as Robin said he looks like a little bear. He came to dinner after both their Exes and the two boys and I went off to see 'Snow White and the Seven Dwarfs', the long Walt Disney film which is the rage out here, and is absolutely delicious. Go and see it if you can. I shall never forget that evening. It was in the middle of the European crisis. When he arrived the Prime Minister said: 'I have been having an awful day'. We all clucked suitable sympathy, and I had a swift vision of him hanging on the end of the telephone to London waiting at any moment to hear the British Empire was at war.

Breathlessly we said, why, the G.G. looking a little bored, when the P.M. said Pat's ill. The G.G. leapt about two foot in the air both ADCs rose eagerly with misery written on their faces, and hung on his lips with bated breath, nervously I said to Pat: 'How near a relation?' Pat gave me a look and said 'It's his dog, he's 15 years old, so it is dangerous.' The story isn't much exaggerated.

I am busy trying to keep up Her Ex.'s spirits, which come down on the slightest provocation. His Ex. is ill too, and has been for about a week, so she isn't in very good form. I am typing in her sitting room, which she seems to like, though it would drive me wild if I had to try and write a letter to Queen Mary which she is doing.

Presently the 'Government House Romance' came to fruition when Patrick and I became engaged. We had only known each other for two months. Laura had received some advance warning in my letters, but was still taken aback by the speed of resolution. She was bewildered by the news that we were truly engaged, particularly as she only knew Patrick through my descriptions to her. She asked for more:

Do give me all details about Patrick – is he in a regiment that goes abroad a lot, ie will you become a Poona-ite? Will you live in

England, Scotland and London (when not in Poona)? Do all the
fascinating things like heart palpitations and secret glances animate
your life now – or is that just in books? I expect it just makes you
sleep more. Joan Pape says that's your great claim to fame. How I
wish there was an air mail service across the ocean. What a world,
talk about Hitler's coups d'état, you beat it by several lengths.

Laura joked that until now she had thought the Black Watch
was a beetle. Having established that the regiment wore a black
kilt, she asked: 'But what does it watch why and where?'

All this was made more complicated by the slow means of
communication. Patrick and I both wrote to our respective
parents, and then had to wait an agonizing ten days for their
replies. The telephone was impossible, not only because of the
expense, but because the reception was so bad that it was
unthinkable to break such news to deaf parents by that means.
Letters went by boat, mostly CPR liners. You read the shipping
news daily in the newspapers to see which boats were sailing in
the near future, and you then aimed your letter to catch that
particular sailing. Eventually we got a sheaf of telegrams from our
families – much to our relief.

I was nineteen when I got engaged – to a young man my parents
had never met. I had a discouraging record for falling in and out
of love regularly which was unlikely to encourage my parents,
and on top of that the heady atmosphere of a Government House
frequently led to romances which were hard to sustain. Secretly I
rather hoped there might be a smidgen of opposition – enabling
me to prove my case. Most ungratifyingly, there was none. The
news caused my father to cable: 'Well done the Black Watch
congratulations and love'. This touching letter followed:

Mum delivered your bombshell to me just as I was getting into my
bath and it nearly caused me to be drowned! I hear on all sides that
Patrick is in every way the sort of man I would have chosen for you.
I am sure he is and I can't say how delighted I am and how warmly

we shall welcome him into the family circle. Money, that cursed and elusive thing, is the difficulty.

We must all put our heads together to see how we are going to manage about that; for as you know hopes that I had built up and on which I depended to make you all comfortable crashed heavily last summer and I really don't know whether at my age I am capable of building up again.

We are all building up other castles, perhaps one will stand up and then I will present it to you and Patrick. One can't live an interesting or useful life without optimism and daring – I have had too much of both all my life, perhaps you have them in better proportions. In any case darling our hopes and prayers are that you shall be happy and we will do all we can to help you attain it. Much love to Patrick. Your loving Dad.

From the point of view of Army regulations, we were marrying 'below age'. Officers in the Black Watch were not encouraged to marry before they were thirty; there would be no marriage allowance. But, encouraged by my father's sentiments, I wrote in the same vein:

We will have very little money, but neither of us need money for our happiness and I am certain we can do alright and we are so in love its all that matters isn't it?

To which my father replied by cable:

Inserting notice of Engagement (in The Times) on Monday delay due in order to avoid clashing with the Test Match love Dad.

A serious letter followed on 16 May:

I am only writing you a short scribble as I am dashing off to Lords to see Bradman make his first record. Harry and I saw him make 257 on Saturday – I have never seen better fielding at Lords and the bowling was always good in fact better than the Australian batting except Bradman and he simply made it all look as if small boys were bowling at him. He had to play steady but when he plays a ball he seems to get every muscle and bit of weight right on to the ball at exactly the right moment so that all ordinary play forward goes to the boundary like a flash – sometimes so quick that you can hardly see the ball go and without any effort at all. He really is a marvel – the best we shall ever see – a perfect artist, and yet a funny looking little man like a jockey – always smiling.

I began to learn something of my future life, about Scotland, about the army there. I worried about dancing a reel with flat feet, but I learned what aiglets were and how to unbuckle the various intricacies of military uniforms.

After Susie left for England, John took up residence for a time in the Citadel at Quebec, taking me in his household. It was a lovely place and later in the war became famous when Roosevelt and Churchill met there for a Summit Conference – at which my sister Vera was to be present. I wrote rather reprovingly to Laura:

By the way my dear little undergraduate-to-be, the Citadel is at Quebec, not Toronto. Don't you remember our history book with Woolf climbing the ramparts (he didn't actually 'cos it wasn't there) and after all you don't think the Tower of London is in Birmingham. As an ardent Imperialist I am deeply shocked at you.

In the end I sailed down the St Lawrence River and went home. I felt quite grown-up, with my future settled, convinced that the rest of my life would be one of unalloyed happiness.

SIX

Married Life

Patrick had filled me in with his family background. I learnt that his, like mine, was a close family. They were devoted to their mother and father but their father had died in 1929. Patrick and his elder brother Bobby had both been at Ludgrove and Eton. Patrick was larger than his brother; Bobby was competitive, Patrick relaxed. Patrick had two surviving sisters. His eldest sister Cherry lived in Invernesshire and was married to Ian Fraser of Reelig. Hope, his second sister, had married Neil Ramsay and had died giving birth to a daughter three years before. Patrick's youngest sister Peggy I had met in Canada. She had come home from Canada to marry Raymond Baring, and Tommy the youngest brother was exactly my age and worked in London.

Their home, Ardchattan in Argyllshire, had been a priory built in the 13th century. It is situated on the north side of Loch Etive facing south with a garden that slopes down to the loch. The view extends across the loch and distantly to the hills of Mull. Behind the house is a large walled garden originally cultivated by the monks. One of St Columba's followers, St Modan, is reputed to have founded the priory, and on the hill there is still a spring of water known as St Modan's wishing well. At the time of the Reformation the priory was dissolved, and the property devolved on to a lay prior, a Campbell, a son of the Thane of Cawdor, who, on being given it by Royal Decree installed one of his sons as lay prior. After that the house was turned into a dwelling and a dynasty of Campbells took up residence.

The chapel became a graveyard after it was supposedly destroyed by Cromwell's troops and amongst the graves was that of Colin Campbell of Glenure. He was the victim of the notorious 'Appin Murder', immortalised by Robert Louis Stevenson in his novel, *Kidnapped*.

As Patrick told his family story, what stood out particularly was not only their family loyalty to each other, but the deep roots they had in Scotland, and this house. Coming from a family that moved from London W2 to London SW1 and holidayed in places from Austria to Wales, I was impressed. Patrick was seriously annoyed at not being consulted when his mother wrote to him, in Canada, with the news that she had re-painted the drawing room.

Their history was not confined to Argyll. Patrick's paternal grandfather, the Rev William Clarke, was the son of Mr Clarke of Comrie Castle in Perthshire. Due to the laws of entail, when the male line of Prestons of Valleyfield died out, William had inherited an Adams house with an extensive estate in Fife, through his mother. He assumed the name of Clarke-Preston. The Clarkes had also married into the Campbells of Ardchattan and once more through the female line and the entail law, Patrick's father inherited Ardchattan, adding Campbell to his surname. Eventually Bobby, Patrick and Tommy decided to reduce that to Campbell-Preston.

Patrick's father, Robert Clarke-Campbell-Preston, was five when his father died. He was brought up as a rich young man, went to Eton and Oxford, shot, fished and hunted, encouraged by his Uncle Colley, his trustee and guardian. He travelled round the world, returning in his twenties to find that his uncle had nearly bankrupted him. Valleyfield had to be mortgaged and the estate went deeply into debt. Just as he was about to get married, coal was found under the estate. The whole property was sold and he and his bride went to live at Ardchattan, where they put down deep roots.

In 1909, when he was nearly forty, Bob married Mary (known as Molly) Thorne, aged 20. She was the eldest daughter of Augustus Thorne, a businessman who had inherited a family firm which operated in the Far East, principally China. Apart from some holidays in Scotland, Molly was brought up in London. Her family consisted of three sisters and two brothers. Her mother's sister, Mrs. Maservy, and her husband had both died young leaving three orphans. The Thornes decided to adopt the children and the Maservy children became part of the family. My mother-in-law always regarded them as her siblings – both the Maservy boys were killed in the 1914 war, as was her own brother Thomas. They were all mourned equally. Her other brother Andrew survived the war and went on to become a Major General. (He married Margaret Douglas-Pennant, a distant cousin of my mother's. When she was consulted on our engagement by the Campbell-Prestons as to the credentials of the Grenfells she said: 'Hilda Grenfell is either driving round Belgrave Square in a Rolls Royce, or pushing a pram with all her possessions in it').

Marrying at twenty and moving from London and a home full of children, their friends and numerous activities, Molly took on a new life in a remote part of faraway Argyll. The nearest village was seven miles away and the only transport a pony cart. To get to the main road on the other side of the loch was by boat. Then there was an elaborate arrangement to get horses and a conveyance on the other side. Cars of a sort did arrive shortly after her marriage.

Social life took careful planning and there were no near neighbours. She was fearfully lonely. One day, frustrated and exasperated and dressed in her long Edwardian skirt, she climbed on top of the garden wall and ran round it like a child. The gardener came and helped her down and looking kindly at her said: 'You're young, you're young, but you'll *larn*!' She did.

Molly took to life in Argyll, and never left it for the rest of her life. As the eldest in her family she knew how to exercise authority. One of her nephews said of her: 'I always felt Aunt Molly should be a Cardinal.'

She took up gardening, this becoming a life-long passion. The garden was an important source of produce. Ardchattan had a large walled kitchen garden, in which raspberries, strawberries, apples, plums and a variety of vegetables were grown.

After Cherry (the eldest of the family) was born, the Thornes' family nanny, Ninny, who had reared Molly and was a lady of great character, moved to Ardchattan with Molly. It was an equally extraordinary translation for her. A nanny who had helped to rear the large Thorne/Maservy family in a London nursery never looked back and she and Molly ruled together until her death in 1942. Ninny was a large plump lady and dominated her nursery wing – the children loved her and all lived in the nursery long after they grew out of it. She absorbed their news, administered first aid when necessary, and chuckled at their stories. Bernard Fergusson, who as a friend of Patrick's, came under her spell, wrote a poem in *Punch* for her:

She came a proper Cockney from the sound of the Bells of Bow
To rule in a Highland nursery at the foot of a Western glen;
And since the day of her coming full thirty years ago
She has raised for the world her brood of Highlandmen.

Lorn is far from London, and maybe she used to pine
For the fleet of prams and children and nannies in the Park,
And see in the lonely wildfowl the ducks of the Serpentine
As she gazed across Loch Etive in the dark.

Strange tongues below her window would murmur in the byre
And in the nursery-scuttle lay unaccustomed peat;
She would watch the train to London toil up towards Stratheyre
And dream of buses in a London Street.

Now in an empty nursery she sits alone and sews
At a window facing Cruachan, grown friendly with the years
Grown friendly with the sharing of nursery joys and woes,
The bursts of laughter and the sudden tears.

Her Highlandmen are grown now and scattered far and wide
In dingy English cities or under an Indian sun;
But dreams of the glen that bred them stray back to Etiveside,
They think of Lorn and home and her as one.

Molly had been brought up to take on civic duties and began these in her new home. She supported the development of the District Nurse, a recent and voluntary organization, and was also associated with the Red Cross. She went on later to the Argyll County Council and became the first woman Sheriff substitute in Scotland.

There was never the upstairs-downstairs feeling at Ardchattan – both Molly and Ninny made everyone feel friends. There were twelve servants before the war. Every morning after breakfast Molly would go round and see all of them.

Having arrived home without Patrick, I had to meet my future in-laws alone. His youngest brother met me in London and put me on the night train. I had never been to Scotland or in a sleeper. The third class sleeper had four bunks and the train to Oban was stopped, on request, at a halt on the line on the opposite shore of Loch Etive from Ardchattan. To drive to the station cost an expensive ticket over Connel Bridge, so trains were always met by motorboat from Ardchattan. As we approached the station I got more and more nervous. How did you dress to meet an unknown mother-in-law? A hat? gloves? high heels or country shoes? The other passengers all joined in and a committee discussion developed. Finally the consensus was a hat, no gloves, but best shoes. The train stopped and they came to see me off. There was a gap of about four feet between train and platform. I hesitated, high heels and a hat. There was a stentorian voice from the platform – 'Jump girl for goodness sake!' Clutching my straw hat I jumped and met my future mother-in-law.

I loved Molly at once. I found her a more relaxed and predictable person than my own mother, a better listener and with a more measured approach to problems. It could be said that she was the mother I had longed to have in the moments when my own mother exasperated and embarrassed us. Eventually I found both fitted the pattern of my life – the one complementing the other.

Staying with Molly I drank in some of the ethos of Ardchattan. On all sides the continuity of life impressed me. The first person I had to meet was Ninny in the nursery wing, having already heard from Patrick how much loved she was. Although her nannying days were long over, she still dressed in a clean white apron every day and a nanny uniform and sat in a well-worn chair beside the fire; the toy cupboard still held toys, now played with by the grandchildren. Bobby who, after Oxford, was working in Middlesbrough with Dorman and Long Steelworks, came up on the night train to view me.

Every minute he had on fleeting visits to Ardchattan he had urgent things to see to. Even so, I was quite startled when he ate his luncheon at breakneck speed and then lay flat on the dining room floor saying he had (not surprisingly) violent indigestion. Molly took no notice and after five minutes he pronounced himself cured and shot off. We appraised each other. Bobby looked like Patrick but smaller. They had exactly the same voice. Patrick's eldest sister, Cherry Fraser, came down from her home near Inverness. On first acquaintance she summed a person up with an unblinking stare. She was small, slim, red-headed, pretty and elegant.

As I encountered the stare my clothes complex rose, was I dressed right for this life? To my mind her and Molly's neat outfits seemed to fit into the background, the tartan skirts and twin sets. The first present Molly gave me was a length of tartan material and the name of the London tailor who knew how to make it up. I was also taken round to meet various people who had lived on the estate for generations. Molly was pleased when the verdict of one of them was: 'She'll do – she's *gude* and solid'. I was not feeling it. I had had to drink several glasses of port in the middle of the afternoon.

The nearest relations to be met were Molly's younger sister Nancy, who was married to (Sir) Hew Hamilton Dalrymple and lived in North Berwick. Hew had been almost a surrogate father to Bobby and Patrick and they were devoted to him. He was stone deaf. Nancy was a charming, friendly and warm-hearted favourite aunt. Fortunately for me, owing to having a deaf father, I never had any inhibitions about shouting at the deaf – it came naturally to me. The first afternoon Hew took me for a drive and quizzed me closely about everything, asking me among other things if I was used to being rich or poor? I was able to answer truthfully – both.

On my arrival in London from Canada, I had found my own family more stable. The gold fields crisis was solved and other interests were ticking over – the Albanian chrome selling well. Nannau still went on – even if with fewer grooms and horses. Harry had a new job in Africa working for the British South Africa Company and left shortly after I got back.

Later on that summer there was the Munich crisis and we all realized we were on the brink of war. While visiting Cliveden, Charles Lindbergh, the great American air ace, was reported to have said that as soon as war was declared, Hitler would bomb London with 20,000 bombers. Gas masks were issued to everyone.

This did not help my family's financial position, though the prospect of a war caused them to put their own problems in the background. I too had the problem of not knowing what plans could be made for my wedding to Patrick. Laura's plans for Oxford grew fainter, and Mary got pregnant which caused my worried father to mutter: 'I wish Geoffrey wouldn't . . .' Then, after what seemed a prolonged crisis, Neville Chamberlain, the Prime Minister, flew to meet Hitler and came back waving an agreement announcing 'Peace with honour' – a scene which Queen Elizabeth told me years later she and the King had watched on their new television set in Buckingham Palace.

When Mr Chamberlain appeared on the balcony at Buckingham Palace with the King and Queen we all surged there, the large crowd cheering and waving. It felt as though a death sentence had been removed, or at least postponed. It may not have been peace with honour, and we sensed it might not even be peace, but it gave peace a chance and us time to prepare – not only practically, but mentally.

I hurried home from the Buckingham Palace cheering and insisted on ringing up Patrick. We could only talk for three minutes. We just had time to decide we must marry before Christmas.

In September my mother decided at last to go to Canada with Susie Tweedsmuir and meet Patrick for the first time. They both wrote brave letters home, Patrick being the most surprised. I wrote to Harry in October to report all these doings:

Poor Mum came scampering home from Canada, complete with principles and prayer books and arrived to find peace which was an awful sell and anticlimax. Poor darling she had an awful time owing to being quite convinced she was going to be blown up on her way over. She even went so far as writing us all farewell letters and telling us all to be brave and remember God if she went down. Luckily we got them just before she arrived and after the peace, so we all rather undutifully howled with laughter. If we had got them before we would all quite certainly have put our heads in gas ovens.

I have come up here for a fortnight and I am being initiated into Scotch sport. It appears to be much more blood curdling and nearly as moist as Welsh sport. The animal involved is a stag. Sportsmen appear at about 7 o'clock in the evening dripping and soaked and exhausted, having fallen in rivers and lain in streams and rolled down mountains and apparently been very near death almost all day. The next 24 hours is spent re-stalking and shooting the stag on the hearth rug. I am enjoying it enormously. Anyhow it's bliss after the crisis.

Looking back now there were moments in the crisis which will never be surpassed for funniness. Daddy of course was wonderful. He was convinced we would beat Hitler in 10 days – much more likely he'd have beaten us in four.

Reg of course with a never ending flow of stories from the highest Cliveden smarties all refuting Daddy's lovely castles in the air about

England's supremacy in every possible way. Daddy would come in saying 'Our Air Force is superb, never anything like it in the world. We'll smash this fellow in a week.' Reg sitting there quietly saying 'Col. Lindbergh at Cliveden yesterday said Germany's Air Force was simply superb and we've only got one old bomber.'

Daddy and I went out to dinner one night and met Nina [Lucas – née Grenfell] and Archie. Daddy said 'These air raids aren't half as bad as people make out. You're always sure it's the man next door's going to get hit. Then you hear Bang and you say "hullo",' and Nina said 'O do you Uncle Arthur, I call that awfully restrained. I suppose even when you feel stinging pain down the side you still think it's the other man.'

Plans became more settled and I wrote to Harry that I found Army leave surprisingly lavish:

I am now getting so excited about Patrick's return, in 3 weeks now, I can hardly control myself. We are being married the week of November 20-27 now and we are starting our life in the Army with the monstrously short holiday of 2 months. I don't know how I shall ever manage on what almost amounts to only a week-end. Katie and Pat are much worse off and I wouldn't be surprised if they didn't die of overwork as they only get 5 weeks. Hardly time to decide where to go, too awful. So if you find me thin and frail when you return you will know we have only had 9 months leave.

We finally married on 2 December at St. John's, Smith Square, (which became a concert hall some years after the war). Family finances were still strained so our wedding took a different format to previous family ones. The floral arrangements in the church showed my mother at her most ingenious. Unearthing several laundry baskets, she darted up and down the King's Road buying bargain dried flowers of a Christmassy nature – with spikes of dried rushes, lots of holly and berries. All this was enlivened by a few fresh flowers.

I dreaded this, but it turned out beautifully – and a lot of modern flower decorating fashion caught up with this idea. A few days before the wedding Hermione gave a large reception for us. Joyce wrote:

We had a very successful family wedding on Friday. Frances looked a darling in her gold and white moiré gown with lace on her head. The wedding was at St John's, Smith Square in Westminster at 12.15. The whole effect was very gay and Christmassy. As a family they do have cosy weddings.

SEVEN

The Outbreak of War

THE YEAR 1939 was to be the last year of normal life as I had known it. As a blissful newly-wed it had a soufflé quality. It is difficult to define our state of mind – or states of mind. In a consciously suppressed state, the war was inevitable, yet there were waves of hope. Coincidentally, this was the year that Joyce's career took off, with her startling success in her first Farjeon Revue. We thought it fun and nice for her, but never envisaged her as the great star she became.

Patrick re-joined the Black Watch, which was stationed at Dover Castle and we settled into a small flat in Waterloo Mansions on the front at Dover. Our income was only £600 a year, Patrick not having yet qualified for marriage allowance. There was a song then: 'Have another glass of port Brigadier, the subalterns will pay, they get ten bob a day, have another glass of port Brigadier.'

On this income we lived in a three-bedroomed flat with sitting room, dining room, kitchen and bathroom. We had a full time cook and a batman, who came down from the barracks every morning to wash, iron and clean Patrick's clothes and uniform. He waited on us at luncheon and dinner, cleaned the silver and helped the cook in various ways.

My brothers and sisters had given us a Baby Ford car as a wedding present at the cost of £100 (we sold it after quite heavy usage in 1946 for £137) and we began to save in order to afford a baby, to pay the doctor and the monthly nurse. The baby would be born in the flat. But I had nothing to do and pined a little for London and the family.

The atmosphere at home was not easy. Our parents could envisage, in their different ways, the nightmare that lay ahead of them and though they both battled with these feelings, my father was as at times ridiculously optimistic, while my mother faced despair bravely. It was appalling for all their generation and there was not much consolation to be gained from their friends. It was worrying too to see their children coping in a different manner again, even to the point of relishing the fight, without wholly understanding the implications. Business affairs, though ever present, were no longer the dominant consideration. Neither of my parents was good at reticence and all these emotions thumped about the home and were difficult to avoid.

Mary had her fifth daughter in the summer, who was to grow to be a lady-in-waiting to the Queen as Lady Susan Hussey. It had become 'de rigueur' for a younger sister to be at hand on these occasions – a role Laura had taken over from me. On being woken early in the morning by Geoffrey saying: 'Mary has five daughters,' Laura, half asleep, thought for a moment that he had been saying that Mary had had quins. We clung onto jokes that year.

I took to writing to Harry out in Africa. On 17 May 1939 I wrote:

Patrick has just departed to perform in the Aldershot Tattoo, an entirely unnecessary bother at this moment, but unfortunately until we have a dictator, our democracy must have its little show, whatever the cost to efficiency. It merely means on June 15 all the reservists are being called up in order to renew their training, and they will arrive to find three very angry officers instead of about fifteen and no battalion at all. Meanwhile all the men at Aldershot, who should be learning about the Bren gun, are being dressed up as brigands to dash about Rushmorre Arena.

The season in London is rapidly becoming an untidy hen party I believe, owing to every honest man being either a conscript or a territorial and unable to attend any dances. But Lolly seems to be having great fun, and dashing from one Countess's dance to another.

Meanwhile we have been in communication with Canada (so socially O.K. we are, doncherknow). The news from that front is that John Buchan, having entirely instigated and effected the Royal visit, Mackenzie King has told him where he gets off, and is letting him appear as little as possible. Considering that this time last year McK was terrified at the very mention of the Royal Visit, and His Ex had to cajole and persuade him, it seems rather hard. But no doubt right. Eric [Mackenzie], the Controller has been made Controller of Lord Derby's seven houses. The fact Susie can't get over is that anyone should own seven houses!

We are bathing in the reflected light of Joyce. My colleagues here think it makes me a little queer, and mention it in awed voices, and look at me as though I might suddenly become a musical comedy chorus girl (in spite of my legs) myself. They all still think the stage a little wicked.

As to politics, I wonder if you are right. The Army say it will be September again if it is, so they are taking the precaution of being to all intents fully mobilised then, with their reserves and conscripts.

During this season, I was determined to enjoy whatever was enjoyable – playing golf at Sandwich, an excursion to the 4th of June at Eton, the Highland Ball in London. Patrick contemplated studying for the Staff College, on the grounds that regimental soldiering was boring in peacetime. That summer my father wrote to Vera: 'We are living in a rather false atmosphere as Joyce won't let the European situation be discussed, and Mummy vetoes it on the grounds it might upset Frances.' So we continued life as if there were no threat of war.

I started a baby. My mother organised for us to meet some local landowners. The first luncheon party we attended was disastrous. We found the company right wing Fascist – several of the guests were later incarcerated in the war for being subversive, along with their friends the Mosleys – and Patrick suffered agonies during lunch, wondering if, as a serving officer, he should leave. But we settled into Army life as a married couple, with frequent visits from friends and family. When my parents stayed, my father produced endless stories to prove that the British Army, Navy, and Air Force were invincible, while the German Army was corrupt, ill-disciplined, badly armed and altogether a rotten show. Patrick produced Basil Liddell Hart and various other experts on our Army to countermand this, but my father swept their arguments aside, even when his defence was weak and outdated. We spoke of our ARP arrangements, but my father then advanced the wonderful argument that no one would dare use air-bombing against the British, because it would have no effect.

Meanwhile, my mother sat murmuring with her holy face: 'Poor darling he's quite wrong. The youth of Britain is rotten, the spirit of England is rotten, Mr Chamberlain is wicked and rotten, we've betrayed God, democracy, Russia and the YWCA.' My parents somehow managed to talk simultaneously for about four hours, but then had the urge to talk separately and ended with a difference of opinion on whether the men who fought in Spain were saints or scallywags. Luckily they enjoyed disagreeing.

At that time, there did seem a fleeting hope that it might turn into a fight between the two opposing ideas of Fascism and Communism. Possibly Germany and Russia would fly at each other's throats and we could watch. The German/Russian pact, signed on the eve of war, drowned that hopeful optimism.

Presently my father became an Air Raid Warden, though it seemed to us that all he did was to sit in Lady Bathurst's drawing room with a 'jolly little Irish lady' during air raids. He was virtually unable to hear the lectures he attended, and when asked questions to which he did not know the answer, merely replied that if they had been in the last war, they would not have asked him such a silly question. Apparently the first question he was asked was, 'If there was a man bending down behind a wall, and a bomb landed on him, what would you do?' My father replied that if he was behind a wall, how could he be expected to know the man was there. The correct answer was 'Go and look for his wife.' To this the jolly little Irish lady piped in with 'How on earth would he know he had a wife?'

Meanwhile I summed up the situation as I saw it to Harry:

Now to come to Mr C [Chamberlain] and his umbrella. Everyone does seem calmer and more cheerful, whether rightly or wrongly one can't quite make out. I suppose we are really having a bloodless war now, and when we are strong enough, we then make Germany and Italy do what we jolly well like. It does seem dangerous though not having a really competent opposition in the H of C who would oppose and criticize usefully instead of waffle like Mr Attlee and Archibald Sinclair.

Mummy has a story about Alan Lennox-Boyd. Apparently they went from Italy to Libya for their honeymoon, where Alan got bit by a mosquito and his face went black, so they went to Addis Ababa. It seems rather a sound place to go with a black face.

Gradually we realised that time was running out. The summer became increasingly grim and my final letter to Harry gave something of the mood of the country during the week before war was declared. It was written on 30 August:

The news certainly is, as you say, bloody. It does look pretty unavoidable this time, but there is still hope, so let's hope. Anyhow there's no use writing about it, because it will all be different by the time you get this. The only amazing thing is the difference in the atmosphere from last year. Everyone is so calm and all the emergency measures have gone ahead so smoothly and quietly, there is no frantic rushing about and hysterics like last year. Everyone knows exactly what to do, and is doing it. All of which makes one feel much safer, therefore the whole nauseous process slightly pleasanter . . .

Patrick has to be in uniform all the time and sleep in barracks, but comes home for meals and his moments off. The Army aren't really working excessively hard as all their machinery now moves so smoothly, till they are actually mobilised, they have little extra to do. So we are just going on with life as usual and waiting.

Maria, at Chewton, is waiting, according to reports from Mummy, for 17 officers, 53 children and 19 blind to be billeted on her. Geoff is manning his anti-aircraft guns at Shaftesbury. Katie is with her, and Pat is guarding bridges at Plymouth. Telephone communication is rather difficult, so we all correspond by postcard.

Daddy, needless to say, seems in far the best spirits, having rows with his precious ARP from which he has now gleefully resigned. He refuses, as far as we can gather, to go to any of their first aid etc lectures, because he claims he passed his first aid at Eton 50 years ago! I can hardly imagine a more dangerous qualification. Mum is Y.W-ing, moving the whole shoot to Bournemouth for safety. She and Daddy thrive on inside information from rather questionably hysterical foreigners. But, as I say, in spite of it appearing far more inevitable we are all much calmer than last year.

PS Patrick is actually a Captain this very day.

During the summer Vera left England to drive across Europe to Malta, then to Palestine and Aden, and across Central Africa to join Harry in Salisbury, Southern Rhodesia. My mother worried constantly about her:

I don't give way to too much 'mutter sorge' about her, or try not, and to tell myself motoring alone in Central Africa is relatively safer than being in London, there are continual noises of aeroplanes overhead flying in mass formation.

Laura's steaming ahead steadily through her dances, sherry parties and girls lunches and dinners and comes home mostly saying 'Gosh'. The Ball of the Season was a huge squash of 1,000 people at Holland House with the King and Queen, which was fun to have been at but a pretty good nightmare. Mrs Roland Cubitt gave it and apologised to the Queen for the squash, who said after Canada and the USA 'it felt like the Prairie'.

Then to our surprise we were asked to a very select Court Ball for

800 for Prince Paul of Serbia which we enjoyed tremendously staying, as did Their Majesties until 4am. The Queen looked lovely and she and the King dancing together looked quite delightful, both are perfect dancers. Joyce and Reg were there, so the tradition of no professional actresses at Court has been broken . . .

I had lunch with Evy Jones, violently anti-Chamberlain, as are Billy and Mima [Lord and Lady Harlech] and of course all the Asquith lot. Evy told me Mima has lost her friends over it, she and Billy feel so bitterly about things. The uncomfy thing is there are such cleavages in families there is an awful avoidance of discussion. In a queer way Hitler has killed free speech – all surface signs look as if war must come. What will August bring? There is far greater steadiness of nerve than last Autumn but one feels agonisedly anxious and the Government look, and are tired out. Chamberlain is obstinate and gives no sign of the Leadership the people long for. Halifax has only just woken up in the last 2 months, Charlie [Grey] says, to really realising that he deals with gangsters, as people so constantly warned him Hitler and co were. Sometimes in the night one wakes choked with alarm – but by day one can push it away.

On 3 September, the day after my 21st birthday, I sat alone in the flat listening on the radio to Chamberlain's declaration of war. I went to church and at mid-day the air-raid alarms went off – the first time we had heard them. I remembered Lindbergh's prophecy in 1938.

No one had a clue what to do so we walked quietly home. It was a false alarm, but it made its point.

The Black Watch were among the first troops to go to France in the British Expeditionary Force. After war was declared they were moved to Aldershot.

I packed up the flat and we spent one last day in it and both cried. It was the end of our idyllic time.

The five years of war were to prove a weird experience. This period was one of suspended animation. Relations and friends were quickly strewn about. Some were lost, others gained. To talk of the future was theoretical to the point of fantasy. The past disappeared.

Everything was dangerous, but even danger became tedious. Looking back on it, I recall an unreal quality. There was strangeness and normality. Laura wrote to me about making our father move out of his bedroom to make way for bomb victims taking shelter in their basement home: 'I so hate having to move Daddy out of his room, he says he's so apt to lose his razor and his lucky threepenny bit.'

Anxiety was heightened by the slowness, even the absence of communication. During the Blitz on London, I longed to telephone to check on the family's fate, but a trunk call was usually impossible. Laura wrote saying how she had tried to ring me, but calls had to be booked and were usually delayed. Letters home took two days, but were lifelines.

Patrick left for war. We had one last sight of each other when his embarkation was delayed and I joined him in Aldershot from Ardchattan. At the end of week the Battalion marched through Aldershot and I found myself lining the street to wave goodbye, just like the women pictured in all wars. I thought the Jocks looked so small in height. There had been a momentary discussion about whether Highland Regiments should wear battledress or march to war in their kilts. Patrick had declared soundly that he had no intention of going to war thus attired, and finding himself suspended on barbed wire by his kilt. The majority of the young soldiers thought the same, and so battledress it was.

After war was declared a number of jigsaw pieces jumped into place. Bobby was called up from his steel works in Middlesbrough – one of the reserved occupations, which gave Molly momentary relief, but a Territorial in the Scottish Horse took priority. So despite the steel works he was called up.

Initially the Scottish Horse found themselves equipped with requisitioned polo ponies. Realising that a cavalry charge was unlikely in 1939, they pressed for a change of role and were trained as gunners. Tommy was called up to his Territorial battalion, the 8th Argylls, and was sent to France shortly after Patrick, which meant that Molly now had two sons in the expected battle zone.

Peggy produced a son in the summer, but found that she had forgotten to resign from the FANYs, a part of the female Territorial Army, and was briefly called up before being released as a mother. Cherry and Ian Fraser also faced a different future when Ian was called up into the Lovat Scouts.

Harry, with Vera, returned from South Africa to join his unit, the Oxfordshire and Buckinghamshire Yeomanry, and Vera moved down to the East End to live amongst her club members.

At the start of the war, Laura was picked up by Virginia Thesiger and found herself an assistant to Stella, Lady Reading, who was busy laying the foundations of the Woman's Voluntary Service (later to have 'Royal' conferred on it). This was a brilliant idea for recruiting women, from duchesses to charladies, but needed an organizing genius like Lady Reading to make it work. The volunteers worked for their local governments, unpaid but on civil service lines, wearing a green uniform, but had no ranks. They were ready to plug any gaps.

Virginia Thesiger, a co-worker with Laura at the HQ, described her duties in a poem 'It's all very well now'. She described how as an old lady she doubted whether her grandchildren would realise the importance of 'what I did to keep my country free'.

How can I convince them that it was in England's good that I went to Waterloo to meet two goats travelling from Camberley?
And drove them in a car to Victoria where I put them on a train....
To Amberley?
Why, do you suppose, when London was burning did I find myself alone with a Church Army lady from Rye?
And why did we do nothing . . . but drink port and lemon
(She had a dish cover on her head, tied with a Zingari tie)?

As the youngest, Laura found herself in an office manned half by efficient trained Civil Service secretaries and half by middle-aged friends of Lady Reading. My future sister-in-law Angela Murray was doing the accounts and her sister was a telephonist. Lady Reading was good at foreseeing where the needs of the future might arise. She planned for the huge influx of refugees from the Netherlands once the real fighting started, and busily set up contingency schemes to cope with workers and victims in the future possible Blitz, etc.

She had immediate access to the Home Secretary and toured the country galvanising local authorities and volunteers into action. This meant that Laura's job had no boundaries – she was amateur secretarial aide (no shorthand), chauffeur, canteen worker, ARP warden, refugee centre organiser. Every day was different.

The next five years she lived with our parents in London and found herself caught between the energetic Lady Reading and the far from relaxed parents. Only Laura could have survived this – often exhausted, often exasperated, frequently furious but for all that balanced and funny. She also managed to keep the scattered family together by writing us round robin letters almost weekly.

Life at Ardchattan was still busy for Molly. I went to live there as it was felt that it would not be good for her to be alone for the winter and besides, I was homeless. Harry went to France during the winter and met Patrick for the first time in a French bar. I reported to Laura:

Patrick does nothing but write and say how much he loves yours and everyone else's letters. But they come so thick and fast he says he hopes you don't mind and understand but he can't answer them all, but it doesn't mean he doesn't appreciate them 'coz he very much does. But now, with nothing much on, all the Jocks write as many letters as they can, and poor Patrick has to censor them all in time for the post, so doesn't get much time to write himself.

We have no less than five spies here now (although one, unfortunately – the best one too with a beard and 'foreign' and dressed as a tramp) has turned out to be the district's best known tramp for years past. So the theory that he dropped by a parachute at dead of night must, I'm afraid, be discounted. But for all that Ninny is sure his beard is false.

During the last week we've had one spy in Oban arrested, caught red-handed with a wireless transmitter in his gas-mask! Which just proves nothing is sacred to the Germans is it? But we all feel a great source of danger has been removed, anyhow. But otherwise we've no news. We haven't even been able to listen to the BBC because Catherine [a guest] told us none of the Right People ever listen to the news now, so we retired squashed, and had to sneak out of the room and listen in secret, like the poor Germans listening to foreign broadcasts.

As the winter continued to disrupt our lives, we were partially lulled by none of the family being in immediate danger. In November it was decided that I should go and stay with Mary at Chewton to have my baby. Mary was the nearest thing to a maternity home. She wrote to Patrick to tell him she welcomed the plan and continued:

Well, isn't this a rum war. I hear you're not finding it deliriously exciting and I'm afraid you must be dreadfully damp. All is quiet also on the Chewton front barring a certain amount of clashing personality on the H.Q. staff. I think soldiers are very sensitive blossoms – they seem to get hurt feelings rather easily, and have to go away and shed tears and drink whiskey and aspirin to resolve themselves a good deal.

Geoffrey is sort of bottle-washer in chief, and the Col. keeps him in good order – he hardly talks English now, its all DHAQMQ's and DADOS's and GSO2's and things. After the scramble of the first fortnight of war when everyone stopped doing what they were doing and started doing something else very badly, things have gone back curiously to normal. The only things that make a difference to life are the lighting and petrol restrictions and neither of these are

Frances as a little girl.   Laura and Frances in Kitzbühl 1922.

Hilda Grenfell (Frances's mother) with her older daughters, Katie and Mary.

Arthur Grenfell (Frances's father).

Sir Robert Baden-Powell, HRH The Duke of Connaught, Arthur Grenfell and his uncle, Field Marshal Lord Grenfell.

Left to right Harry, Vera and Reggie (all three in 1911).

The dining room at Roehampton in 1912, with the Titian beyond the table (on the left).

Joyce photographed by Sasha shortly
before her wedding, 1929.

Patrick as ADC to the Governor-General of
Canada, 1938.

Lord Tweedsmuir (John Buchan),
Governor-General of Canada.

Lady Tweedsmuir.

Patrick and Frances's wedding in 1938. Frances's sister Katie is in the doorway.

Patrick with Mary Ann in 1940, shortly before he went back to war.

Patrick with Mary Ann and Robert in 1949, after he came home.

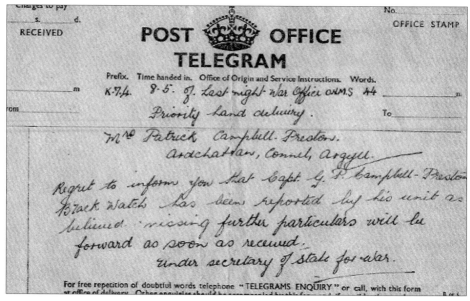

The War Office telegram announcing Patrick as missing.

An eyewitness sketch of the Warburg escape over the wire.

Patrick with Martin Gilliat and Mike Grissell while imprisoned at Colditz Castle.

A group at Colditz, including Patrick, John Arundell, Jack Fawcus, Colonel Stayner, David Walker, Peter Dollar, Colin Mackenzie, and Douglas Bader.

The 'Immobile' Wrens: Frances at the back, on the right.

Frances fishing on the River Awe in 1941.

Princess Elizabeth greeting Hilda Grenfell.
In the background, Florence Campbell and Clementine Churchill.

entirely unpleasant. A bicycle is a grand vehicle I find and I'll never be dislodged from one again – you can smell and see and hear from it, none of which you can do from a car.

After Christmas there was a major freeze up. Trees came down from the weight of ice on them, telephone lines froze and the poles crashed down. All leave from the BEF had to be stopped because of transport difficulties.

Mary Ann was born on 15 February 1940. When she was ten days old, Patrick came on ten days leave. In those days birth was a ponderous business. After producing a baby you stayed in bed for at least three weeks, did not put a foot to ground for a fortnight, and rested and slept every afternoon. For Patrick the change from troops preparing for war to a maternity home atmosphere was a shock. Not having been together during the process of pregnancy, it had meant nothing to him, and he found himself with an apparently invalid wife and a bundle called his daughter.

This leave had an element of frustration and despair. The Germans were on the point of invading Norway while the Black Watch were transferred to France from Belgium to join the 51st Highland Division. On his return he found himself in a small village in France, having to get up early as the troops had suddenly adopted the habit of lying in bed so, as he wrote to Laura: 'We have had to have a beat up and get them up at 6.15.' He ended sadly: 'That 10 days at home was perfect, but it was far too short and seems ages ago now.'

In April, Mary had a visitation at Chewton. Queen Mary, the Dowager Queen, had been evacuated to Badminton to stay with her niece, the Duchess of Beaufort. Queen Mary was still an active lady and her Household was pressed to find ways to entertain her. Mary was informed that Queen Mary wished to come to tea. As an avid collector, it was always said that if Queen Mary saw something in your collection which she coveted, she was apt to put some pressure on a loyal subject to give it to her.

Mary and Geoffrey had some valuable miniatures and it was known that the Queen was knowledgeable about these and that she collected them. Mary took the precaution of hiding hers in the linen cupboard and substituting copies as a safety measure. We were aware that Mary's two eldest children, aged 8 and 5 had seen this operation and we were on tenterhooks all afternoon in case two voices piped up to inform Queen Mary of what Mummy had been up to that morning. I wrote to Laura:

The Queen's visit went off most successfully and nothing unforeseen happened. Poor old dame had an awful tummy ache, and we thought looked far from well, but she was most cosy really and not a bit frightening! We presented all the children, including Mary Ann to the Queen and they were as good as gold. Mary Ann gazed at her quite calmly. Susan I must admit, gave the toque one look and bellowed.

In the spring my parents had gone to the Balkans to visit the Alatini mines. My father got pneumonia, and my mother had a tough nursing job on her hands. After a long month they returned. Laura wrote saying our father had been taken to see Plesch, who much to Laura's relief, made no outrageous suggestions, merely recommending rest and that my mother should apply goose fat between the shoulder blades to keep out draughts.

In May 1940 Hitler ordered the invasion of Belgium and France and the war started in earnest. I decided to return to Ardchattan to be with Molly, now obviously worried about both Patrick and Tommy. This new war was especially gruelling for her since she had lost three brothers in the previous one. The presence of Mary Ann in the house gave her new things to think about. My mother came to stay, and we heard Joyce on the wireless. Her first sketch was so bad that my mother apologized repeatedly to Molly, and would not let us listen to any more.

I felt bad leaving Mary, who had been feeling ill and crying on my shoulder when she found herself pregnant again, this time with the long-awaited heir.

There was no news from Patrick, though it seemed that he and Tommy were in comparatively safe zones, and not yet in the real melée. Then my mother-in-law got a letter from Tommy saying they were 'having a more exciting time than usual'. It sounded as though he was enjoying himself and he said that Patrick was quite close and having an even more exciting time than him and doing very well. I consoled myself that we had the better men in the end, which was eventually all that counted.

The evacuation of Dunkirk took place soon after my return and anxiety was focused on Harry who was somewhere in the battle. Days passed but then he materialized at Chewton, looking all right, but occasionally with a haunted look on his face in unguarded moments. Mary reported:

He hasn't a good word for anyone except, rather fortunately, Lord Gort himself, whom he saw on that awful beach behaving most awfully well and trying to get things organised.

It has been a ghastly disillusionment to them all, and the authorities will have to be very careful to explain to them exactly what happened, else they'll never trust anyone again. The original trouble was the black French troops who ran like hares at the very outset and let the uncontrollable flood in. The Belgians didn't seem to make much difference as far as Harry could tell as everyone was in full retreat by then.

It's all terribly depressing – but someone must have done something well somewhere to have got them out alive. They can't get over being stripped of every vestige of their equipment and think it will take months to re-equip.

Almost immediately bombing started around Chewton, aimed at Bristol. Chewton Priory was requisitioned, soon to be taken over by troops. Looking back to the summer and autumn of 1940 when an invasion was a real possibility, I find, with hindsight, that my blood runs cold. How much at the time did we really envisage it happening?

After Dunkirk Harry was acutely aware of the possible horror but kept his thoughts to himself. My father seemed not even to have contemplated it happening or succeeding. Laura wrote of one friend: '. . . She is jumpy, there's no getting away from it. She talks incessantly of bombs etc, in front of the children and hates when Bill can't sleep in, in case parachutists land in her garden'. Laura seemed to have thought that an odd reaction. Joyce wrote to her mother:

> *Thank you so much for your call – we are ALRIGHT and this bloody lie of a war can never be true, by the time you get this we may have been bombed, but I've a sort of feeling I'll always be OK. At this moment Virginia and I are sitting out in the garden, Reggie is spraying his roses, and Nan, the retriever, is wandering about. There are just a few clouds ... otherwise it is perfect. You couldn't guess there is a war on, it's a very peaceful Sunday. We listen to many news bulletins, but that's a passing fever, and as soon as we get used to fighting in the Netherlands we'll give up.* [At that time Harry was heavily engaged fighting].
>
> *There is a certain satisfaction with the new Cabinet and Winston as PM. Aunt Nancy wishes it was Lloyd George – but he is going on 77!*

Ardchattan presented a different scene. We slept peacefully in its silence and had no air raid sirens with which to contend. It is extraordinary to think that we then had a cook, a parlourmaid, a housemaid (if not two), several dailies, and I had a nanny. In the garden there was a gardener and a helper for him.

Some restrictions were beginning to be felt. The coal for Ardchattan always came by boat, once a year. This had to be reorganised and meant that coal came by road and in smaller quantities. So fires in bedrooms had to stop and we moved into one sitting room, which also served as the dining room. This was quite revolutionary. We used the dining room in the old part of the Priory with its thick walls and small windows to keep the heat in.

The other commodity that came in bulk was flour. There was a large steel-lined chest in the kitchen which was filled up once or twice a year. By the time you reached the bottom of the chest the weevils and the flour were more or less in equal residence. With rationing, flour bags replaced this store. The rabbit population made meat rationing much less irksome.

It became a war duty to stalk for venison. Bobby had a pool at the mouth of the River Awe where we caught sea trout and the odd grilse and I became an ardent fisherwoman. The cold at Ardchattan in the winter was even noticeable when I was in my twenties. There was no central heating, just a range in the kitchen and a fire in the sitting room and nursery and an airing cupboard. By the end of the first winter I counted the blankets on my bed and found I had ten. Getting up in the morning required a great act of will. For all that no one seemed to get seriously ill.

Molly was unendingly generous and hospitable to my family, who came whenever they could and went back restored by the rest. Harry, looked on as the realist in the family, came on his leave. He and I went for a walk on the hill and he told me that he foresaw the war becoming a stalemate, ending in a compromise peace. He warned me that I should relinquish any hope of seeing Patrick for fifteen years. It was a lovely autumn day and we were looking at a lovely view. Somehow, it was difficult to believe this.

Oban had become an airbase for sea-planes patrolling the Atlantic. It soon became a naval base.

Letters from Patrick continued to trickle in during June. They were always quite out of date, and said little due to the censors. His mood seemed to alternate between cheerfulness and gloom. Once a week we went into the canteen at Oban, and talked to the airmen, many of whom looked like poets, albeit physically fit ones. One or two tiny men came swaggering in, looking like little cockney sparrows. Local ladies cooked by day, and Molly washed up in the evening, puzzled by the cups 'with the most extraordinary sediment in the bottom'. This was camp coffee – the precursor to instant coffee.

As the dangers grew, the impact of which was so much more immediate in London, my mother's religious faith was her strength and she longed for us to share it to the same degree. She was never able to express herself succinctly, writing instead deeply emotional letters. Taking her literally, I concluded that her message was that we should probably all be killed, so cheerio, but we would all meet again in Heaven.

I remained supremely confident that Patrick would survive and I wrote to Laura to say that I loved our mother dearly but thought her quite dotty. I had been embarrassed that she had written to Molly in the same vein, because Molly was not used to such emotionally charged letters and was puzzled as to how to respond.

EIGHT

Prisoner of War

WITH THE fall of Belgium the hapless King Leopold III was made a scapegoat, although Harry said the failure of the Belgian troops had little to do with our disaster. 'Aunt Lola says the King of Belgium's mother is German and I suppose has been nagging him for years,' reported Laura. Refugees from Europe began to pour in. Laura was one of those coping with the problems of housing them at Alexander Palace, blacking out the windows, and dealing with the lack of beds.

Life at Ardchattan had not yet shown much pace. In July I joined the WVS:

> I try and make people collect scrap, which is quite easy, but trying to get people to take it away is not at all easy, as they all say it is the next man's job, and they haven't got any petrol . . .
>
> By the way your old WVS in London is being very very poopsy. Half our district here lies the other side of Connel toll bridge, and if I am to do this job properly I must go across said bridge in my car, but refuse to pay 10/- every time, and so I have registered my car as a WVS and told them to buy me a season ticket at £2.10 a year. Edinburgh agree with me, and London say I must go by bus! The nearest bus is the other side of said bridge 6 miles away, and goes to Oban, which is a separate WVS area, and as such does not want visiting by me anyway. So tell London the West Highlands is not Tooting Bec, with my love.

One of the lessons learnt by the Dunkirk experience was that the fleeing refugees, with their belongings piled on any form of transport available, had clogged the roads so that the army often could not move. Lady Reading's opinion was that as many people as possible should be encouraged to leave the south and east coast at once rather than wait for the expected invasion. Laura noted in her diary that Lady Reading persuaded Sir John Anderson, the Home Secretary, to issue an order that 'all children will be evacuated on Monday within 25 mile zone from East Coast to Swanage. From London by Southern Railway or GWR over the next six days.'

Ella Allison, a Black Watch wife, had become a close friend at Dover, and had stayed there, her children being at school in the area. One day, with no warning, the children were marched from school, put on a train for an unknown destination, and turned up in Newport, South Wales, after an eleven hour journey. A few days later their mother found them there, billeted out, bewildered and miserable.

Lady Reading also encouraged the acceptance of offers from Canada and the USA to take in families, or children on their own. Laura supported this, urging Geoffrey to send Mary and her large family there, and also suggesting that Katie and I went too.

I immediately decided against. By this time Patrick was missing and with the possibility he might escape and turn up, there was no argument that would persuade me. Ardchattan seemed a safer place than launching off into the Atlantic.

Katie moved to a small house at North Aston next door to Hermione – so she was not homeless, as Mary was about to be. The financial arrangements were sketchy. No money could be taken from this country, and it was necessary to find a sponsor in Canada to finance you. Susie Tweedsmuir found herself being asked to help with contacts. So in the end, under great pressure, only Mary went, taking her children with her, and writing me a miserable farewell letter which ended: 'Just heard we have to sail Wednesday and go to London tomorrow for medical exam. Oh darling, it looks as if I'm for it – and I long so much to be with you all through this beastliness.'

This decision had to be made very quickly. The visas, forms and journey took about a fortnight to arrange. Her journey was a nightmare. Euston was pandemonium, the train dirty, uncomfortable and crowded, with no food and filthy lavatories, as was inevitable in wartime. When they came to leave the train, they were turned out a long distance before the checkpoint for passports. They had to carry their own luggage, walking along sleepers, the children carrying what they could.

The queue was too tightly packed for them to put their bags down and Mary felt like a refugee on her way to the Isle of Man. When at last they were safely on board, the CPR officials were kind and efficient, but had difficulty in feeding the many, who like them, had only eaten scraps in the past 24 hours.

A week before Mary left, a ship carrying refugees had sunk, so we were deeply relieved when the news came that she had arrived safely in Canada. A small part of me felt guilty that I had not dared risk that voyage, though I had many reasons for staying.

Mary produced her long awaited son in Canada. It was bitter-sweet that this event happened so far from us all. It had been promised that if and when the heir was born the church bells at Chewton would be rung. By the time he was born the ringing of the bells was strictly forbidden, as this was only to be done to alert the area to a German invasion.

Left behind in England, Geoffrey found himself in a desperate situation. All of a sudden his wife and family had gone, and his home had been requisitioned. It had all seemed so secure such a short while before. He and Laura went for a weekend with Joyce in her cottage. Joyce was about to return to the stage, Farjeon putting on a short programme called *The Late Joys* at the Players Theatre. This was a chance to try out new skits and sketches for the Revue in the autumn. Laura was amused by a 'delicious poem in dialect called Yokel Defence, an inspiration in itself', which she sent to *Punch*. While they were there, they heard what they thought was an explosion. They put out the lights and went out to have a look, at which point a plane flew across the evening sky and was picked out by three searchlights. Since it made no attempt to evade the lights, they concluded it was on an exercise.

The three of them lunched at Cliveden. Besides their hosts, the Astors, there was Dr Tom Jones (the retired deputy Secretary to the Cabinet), Bob Brand, David Astor, and two American journalists. Geoffrey did not make a hit with Lady Astor. Every now and then she dug him in the leg and bawled out 'Waldorf, this loon ought to be sitting next to you, he only wants to talk about cows.'

Then she produced a letter from her bag which she read out so fast that one word in six was all that any of them could hear. Apparently Geoffrey half enjoyed the repartee, while being slightly agitated by the noise and commotion. Lady Astor began by being disapproving of Mary and the children going to Canada, though she relented when she heard there were five children under eight.

The American journalist, Ben Robertson, travelled back to London with Laura and Geoffrey. He described how he had come via Lisbon and had seen the refugees pouring in from France in every kind of vehicle from Rolls Royces to wheelbarrows. Meanwhile, the Portuguese were dancing in the streets celebrating a festival. Now he was in London to see the bombing.

Meanwhile we lived in a situation where you never quite knew if you were to face tragedy or comedy. One day the Local Defence Volunteers were ordered to stand by as parachutists were expected. Our LDV at Ardchattan were a gamekeeper and a gardener, previously in the Black Watch. The gamekeeper asked my mother-in-law what he should do. She told him to get his gun and ascertain his orders. He turned up later, bearing a rifle and said his orders were to wait with the gardener in the back yard. The gardener's first reaction was to put on his best clothes. So we spent the afternoon with two unhappy men, prowling about the back door. After about two hours the all clear went and all was well.

We resolved that next time we would not have two men

prowling about the back door, lest they shot us before the arrival of the parachutist.

All this time Patrick and Tommy were fighting in France. Patrick later wrote an account of the battle. Initially they were stationed on the Maginot Line on the Somme. Although the fighting was fierce, the Maginot Line proved to be impregnable, only to fall later when the Germans turned its flank. Towards the end of May the 51st Division was moved to support the French in the defence of Abbeville. Here they faced the real German Juggernaut and were forced to retreat, along with the French. He described how they fought by day and fell back by night, so were out-gunned and sleepless. The Germans could afford to rest their troops by night.

The evacuation of the Division was never put into operation. Our Government was attempting to boost the morale and resistance of a falling France and felt that if they rescued our troops, the French might accuse us of abandoning them.

We soon realized that the situation was desperate as hopes of another evacuation, as at Dunkirk, faded. News percolated through that the Highland Division had been captured at St Valery in Normandy. The first rumour was that Patrick had been seen wounded and very angry, and been evacuated to either Cherbourg or Brest. Laura said there were hospital trains in the country with patients who had not been identified and that he might turn up on one of these.

In July Tommy arrived back with the news that he had found Patrick's batman, with Patrick's kit, including a sleeping bag and a brand new typewriter which I had sent him, on the boat, but no Patrick. We began to hope that he was a prisoner, but had no way of knowing the truth. Two companies of the 8th Argylls had escaped through the German lines by night. They were led by Lt-Colonel Lorne Campbell (later a Brigadier, a VC, whose son would later become my son-in-law), and they were evacuated from Le Havre.

The bombing in London and the South began in earnest, the

cause for further anxiety as so many of my family, friends and relations were in the middle of it. These stories ran parallel and the changes in our lives were so quick that it is hard to tell them in the correct chronological order.

I heard no more news about Patrick, but snippets of information reached me. His aunt, Nancy Hamilton Dalrymple, met the Chairman of the Prisoner of War Department of the Red Cross, who gave her what she called a 'cheering' account of the treatment of prisoners. They were allowed to see an American representative alone, which implied that news of them was reliable.

One of the refugees who turned up at Ardchattan from France was Paul Maze, the painter, with his daughter Pauline. Paul was famous for having taught Winston Churchill to paint, and his work includes many scenes of the Guards marching at Trooping the Colour. He and his daughter had been living comfortably with M. and Mme. Balsan (the former Consuelo Vanderbilt – Duchess of Marlborough) in their chateau on the outskirts of Paris. As the Germans drew near, they decided to leave and make their way to Bordeaux. The Balsans took another route and left Paul to escort a home of 100 babies, evacuated to the chateau grounds, to safety in the South of France.

Paul was the stepfather of Ernest Nelson (our nearest neighbour across the loch) and an old friend of Molly's. The account he gave of his journey was hilarious and he was rather annoyed at our laughing. He decided to try and shake our composure by assuring Molly that when the invasion started, the Germans would descend disguised as nuns, armed with machine guns and wearing large boots. Molly pointed out this would not go unremarked in a Presbyterian county.

Paul was separated from his wife, who was living in a cottage on the other side of the loch. We thought he was trying to get money and clothes out of her. He had fallen for a charming cottage with no roof or drains, but in the meantime was writing long letters to Molly, ostensibly about Patrick, but in fact hoping to come and stay with us. His reputation was such that Molly was not having that, lest the neighbourhood thought he was living either with her or with me. There was news from Germany:

We heard yesterday that two of Tommy's men have escaped from the Germans and are on a ship in the Clyde, which is rather exciting. We have heard no more of them though. The father of one of them was going to meet his son, and said he would wire us if he had any news of Patrick. But as he hasn't wired, he can't have any. It wasn't very likely he would. But it doesn't look as if they can be in Germany, as I doubt they could have escaped from there. The morning papers have just come, and I see a description of their escape. They seem to have been to Spain! How on earth do you get from Spain to Scotland and from Belgium to Spain when the only part of the world one knows is the Highlands? They are tough these boys there is no doubt.

Argyll became a place of refuge for many, including Curzon's daughter, Lady Alexandra Metcalfe, who arrived in July and immediately set about trying to entice our servants away. There was considerable activity that summer:

What a world! The war office have just about torn it this time, but all this is desperately secret so you'd better not mentions it much. But Tommy and all his men, only just home from France, having had a bare 48 hours leave, are being sent for God only knows how long to Singapore. The wretched 4th Black Watch left for China last week. These men all feel pretty bitter. They are all the remains of the 51st division, and the Scotch are just as proud, and with just as much reason, of their 51st, as any Guardsman is of the Guards brigade. They fought longer than anyone else in France, they had 6 solid weeks of it.

They suffered very heavy casualties and were given an impossible line to hold, yet not one single one of the officers or men have had any form of recognition at all. This is probably only the slow moving ways of that most hopeless of departments, but there should be no slowness now. Now they are being sent on garrison duty to the east, after being told their precious division is finished. To send territorial battalions, recruited to defend their homes at this moment is pretty bitter and hard for these men and their women. They all come from the villages round here, so of course all the women get together and talk, and I can tell you when they realize the men have not been allowed to breath a word or allowed home, if it is true, feeling will run pretty high.

Haw-Haw's latest stunt has been buttering up Scottish nationalism and trying to divide Scotland and England. You may think it nonsense but all I can say is there is a strong feeling up here and among fairly high up officers, that the English generals in London don't care a fig for the Scotch soldiers. It's absolutely monstrous, and personally I feel almost glad Patrick is in Germany, they may care for him as much as the war office. Only had Patrick come home and been sent, I should have been pretty angry, but as a regular soldier I should know it was in his contract so to speak, and have lumped it. But to send territorials and without giving them a chance to settle affairs for their wives and people, is absolutely monstrous. We are all so angry we can hardly speak. It is pretty hard luck on poor Mrs C-P, having just got Tommy home safe, as heavens only knows when she will see him again. They'll probably leave them out there for years after the war.

My mother-in-law returned from some WVS work, having visited two villages, from which some of Tommy's men had gone to war. She found the villagers bubbling with anger. A deserter had turned up and the entire village were organizing themselves to hide him, explaining 'Och he's only a wee boy, and he's fought that weel out there.' There was great excitement: 'It's as gude a' the '45 again,' declared one woman. My mother-in-law found that they were all listening to Lord Haw-Haw on the wireless in the hope of getting news of their relations. More worryingly, the wife of the local minister told her that the 51st Division had been so badly treated that in her view: 'The only people who will benefit by this war are the rich. We'd do just as well under Hitler. Look how they treat our men, they don't care.'

Although this was foolish talk, it was understandable, given the way the authorities treated the relations of the serving soldiers. Laura reported these views to Lady Reading, who relayed them to the War Office. (Laura even telephoned me to report this). A few days later I wrote to Laura:

I think you have done the trick as everyone is mollified and as pleased as punch. We had a delighted letter from Tommy saying they have been told they were on a hush-hush job and would only be away six weeks. They had been especially selected because of their excellent record in France. So tell Lady Reading it was obviously her.

They all received a letter about wartime pay – even those like me, whose husband was missing. This was hard to understand but caused many to think they would be left to starve. They never went to Singapore, and rightly or wrongly, Laura and I smugly felt that we had caused something decisive to happen.

I hoped that if the Germans heard that Patrick had American friends, he might be better treated. News of the various prisoners was coming through, and I was confident that I would soon hear news of Patrick. One of the prisoners had devised a code with his mother, that if he wrote home about the weather and scenery, this meant he was being well treated. But it was hard:

I must admit I would like some news although I am sure he is alright. I am afraid those beastly Germans will be telling them of dreadful things which are happening to us. I do hope they have the sense not to believe them.

I did not get the standard War Office telegram reporting him missing until August. As far as I was concerned, this merely stated the obvious, but for Molly it was more chilling. In the 1914-18 war this was invariably followed by a 'Killed in action' notification. Molly never voiced her fears or misgivings to me. Her courage and support was of rock-like quality and she kept me as sane as she could.

But then Major Thomas Rennie[2] of the Black Watch, who had escaped on the line of march as they went through France, arrived home with news. He did not know if others had followed him, so some slight hopes remained. These were not as important as knowing they were safe. I was excited and relieved:

> *Oh the excitement, joy and God knows what, I can hardly bear it, it is so marvellous. I rang Thomas Rennie up as Dad arrived. I wonder if he told you what he told me about Patrick coming after him? At least he said he hoped I would see him soon too. Somehow I know Patrick will turn up, although it may take months. I wonder what you all got out of Thomas. I think he's one of the world's nicest men, but not gifted with the gab. I hope you have written and told me all he said. All the nice people sound safe, which is absolutely grand. I hope the whole damn regiment escape.*

My father was soon on the track of Major Rennie, urged me to be patient, assured me that Patrick would be sensible, and comforted me by saying that Patrick and his Division had covered themselves with glory. He managed to see Major Rennie, and thought him 'a brave and gallant gentleman in the best sense of the word'. At last there was firm news about Patrick:

> *He told me the Germans moved the prisoners partly in cars, partly on foot. When he escaped he was actually marching just ahead of Patrick, they were of course in column. At night the officers were generally put into barns or buildings with the men camped in fields surrounded by wire. They didn't get much food from the Germans,*

2. Thomas fought on through the war and ended up as a Major General. He was killed in 1945, leading the 51st Division into Germany.

two small meals a day, but the French village people pressed food and fruit and sometimes tea and coffee on them, in spite of their own evident poverty. He slipped into a wood and after trying to get to the coast decided to strike south and by some marvellous ingenuity they found their way through France into Spain and through Spain into Portugal and arrived yesterday. He looks as fit as a fiddle, he says Patrick's wound was very slight. He thought it might have entailed one stitch, I think in his forehead. He had lost a certain amount of blood but was none the worse for it and marched with them alright.

On 21st June they had got as far as Lille. He doesn't of course know to what camp they were going. I think therefore you may feel comforted in the knowledge that he is not badly hurt and a prisoner. I was afraid there might have been a rough and tumble before they took him. You will, no doubt, see Rennie who goes North tonight and he will as soon as he gets a spare moment tell you all their story. It was very good of him to let us see him.

Reggie also wrote to me, full of optimism:

Laura has just told me that it is practically certain that Patrick is a prisoner. So this letter is to send you all my love and to say that if Joyce and I can do anything for you, please let us know. We would so love to do something.

It is terribly bad luck, but after all your anxiety, I hope that you are able or almost able to look on it as good news. Don't imagine that frightful things will happen to him. We know quite a lot at this Ministry and our censors see a good many of the letters written by British and other prisoners in Germany. We don't tend to admit it in public, but (and this is absolutely honest, I promise you) the Germans are looking after their prisoners very well. They are an odd race, the Germans, but the one thing they do admire is fighting courage and they are definitely better disposed to people in ratio to the resistance they have put up. Well, in this war, the British and perhaps especially the 51st Division, should be at a considerable premium. He will be well looked after – but it won't be like staying at the Ritz. I don't expect that poor Patrick will have actually put on weight when you next see him – but then there are cads who would say that that didn't matter. Never mind, Fuffs, when we do all see him again, we'll give him the freedom of the restaurants and it won't be our fault if we can't visibly see him regaining his figure.

Poor Patrick and poor you. It seems hardly for me to say that it might have been worse, but I do say it all the same and I hope, Fuffs, that you can really believe it. It may be unpleasant, and when you next see him he will be thinner, but he'll still be Patrick, exactly the same, and you will see him – for now he is out of the WAR for the duration. What fun it will be when this WAR IS OVER – and it will be over soon, much sooner than most people think. I am absolutely certain that the Germans will crack up and have had enough far earlier than last time. If they don't beat us before October and they won't – they'll be making peace by this time next year for sure. Hitler knows that perfectly well.

I suppose that I did not accept either Reggie's prognosis of a quick result or Harry's of a fifteen-year war. With hindsight, I think I ploughed my own furrow, thus protecting myself from either extreme.

At last, in the late autumn, a letter arrived from Patrick, the first since his captivity. It came from the chilling address – Vor-und Zuname Capt G.P. Campbell-Preston, Gefangenennumer 1225, Lager Bezefchung Oflag V11C, Deutschland.

Patrick was then 29, a young man who had enjoyed life. Sports and exercise being almost a sacred part of that life. Now he was facing incarceration and the loss of all that he most enjoyed and valued. He fully realised that this was not going to be a quick war. He wrote of the casualties – two officers killed, and five sergeants and corporals. This was relatively light – 'the German Panzer Division were magnificent,' wrote Patrick, 'as were their Air Force. I saw 3 British planes in 6 days!' He described how he had been slightly wounded in the forehead, his battle dress was ruined and blood-soaked, and he had no clothes. This last indignity was particularly irritating to him since the only address in London he could reach unerringly was his tailor's. He continued:

Our ration today is coffee, cabbage soup, 10 potatoes and 2 inches of bread. Life palls here at times, however we might be worse. David Walker and I Highland dance and now we get some exercise playing basketball. But I can see no end to this rot.

Deprived of news of us, he naturally asked many anxious questions about his family. At last, at Christmas, he got 24 letters from me.

NINE

Vera in the East End

IN THE First World War it had been found that in the Zeppelin raids thousands of people had crowded into the underground stations at night and been too frightened to come up the next morning. This led to a pre-war commission foolishly deciding that if deep shelters were built and underground stations used as as air raid shelters those who took refuge in them 'would grow hysterical and never surface to perform their duties'. As a result, none were provided. Vera and Irene (Lady) Ravensdale used all their connections in Government to try and rectify this. They frequently stormed the Home Office and any other relevant authority.

The East Enders proved that their courage was unbreakable. Vera ran an Emergency Feeding Centre at Paddy's Goose Club, just above the burnt-out Docks. Into one room of this her team moved their beds, so as to be near the dug-outs. When fire was raging in the Docks, any idea of a black-out was impossible, and the heavy bombs and screaming bombs not unnaturally played on peoples' nerves. Despite no water, gas or electricity, the East Enders never complained. Sometimes there would be as many as 500 of them in the crypt of one church.

Vera supervised hot tea, cocoa and served 200 hot dinners a night. The Council kept them well supplied with food – soup, potatoes, stew in containers, and quarter loaves for sandwiches, filled with corned beef, cheese and jam. The children got fresh milk. Vera would start at 4 a.m. to cope with firemen who arrived for refreshment. Vera was also involved in rescue work from the shelters. She was soon known as 'the lady in green trousers' on account of her green siren suit. One night 450 people arrived in lorries with piteous bundles in their hands, the occupants of two blocks of flats. She pressed the Council to arrange the evacuations and eventually some 700 were sent off in fleets of buses. Amongst them was a girl who had lost five members of her family when a bomb hit their block of flats, killing 70. Vera gave her first aid, but she later died.

Communication was difficult and at times impossible, but she worked on amongst the smouldering buildings. She arranged clothing and feeding and was forever impressed by the bravery of those she encountered. When their shelter was full, the overflow slept in blankets in the big hall, including a woman of 95, who never complained.

After a particularly bad raid, Vera was faced with a situation which she thought could have led to panic or even a riot. The men were threatening to form a deputation to Whitehall, demanding evacuation. Vera stepped in and after much pressing commandeered some buses which resulted in their evacuation.

In November 1940 heavy rain filled the shelter and trenches at Shadwell Park. Undeterred, and without any official endorsement to do so, Vera soon commandeered five strengthened basements in Dr Barnardo's offices, thus housing 150 people, and then the ground floor of another big building which took 200 more. The ground floor was not as safe as the trenches but it was a solid building and at least it was dry.

During one of my visits to Ardchattan I travelled in a four-berth sleeper which, as so often, resulted in conversation with fellow travellers. A lady told me how she had been in Shadwell during the Blitz and had witnessed an occasion when panic had nearly taken hold, but, she said: 'There was a splendid lady in green trousers who singly handedly averted a riot.' I felt very proud.

The German Blitz started with indiscrimate bombing. We lost many friends in these raids, especially in Kent, which was deemed the flight path to London. In August the Blitz was in full fury. Returning by sleeper from a visit to Ardchattan, my father was delayed for three hours by a raid at Warrington. His office clerk told him about the second Croydon raid, saying that if it had not been for the damage, 'it was the best show he had ever seen. Our Spitfires raced into the attack, chasing the Germans away.' A few days later my father got shut in an air raid shelter for an hour, trying to visit Harrods. When my mother came home the same night, she told him of an air raid then going on, but of which he was unaware due to his deafness. He reported:

> Of course my first action was to go out in our little garden and watch the searchlights, they made quite a good show, now and then it looked as if they had spotted a machine and twenty or thirty beams raced across the skies. We could hear the planes but couldn't see them. Wooster, who is as deaf as I am, heard the guns in Hyde Park go off, but luckily it was only his imagination and so at 12 midnight to bed.

My father was clearly determined to give the impression that much of the Blitz was quite fun. My mother was more honest. She frequently admitted to being frightened and so threw herself into frenzied activity. In September she wrote to Harry, telling him that the big anti-aircraft barrage had begun:

> The Ajax and the Cossack are said to be up the river and this and the mobile guns moving up and down the Commercial Road comforted the E. Enders all a lot. We have a specially heavy barrage here because of Westminster and Buck. Pal and Chelsea and Victoria, all of which get special unremitting attention. Chelsea was so bad (I was sitting with Grandmums when a bomb brought smoke and smell and dust into her room and the noises were incessant) so I moved her out to Ockham [Surrey] – where she arrived safely and is alright, tho' two houses nearby there, were burnt. The whole of this part and indeed the county is fairly peppered. Every one has had a bomb within half a mile and it does little harm relatively except in the poor parts, where instead of houses streets go down. 23 and 46

Eaton Square and 65 Pont Street were hit today and V's flat had 2 incendiary bombs which did no harm tho'. Buck. Pal has had it twice, and bicycling to Vera's Club through the City and along embankment there were continual Police 'diversions' for unexploded bombs. The big buildings behind Thames House are burnt out but standing – ditto Bryanston Square, west side, which has sent Lola packing off to Yewdon but so far we are all well able to stand it and I can't stop Dad going out to look around when the barrage begins. I got caught in it proper getting back from Reading. Our train was kept a few miles from Paddington for nearly 2 hrs 7.30-9.30 and the barrage began as we at last drew into the station. There was a line of taxis and I asked an ARP man where the drivers were – 'very tight,' he answered, 'In the shelter lovey, and you go too – where d'you want to go?' so I said 'Home'. 'I don't blame you my dear' he said sententiously.

When I go to Sloane Square – in the underground I had to run for it to this house, through the barrage. It's a good thing to have to do that once – as for ever after a house or any shelter feels so much safer. Later – Since starting this we've had an extra go of 'breadbaskets' meted out to us here – with 2 fires started in this very block, and mews, Linlithgows' house . . .

Laura found she was spending most of her time in shelters, but still had not heard an explosion loud enough to scare her. 300 bombs had fallen in the Westminster area, causing only 15 casualties. But Vera had a grimmer story to tell:

It was a pretty ghastly sight – blazing fire and debris everywhere, 1st aid parties and stretcher parties working to liberate the people and take the injured to hospital. Five wardens were killed though only 3 bodies.

Flares were continually dropping and there was constant gunfire. Back here by 3.15 when there was a big bump and all too soon we realized from a new fire that it was by St George's Church and one of our Crypt Shelters. I must say my heart sank. I knew there were

200 people sheltering . . . we sallied out with fresh cups of tea and arrived at the Mission Hall just as most of the people had been got out of the Crypt. Everyone got out safely, but it was getting pretty thick with smoke when we got the last out.

My mother initiated the idea of requisitioning basements in Chesham Place following a meeting with Admiral Evans, the Chief Commissioning Officer. The plan was to include much of Belgravia, including Lowndes Square and Belgrave Square. This had the effect that the basement at 36 Lowndes Square was requisitioned by Westminster City Council, thus alleviating the need for my parents to pay the rent. They provided a dustcart for my mother to remove some family furniture, as she explained to Harry:

We were in the midst of planning this when the alert went. V had just arrived to stay – we were in our downstairs room when boom! went the guns – rattle rattle the bullets and Zoom! an aeroplane surely just about to land on the house? It was a crashing German bomber which crashed on the edge of Victoria Station followed by a crashing Spitfire. Everyone even our hitherto shivering servants out in the street cheering.

When the 'all clear' sounded, they continued to move furniture. The men had not eaten since breakfast, so they all went off to a café in Pimlico for tea and cakes. Meanwhile the guns were still firing and the planes flying:

Dad so thrilled he can hardly sit still and keeps going out and trying to see the local craters. Buck. Pal. has been well peppered all round and struck twice. I guess the King and Queen would like it all to go and give them chance to build a nice new Palace. Q Anne's Mansions and wall of Chelsea Power Station hit and Duke of York's School. So we are thoroughly in the midst of it all.

Laura described the further happenings:

Mummy had woken up the Westminster City Council and got them to commandeer Mrs Somerset Maugham's flat and basement. On Monday before any people came, we were struggling to get it ready, and I came home with a load of blankets and mattresses from the WVS clothing depot, and arrived here very dishevelled in that old Ford van from White Lodge, when a sort of deputation of little men in enormous black Homburg hats, came along the pavement towards me. At first I thought it must be a wedding or a funeral, but it turned out to be the Town Clerk of the Westminster City Council, who thinks no end of himself, and behind him, Malcolm MacDonald [Minister of Health and son of Ramsay MacDonald], *and all the biggest wigs on billeting. They shook hands with me, and I shoved them in a very bare room, and rushed off to find Mummy.*

They stood about and wandered in and out in a very aimless manner, and rather missed the whole point as none of the East Enders were there then. They came the next night, after Mummy had done the most stupendous day's work. Daddy is enjoying this awfully, though he hates having his dressing room 'cluttered up' with people Vera and Mummy collect to come here from worse areas for a night's rest. He and Min have the same outlook and are firmly convinced that people should remain where they belong, and if they have been bombed out of there, they should go somewhere else but not here. And Min is very indignant that V. should be sending up people who have been working 24 hours out of 24 down there for a night's sleep, (even in the passage where two are tonight) as she can't figure out that anyone is worse off than we are, although we have light, heating, gas, our own bedrooms already fitted in the basement, security and everything else that others haven't got.

We had the nearest bump I've heard yet, last night, and much to Daddy's dismay, he was unable to locate it during his daily tour of inspection. It upset Mummy a bit, because she is so tired, and she would get up and wander about in her trousers, fully dressed, and make me get out of my nice warm bed and put on some clothes and sleep with my shoes tucked under my chin so that I would know where they were.

My father conceded willingly that something should be done, but he was not going to concede that the East End was worse bombed than the West End. He explained gleefully:

Their first night coincided with a big German attack on the West End, the guns were going off merrily and loud and they hadn't heard guns so near them and were terrified and soon left their rooms for the basement. The destruction no doubt looks much worse in the East End because their rotten houses collapse, but I think much bigger stuff has been dropped round here.

Laura's version was:

I expect Town Clerks will take cover soon when they see her coming – she is quite unscrupulous and when they won't let her do what she wants in the time she thinks it should be done, she rings up Malcolm MacDonald's secretary and fixes up an appointment for such and such a day or time and then goes back to the Town Clerk and says 'Mr MacDonald is coming to see the house', wherever it is, and expects to find it full of evacuees so will you requisition it, arrange to have the basement shored up, electric light etc? It worked like magic here, and is being tried in Paddington where they were more reluctant to do as she wanted.

The sleeping arrangements in the basement flat were nightly a source of argument. Laura had a bedroom in a passage which joined the house to the mews. This was not bomb proof, but comfortable and every night Laura had to fight to be allowed to sleep in it. Otherwise there was a double room and windowless dressing room and the passage. Sometimes she lost and had to sleep with my mother, while my father slept in the inner bedroom:

With the early morning tea Mummy produced an armful of books and started reading especially chosen fragments and not only that, she kept asking me who wrote that, when and where. My literary and Biblical knowledge as far as texts go is strictly limited and every time I plumped for the Old Testament it was John Buchan or vice versa with occasional bits from Milton or Wordsworth thrown in to muddle me up.

The final score in Chesham Place was that every empty house was requisitioned with over a hundred homeless people there at any one time. Whole families came. Wardens from the YWCA organised it and the exquisite dining room of Mrs Somerset Maugham became the communal eating room. The next year, to everyone's great pleasure, the Queen came round to see it.

My mother was of the school that disapproved of women in trousers, but, having taken to bicycling was forced to adopt them. But she compromised, wearing a dress which she pinned up all round her, and over which she put her trousers. She then set off to her destination, be it the YWCA or to see the Minister of Health. On arriving, she dived behind the door, removed her trousers, undid the pins and sailed into the interview, in her dress.

Joyce wrote to her mother in America:

I don't know what the world would do without the likes of Vera and Hilda Grenfell. They look dead tired both of them. Vera hasn't had her clothes off for a week, and is living in Shadwell where things have been bad. Hilda is the quiet persuasive sort who looks harmless but cuts through anything when she's got a mind to do so. And, rightly, it's struck her lately to get the cellars of large rich houses in Chesham Place requisitioned by the LCC turned into hostels for the homeless of East London. She wiped away red tape and got the thing going in two days. She got YWCA workers in charge and is making an excellent job of it. Vera is helping to feed 1000 people a day in Shadwell, and to evacuate at the rate of 3000 a week.

TEN

The Second Winter

THE IRONY of this second winter of war was that British soldiers were relatively safe. They were being retrained and re-equipped, having been virtually disarmed during the retreat to Dunkirk and evacuation from the beaches. On the other hand, the girls were in the Front Line. Bobby was guarding the East Coast based in Scarborough and spent his (not infrequent) leisure time shooting pheasants at some of the best shoots in England. Tommy was in Perthshire where the new 51st Division was being raised, and enjoying his social life there. Harry, who had transferred to a gunner regiment, was training happily on the Yorkshire moors and shooting grouse, while Reggie and Patrick's brother-in-law, Raymond Baring, were with the 60th Rifles at Chisledon in Hampshire.

By his own account, Reggie did very little. About once a week, at night, he took a patrol to a chosen area between 4 and 6 in the morning. They beat the neighbouring woods to see what would come out – mostly pigeons and rabbits. His Regimental Sergeant Major appeared to treat the war as merely an incident in the background, giving lessons in army drill, but reckoning that the 60th had always shouldered arms perfectly and always would, war or no war.

Nor were there any bombs at Ardchattan. The highlight of the summer was the prospect of a visit from Bobby. His imminent arrival gave Molly the excuse to tidy the house and even the farmyard in honour of the laird's arrival – rather as people do now when a Royal visit looms. She prepared to fly the flag on the flagpole on the lawn.

Bobby brought two guests with him – Tony Murray and his wife Angela. Tony was the heir to the dukedom of Atholl, and a fellow officer of Bobby's in the Scottish Horse. Angela had been a Pearson – she was Lord Cowdray's twin sister. She knew Laura in the WVS office, her younger sister had 'come out' with me and they were both friends of Reggie and Joyce. Both having come from a family of brothers, Angela and I shared many jokes about them. Above all we were amused by the flag and flagpole.

Nearly five years later, in the last month of the war, Tony Murray was killed. Several years after that Bobby married Angela. Her first act as bride was to remove the flagpole.

Meanwhile London endured the Battle of Britain, as my father related in two letters that September:

On Wednesday I left my office after hearing blood-curdling accounts of escape from Newton and Miss Thorn and others. One man told me he found his wife and daughter in a terrible state of shattered nerves on his return home last night. They had had 5 Messerschmits crash within a few hundred yards of their house one after another, some in flames. All made a tremendous crash.

They described the scene as awe inspiring and felt the heavens and hell were falling on them! It wouldn't have had that effect on me. I started to go to visit the girls in our radio factory – my taxi took me SE instead of NW. I thought it was because the roads through the City were blocked as exaggerated stories had arrived of Cheapside and King William Street being in ruins. We crossed Westminster Bridge which was intact in spite of rumours to the contrary and shortly after came to signs of fires and crashed buildings, then found out that the taxi was taking me to the Elephant and Castle instead of the Angel. We returned over Blackfriars Bridge up King William Street, past the Bank of England. Some bombs had played old Harry near Cannon Street and I think it makes more of an impression in one to see these great solid buildings, wholly devoted to peaceful trading purposes just ripped in two. I suppose having known these great offices for nearly 50 years in all their might and majesty, it seems almost unreal to see them crashed to the ground. Near Old Street a block had come down and was still smouldering . . .

Where [the Duke of] *Westminster himself lives (shut up) hadn't a scratch tho' it is practically next door! The big block of buildings used by Ministry of Economic Warfare has all its windows smashed. It looked from where I was as if it had had a direct hit on the main entrance. Lansdowne House (of old) is also messed up so Berkeley Square shows deep scars. Bruton Street has had several direct hits and several houses are on the floor across Bond Street. A whole block between Conduit Street and Maddox Street has been gutted and houses flattened, several bombs falling right in the middle of the block. Liberty's windows opposite all broken, then I arrived at Oxford Circus all barred off on the left the whole of John Lewis shop from Oxford Street to Cavendish Square completely burnt out and smoking hard; it was quite a wonderful sight to see 8 huge jets of water being flung to the top of these shops, dousing the ruins. The fire extended almost to Selfridges.*

I had to turn up Great Portland Street (I wanted to get to Wigmore Street) and found a block with Langham Hotel, Queens Hall part of the BBC wrecked. After quite a long detour I got to west side of Cavendish Square, an unexploded bomb rests in the square facing Teddy Grenfell's house no. 4. where the Hoppner picture of my grandfather and his mother (a St. Leger) is being housed. So far the centre of the square is wrecked but No. 4 untouched, then I came through Brook Street (minor cracks and crashes) and again into Hyde Park where I watched for over 20 mins a wonderful show in the sky. For some atmospheric reason the exhaust of aeroplanes was laying out 6 lines and one extra line of white smoke rather like sky writing. Large circles and then sudden steep risings appearing and disappearing behind clouds.

If we had known what the game was it would have been exciting but we couldn't see the planes. It was evidently several of our Spitfires hunting a Bosch. I then realised the raid was still on, however that didn't deter any of us from watching and hoping to see something dramatic happen but heavy clouds blew up and our friends and foes disappeared. Then the all clear sounded and I went in to lunch. There were so many people watching the John Lewis and other fires and smashes that one couldn't believe there was an air raid on. I think most of the young men and women had been stopped at their work in order to take to the shelters but had taken the opportunity to go out and see the sights.

This wanton and wicked destruction which cannot in any way influence the outcome of the war makes one boil with rage when one realises too, that when we have beaten down this blackguard race of Prussians there is no way in which we can get compensation for this wicked destruction. I should sterilise every Prussian for 25 years and kill out the breed.

It is amazingly interesting, amazingly tragic and the people's reaction amazingly grand.

We had an absolutely topping morning, a real good dog fight right over our heads, our doorstep strewn with cartridge cases. One Spitfire vs two German bombers and our man got a left and right, a third bomber high up beyond the clouds was hit either by our pilot or our A[nti]A[ircraft] and his bombs must have exploded as the machine was blown into 10,000 pieces. Of the other two, one had both wings and his tail shot off, part of his fuselage fell on the jeweller's shop at corner of Victoria Station just opposite the cinema, one wing near a pub.

Our man's machine crashed and landed in Buckingham Palace Rd near Ebury Bridge, it cut a water main and apparently sent up a huge fountain but by the time I got there everything was in order. We have since heard that the crowd hoisted the Serg. pilot and carried him shoulder high until he prayed them to let him walk. He was furious at losing his machine but one Spitfire for 3 bombers over Belgrave Square not a bad record. We hear one German was taken alive, which surprises me as the temper of the crowd was very bitter and hostile. Fancy our seeing a man bale out and come down in his parachute from our doorstep!

During a short interval of peace this afternoon I walked past B.P.

to Westminster and then back by the Mall. The attack on B.P., was a very determined one. I wonder if they weren't going for the Admiralty. There are at least 3 big bombs in the park just opposite Wellington Barracks, 2 on Queen Anne's Mansions which are cut in two. One immediately in front of the Palace, 3 on the Mall side. I got to Constitution Hill at about 5.45; bang went a big bomb, several men in front of me went straight down on their faces leaving their less well trained ladies standing up! I comforted a baby and its mother saying it was the time bomb in Eaton Square but it was according to the wireless yet another bomb shot at the Palace and went off just over the garden wall. Several houses in Grosvenor Place were left with no windows. I was glad to find my nerves had not deteriorated.

All's well and tails up tonight old H is done for.

My father was considerably annoyed when Harry arrived on leave a week later and witnessed no raids. He arrived on the first quiet night in fifteen. But my father took him down to collect Vera and see some of the damage near her club and the docks. Meanwhile my mother had 100 beds delivered to her for her scheme. This enabled her to run three more houses. She wrote from their subterranean bedroom at 26 Chesham Place:

The overcrowding of shelters in E. End is an awful problem. Oh things go so slow this reception end – when once one has seen the 100's wanting housing.

The gun barrage is so noisy it is difficult to distinguish between bangs and crumps. The former so comforting, so one always tells oneself it's that.

I sleep on top of my bed in jersey and slacks and Dad has his day clothes disposed near by him and won't cover his shoes up as I tell him to, in case of flying glass. That's my one idée fixe – stepping out onto a carpet of glass, so I keep my shoes under my pillow.

Of the 3 other houses 29, 33, 35, 29 and 33 are ready for 60 more. Two children have developed diphtheria and have been sent on to hospital. One to Lewisham, the other to Shooters Hill, both badly bombed areas, their poor parents feel so anxious. I am the link with Ministry of Health and City Hall – all its services on which we have to call . . .

The benefit of this state of affairs is one stops agitating to get ones alien refugees out of internment, they are safer and happier in Isle of Man – tho' the loss to England of some of their scientific and technical skill is great. The Comic things one notices are the machine gun post at the Chelsea Bridges are camouflaged to look like sort of Wendy houses, artless little things with green shutters – at Admiralty Arch they look like ginger bread houses in a pantomime. The Home Guard at the Admiralty are old pets of at least 80, I think covered with medals, either ancient Admirals or full Generals, but so alert and happy looking.

Also the porter at Marlboro' House in his green and gold braided frock coat etc with a tin helmet on top looks too comic for words. As do I on a bicycle with my helmet filched from WVS for me by Laura. It cocks up on the top of my bun in a most odd way. As I'm congenitally and aurally unable and too inattentive to hear or distinguish 'Alerts' from 'All Clears' I'm shouted at by ARP wardens to put it on as I bicycle along with it forgetfully on shoulder. When it is on I'm smiled at by all passers by!

Lavinia Shaw Stewart [a young cousin] with her ambulance has done magnificently. The very first night she had a horrid job, being rear attendant she had to help taking in awful cases from a crump in her district. The War is simply the making of her. When duty allows she dines with her young man at the Ritz and gets caught by the Siren and so stays on there sitting up in a very posh air raid shelter with various celebrities, including King Zog of Albania, his wife and sisters, for whom a special lavatory is reserved on which they sit in state, being crowned Heads and to relieve the strain of curtseying!!

Dad is furious that no one paid any attention to his ARP scheme of seeing that a squad of watchers and people in charge of keys of empty houses and flats was not adopted. He has been proved *awfully right as the wardens never saw the two worst fires.*

A few weeks later my father reported:

I send you a timetable of our ordinary merchant banker's day in Sept 1940. I came up from my basement dressing room to breakfast about 10 mins to 9, had one little bit of bacon and some toast, eggs not obtainable which was amazing as I passed a man (a gent) in Oxford Street yesterday selling eggs from his motor car and like an ass hadn't realised there was any difficulty in getting eggs. However I had a very pleasant breakfast with Laura when in spite of my deafness I heard guns shooting overhead so I asked Laura if the sirens had gone off and she said just a minute ago. So I said well there must be planes overhead. I was dressed except for shaving and in a dressing gown. Bang. Bang. Bang. I said we must see this; Laura with great sense got her tin hat which I believe is made of reeds or some Eastern grass! And brought mine and we went out into our garden. So I had tin hat, field glasses and dressing gown. Bang Bang Bang and hundreds of little puffs of shells miles up. 'There they are,' said Laura, 'there there there, lots of them.'

It was a very difficult light and I only saw one, then the bangs stopped and more and more aeroplanes going like stink from South to North, evidently our Spitfires. Laura thought she saw a machine come down. Later reports confirm that 2 were brought down. We felt we had had quite a good start for our day's work, Mum had taken a long lie in and was very disappointed at having been underground during the fun.

10.15, no Mr Newton, no secretaries, but I had to go off to the Bank of E to clear up an account between that august institution and the Yugoslav National Bank. I got to the Bank after looking at a nasty gash to 'Bow Church' where the Bells ring, or rather used to ring.

At the Bank after considerable hunting in the deepest or 4th level I eventually located the department but found the man I wanted had just gone off to the Treasury, so I have to return another day. It's odd passing down passages, one a complete Red X unit standing by, basins etc all ready, beds dumped anywhere in the passages and stairways. Grenadiers with fixed bayonets at the entrances who look you over on your exit as well as your entry.

Having heard my factory girls at Islington had had a bad time I went off to see them. A week ago I had left their street all neat and tidy and no sign of war. I found it today all flat, forty or fifty houses just completely collapsed. Every house around the factory demolished except the factory. I found them all in the shelter below in very good spirits. I can't help thinking they have enough humour to think it rather amusing that the Herr Erber of Vienna is paying them so much an hour while they stitch and sew in a shelter from shells directed on London by his Boche cousin!

I had lunch with Erber at a Lyons Café at The Angel. I asked for two poached eggs on toast. I was told I couldn't get toast as there was no gas available in that district, so I had Irish stew and it was quite good. After lunch I took a bus for home and got a front seat on top. Hilda had made me take my tin hat which is made of tin! And very thin tin too. When I had just started off went the Blitzkrieg signal again. Nothing happened until we got near Aldwych when the man next to me jumped up and said 'Gawd look at the planes,' so Gawd looked at the planes. 3.20pm by my watch, then on went my tin hat, bang bang, a magnificent barrage it delivered to bursting on top and around a mass of planes. I decided to get to the ground and find a better viewpoint so dived down into the street and saw a splendid sight. It was most awfully difficult to see how many planes there were, the crowd round me thought there were a great number. I thought only five and I think they got mixed between the planes and the white puffs. I certainly thought I saw one hit for certain and gliding down and I thought I saw another dissolve into smoke, everyone delighted. When I go near St James I saw dozens of people climbing up an iron staircase trying to get on the roof of a very tall building so as to get a good view. These thrilling moments only last a very few minutes.

I got back to the office and said to Newton, 'By George that was a topping sight, did you see all those planes?' 'No,' he said. 'I heard them though and so dived down to the cellar!' I wonder why people want to live to so long? I feel quite bucked up by my day and I am sure he has gone back with a tummy ache and terribly ungrateful to Hitler for having provided us with two first class shows. They say Boche aeroplanes have been tumbling down all over the place.

ELEVEN

London under Fire

O N 14 OCTOBER 1940 the mood changed as tragedy struck our family. Our uncle, Lionel Hichens, who was living in Oxfordshire with his family, came up to London one day for a meeting and was killed in that night's raid. My father told me what happened:

Yesterday and today have been two sad days for us all. One of the best killed. After seeing the room at Church House I am quite certain he was killed instantaneously and did not suffer and that's a small comfort. And I am glad to think that Hermione being away in the country has been spared much suffering and that I have been able to arrange things here for her. The odds against a direct hit are so great that one simply can't understand why he should have been the exception. He had promised Hermione he would go into the shelter at night if there was a raid on, but it is evident that he and the other 5 people who were staying there had just foregathered before dinner and at 7.45 down came the bomb.

I don't know why I had felt apprehensive all day that something was going to happen, so when Mum came in late for dinner, having been out fussing over her refugees, I was quite cross with her and told her I had already heard a bomb which had probably hit a great number of people and it must have been that very bomb. A little later we heard a tremendous noise like tearing calico and crump which shook the house. I thought it was going to hit Laura's old room here (she now sleeps next to us). It apparently landed in Wilton Mews, knocked down several houses there; and this is absolutely true the explosion was so great that debris, clothes male's, female's, were thrown right over the top of the high houses on East Eaton Place and landed in Eaton Place. Some of it is still there today. I wouldn't have believed it possible.

At the coroners H.Q where I had to spend some hours this afternoon to settle the question of Lionel's identity the man next to me told us his wife was the only occupant of one of the houses in the Mews. He had only left her for one night, came back at 4 o'clock next afternoon to find his house had disappeared and there had been such a demand for demolition squads that the debris of his house had not been touched. I tried to comfort him by telling him that the down draught of a big shell knocks you completely unconscious, as I know from two personal experiences in the last war, and so his wife, like Lionel, could not have suffered. Then a young officer on my left told me he had come to identify two brothers!

So darling you see Patrick is right, it is simply folly to come to London. He would never forgive me if I let you come and I am sure Molly will never consent to your doing so. We have a rough sea on at the moment so don't think of coming up. You will only see one tragedy after another and if a mine lands anywhere near you, you will get blown back to Ardchattan much too fast to be comfortable.

The temper of the people here is rising and they won't be satisfied unless the German people are made to suffer the same destruction and ruin which they are facing here. I don't suppose we have enough planes etc to knock out the people and the military objectives and so the military objectives must have the preference but these people who write about reprisals being wrong will bring about a revolution here and are playing Hitler's game. To win we must pay him in the same coin and we must make his people and his towns suffer and crash. I would like to hear that Cologne, Munich and Nuremberg, Berlin and Vienna have disappeared so that history would say these ruined cities are witnesses of the wickedness of the German Prussian race and then let Milan, Florence, Venice and Rome put up a tablet to the memory of Musso.

I can't qualify for Y.W!!!

Despite further agitation on my part about coming to see my family in London, I was told forcibly by not only my father but also Laura that it was too dangerous to risk. By December the day raids had eased off considerably, and they grudgingly gave way. It was agreed that if I slept out of London, I could come into the city by day. Angela had a large house at Hemel Hempstead, already full of friends who worked in London by day. She took me in.

All went well until my last evening. I was due to catch the night train from King's Cross. My father was disappointed that I had not even had the fun of seeing a bomb. But, as we waited to go to the station, the raid started and bangs began. Unused to this, I wished I had never left Ardchattan. Laura comforted me by assuring me that they were a long way off, and I was ashamed to feel relieved that someone else was being killed rather than me.

Matters became more worrying as we took a taxi to the station. At Hyde Park Corner, bombs were dropping in the park and one came over the top of our taxi and exploded in front of us. The taxi turned on a sixpence to take an evading route. My father urged him to drive straight down Piccadilly to give us the chance to see more bombs. But the driver must have read my thoughts and I was relieved when he took no notice. I thought of the words of a young soldier friend, who had told me that when first in action he had found himself praying: 'Please God don't let that bomb hit me. After all it makes no difference to You, but it makes the hell of a difference to me.'

The taxi driver got us safely to King's Cross. Laura and my father were not allowed onto the platform and I sat in the train looking at the acres of glass in the station roof and hearing the bombers overhead. To this day I feel a surge of relief when the night train from King's Cross leaves the station.

My father later wrote that he and Laura had waited at the barrier until they heard my train leave. They helped a woman and two small children away from the glass roofs to the relative safety of an arch and helped her with her problems. My father was delighted that he had got me 'under fire' as he put it. I could not entirely share his excitement as he described the various flares he saw on the way home:

The whole park was lighted up like Fairy Land, several flares 15 to 20 feet high. By the time we got to Hyde Park Corner and looked through the gates I realised the Eton 4th of June wasn't in it. So we stopped the taxi, got on our feet and dived into the park. It really was a wonderful sight. We counted 8 to 10 big flares between the Serpentine and Marble Arch and several incendiaries and by the time we got to the Achilles statue we had an incendiary of our own. A small affair which Laura, another man and 2 young soldiers put out with sand and mud. The flares soon burnt themselves out but it really was a sight worth seeing and all paid for by bankrupt Hitler!

We then turned for home, the horrid red glow of the big fire behind us – somewhere between Edgware Road and Baker Street – getting bigger and bigger. I hope you didn't see it! By the time we got to Hamilton Place traffic had started again up Piccadilly and yet the incendiary bomb which interfered with our journey up Piccadilly looked as if it had landed right in the middle of the road . . .

My father thought that Hitler's bombers would soon follow. He told me that my mother had returned home twenty minutes later, having ridden her bicycle from Marble Arch to Hyde Park Corner:

If she had been 25 mins earlier she would have been right in the middle of it all. So I first gave her a wiggin' for being out during a Blitz and then confessed to taking Laura into the middle of the fireworks.

His enthusiasm undimmed, my father went out the next day and established there had been three bombs, one of which had fallen less than 150 yards from us, and two behind the RAF Club, a mere 100 yards behind us. As a result Hyde Park was roped off with notices of 'unexploded bombs' exactly where he and Laura had extinguished the half burnt out incendiary bombs and where my mother had cycled home. With some excitement he told me:

There were ten flares dropped and many incendiaries – at least eight in one small place between the Serpentine and Marble Arch so you can, later on, tell Mary Ann how you defied the German bombs on either side of you and yet you won through to Kings X and caught the 9.15.

As the Blitz went on night and day, so fear of invasion increased. Rumour fuelled rumour. All the signposts in the country had either been removed or misdirected in the hope that, on landing, the Germans would turn left when they should have gone right. The road down Loch Awe side, our main road to Glasgow or Edinburgh, had concrete blocks half way across the road in alternate directions in order to hamper tanks driving down the road, which made ordinary driving like taking a slalom course. The local Volunteer Force was renamed the Home Guard and were by way of being trained.

In London my father spotted men in bowler hats, their umbrellas representing guns, being trained in Belgrave Square. Our local Home Guard had a tragic story. Each patrol had been issued with some genuine hand grenades. One local commander having never seen such a thing in his life thought he should demonstrate it to his men. He aimed to throw it over their heads so that it would explode safely in the loch, but it landed amongst the platoon, killing two of them.

In the autumn there was suddenly a countrywide alarm. Rumours darted about. German troops had apparently landed, different locations were cited, the local Home Guard was called out, and a shepherd who was living up Loch Etive and had fought through the 1914-18 war, was awoken at 3 am and told to report, bringing food for five days with him. Snorting with indignation at the inexperience of this post-war generation, he arrived with two potatoes. Connel Bridge was closed. After a day life returned to normal but the rumours from London remained dramatic. On 26 October my father wrote:

> *Rumours here put the German losses on 16 Sept at 100,000, but I'm told the Air Force are inclined to exaggerate the results of their raid as Naval and Army chiefs had wanted the Germans given a bit more rope and to have let them come out and then had a spectacular victory. Which scheme was rather spoilt, but if we really did inflict such losses on them why not give it out. There seems little doubt that the Germans are beginning to realise they have lost the mastery of the air. Their intrigues with Spain and Vichy France look like the last throws of a desperate gambler.*

Christmas and the New Year of 1941 were not much celebrated and the years went on seamlessly, except for Laura's Christmas letter to the whole family. She kept us in touch with her typed letters written over carbon paper, and circulated round to us all. At the end of 1940 she wrote:

> *The most extraordinary things have been happening to me lately. I would never have dreamt in my wildest moments that I would have been dining with the Trees* [Ronnie and Nancy Tree, who owned Ditchley Park – she was Joyce's first cousin], *spending Christmas at Cliveden, dishing out custard at the party at the Canadian Hospital, collecting a consignment of toys from Coppins* [home of the Duke and Duchess of Kent].
>
> *In comparison to this, the fact of the Blitz going on outside, and not spending Christmas with all of you somehow seems quite ordinary, but horrid. My American journalist friend* [Ben Robertson] *was returning to America for a month, so I asked him here for a farewell dinner. He rang to say he had to go the next day, and the Trees, with whom he had been staying, had asked him and me to dine with them at the Ritz. I spent hours putting on my best clothes, never dreaming for a moment that I could ever be over dressed in such company, at such a place, but of course when I got*

there they were all dressed (ultra expensive) in woolly frocks and coats and even hats.

The company consisted of the Trees, Leonora Corbett, the actress, Helen Kirkpatrick, the leading journalist here at the moment, Ben, and Mr Kirkpatrick of the Foreign Office and a man called Anthony Head [then Assistant Secretary CID – later Lord Head].

When we arrived the room was full of everybody practically, but they drifted away and we sat down just the above company for dinner. What a dinner too! Leonora Corbett looks quite lovely and is just what a leading actress should be. All the tricks, great wit, but if the conversation strays from her, it's just hauled back again. I'd never believed that sort of character when I have seen it in films, that it is true through and through and couldn't be exaggerated. I was fascinated. The great thing seemed to be to hold hands, and fight terrific mock battles over the corpse of any male within sight. You can imagine I stayed as mum as any dormouse.

The conversation ranged from the most inside political discussion to 'Nancy darling, look at Ronnie, aren't you jealous he's holding Helen's hand now?' All in the same breath. It needed careful attention to keep the different sets of personalities separate and at moments I wondered whether I was getting real Daily Mirror gossip about all the cabinet, then I found the conversation had switched back when I wasn't looking and returned to the present company. All very confusing.

It was very good entertainment though, although rather nerve wracking at the time, as I felt so much like something the cat had brought in. Actually apart from the amusing side, it rather got my goat to think that a certain section of our politics is dealt with by such people in such a manner and I can't help but believe that Ronnie Tree is one of the very stupidest men, even though he may have a heart of gold (solid 18 carat at that too). All the little personnel string pullings and intrigues that they talk about in the most off hand way make my stomach turn rather. I couldn't help saying to Ben in the taxi coming home that nothing could be less English than that, and Cliveden, and I rubbed it in hard, as I think it is a pity that most of the American journalists only see England from there, which though pleasant, couldn't be less typically British. After that dinner, they certainly won't go back and say that we are starving.

I went down with Joyce for Christmas day, and after spending a lovely cosy Christmas Eve with her at the cottage, we went to Cliveden after breakfast on Christmas Day. I'm always painfully aware of a hole in my stocking, a spot on my skirt, a smut on my nose and untidy hair when I go there. There were innumerable officers, all very young and very Eton and Oxford who are billeted there. Added to these were several American Naval attachés, various other friends of different ages and, thank heaven, there was Dinah Brand, and Jim.

Before church Dinah and the others opened their presents and never in all my life have I seen such a display. Bottle on bottle of the most expensive scent, at least two dozen pairs of the very best silk stockings (from Lady Astor) several pairs of stockings for country wear (from Lady Astor) several super expensive Flap Jacks [powder compacts] (the best from Lady Astor) and several very luxurious cigarette cases, a pair of terrific bedroom slippers, and goodness knows what else: you've never seen anything like it.

We went to church at Hitcham which was very nice. Back to an enormous dinner we sat down thirty. I had an officer on either side and made the very best ex-deb conversation I could. In the afternoon I had to return to my character of member of the WVS and in that capacity drive over to Coppins to collect some toys graciously given by His Royal Highness the Duke of Kent. I drove over, got lost about three times, and was then sent from the front door to the back, where I received very haughty treatment at the hands of the butler.

I crawled away with a fort and a huge box of toys in the back of the car, which I then took and dumped with the Caretaker of the Slough Town Hall. Goodness knows what has happened to them now. I returned to have tea with Joyce at the cottage and immediately after we had to get dressed in long velvet frocks for the party at the Canadian hospital to begin at six. Off we went all dolled up. There were about three hundred men, they each had a mug, a plate and spoon and their form of applause was to bang these against each other and whistle.

Joyce led the proceedings to great applause. Lady Astor did her bit and a band came up from Skindles for about an hour. After a good deal of singing and music it was announced that there was to be a meal of hotdogs and Christmas pudding. Unfortunately some hitch occurred (I don't think the chef had ever met a hotdog before so wasn't going to try) the rolls came first and then there was a time lag before the hot sausage arrived to go in it. With the result that the soldiers in the front ate their rolls without sausages, procured a second roll and stuffed that with a handful of hot sausages, the men at the back who were the less well ones anyway had to go without and there was quite a lot of shouting and exhorting from all concerned.

You'd never have thought dressed in my blue velvet bridesmaid frock with all me jewels (!) on, I should have seized a handful of very hot and greasy sausages out of the pan and passed them over several rows of Canadian heads to the back row. I've never been so greasy in all my life. For the next course I thought I would seize the pot that looked as though it couldn't run out, so with two staunch men carrying the cauldron I wielded an enormous ladle and dished a sauce (which was said to contain rum) on the plates on which a dollop of Christmas pudding had already been put. During all this, Joyce had slipped away to sing to the bed patients in her ward and found a co-star in a Cockney who came out with a glorious series of songs.

After the party we went up to Cliveden again, washed off some of the custard, and sat done to an enormous dinner – forty strong this time. After dinner we went into the Long Drawing Room and after some community singing of all sorts, Joyce at the piano, they started to do charades. Hugh Fraser did a brilliant imitation of Laval in flowing French, somehow managing to look just like him. Jakie [Astor] did a very good Colonel Blimp. Joyce then did her canteen

*lady and then a new sketch, 'In the Lending Library.' As we had to
start fairly early the next day, she had two performances, one on
Boxing Day morning as well as the afternoon, we didn't stay on
after. It was great fun.*

*Nothing could have been a greater contrast than the party I went
to the next day, in the capacity of chauffeur to Lady Reading. I took
her to two hotels where Gibraltar refugees are housed, where they
were celebrating Christmas. I have never seen so many children in
proportion to grown ups.*

*On Boxing Day we had lunch party here. Mummy contrived a
sort of fork lunch quite beautifully. The Wyndhams3, Ann Talbot
and Roger Makins* [later British Ambassador to the US] *and V came
too.*

Early in the New Year of 1941, Laura wrote to me:

*I can't think what you've done to Mummy. I really am quite nervous
about it. This time next week I shall be standing quite nude in the
middle of the street at this rate. The 3d bits I'd saved for Mary Ann
were 'borrowed' as a Christmas present to Edna Woosley. The Diary
I bought as a present for Dad has also been pinched and I gather I'm
to get another like it, for her to give him. There've been two taxis to
pay for, a bottle of Sero-Calcin was 'borrowed' for the secretary at
the Y.W. who was presented at the same time with some whisky and
orange juice transported to her in my best knitting bag. That just
about reduces my worldly possessions by half. But after all if she
hadn't taken them a bomb might have!*

All through the next six months the Blitz continued. My father
sent us detailed news of every building damaged or destroyed in
the various raids, while Laura reported more comfortingly on

3. Hugh Wyndham (1877-1963) was married to Hilda's first cousin Maud
Lyttelton. In 1952 he succeeded as 4th Lord Leconfield and was photographed by
the Press buying a ticket at Sloane Square Underground, as he was travelling to
Westminster Abbey for the Coronation in the full robes of a peer of the realm.

young friends home on leave and their parties in nightclubs, the American canteens, and the energetic activities of Lady Reading.

In February she took Geoffrey to stay with the Selbornes. Lord Selborne, known as Top, was the father of Laura's great friend, Mary Palmer. He gave Geoffrey his views on the war:

Top said the powers that be were pretty sure there would be an invasion attempt, and as the opinion of almost everyone was that whoever invaded would be bound to lose, we were hoping that they would do it before we had to.

TWELVE

Life in the Wrens

IN THE SPRING OF 1941 the Government ordered the registration of all young women with a view to calling them up in the services or allotting them to other jobs. It was not quite as rigid a law as conscription for the men as there was leeway for choices.

This put an end to domestic service as we and our parents had known it, and I was faced with losing Mary Ann's Nanny, or finding full time war work myself. I had been getting rather desperate at not having enough to do. So we decided I should try to join the Immobile WRNS, who were recruiting in Oban. We lived at home but worked by day. In June I gave an account of my new life as a Wren:

It's no laughing matter being a rating in HM's navy, at least it doesn't sound it. I expect you are all thinking me dotty to do it, but I've thought the whole thing round about 90 times and I'm sure I'm right. I heard a terrifying story which I don't think unreasonable of a woman who looked after her baby during the war and didn't see her husband for 3 years. When the husband came back the child was about 4 or 5 and having always done everything with the mother, she resented bitterly being handed over to a nanny when her father returned, and she's never forgiven him or got on with him to this day. Can you beat it? Anyhow there are the majority of my reasons for anyone who cares to know them. I have a few more for anyone who remains unconvinced.

By great luck I've landed a job with the WRNS in Oban. I can live here and come back every night. The hours are 9-6 and I get off after lunch (laugh this one off) on Sunday, that's my only time off. I occasionally get a whole Sunday. I have 3 weeks leave spread over a year. I work in an office and it's highly confidential and terribly important and only the very very honest can do it. One day I get a uniform. It's said to be very strenuous at first, but easy once you have the hang of it. God only knows what it is. I work under a navy officer (male) who's apparently terrified of the females in his office. I hope to jump a good deal of time off out of him. I gather he's the equivalent of a ½ loot.

I start work today week, 7 July, and get £2 a week. My word, sounds as if I deserve it too. I am backing on getting extra petrol so that I can drive each way, otherwise it won't be so funny. The WRNS are trying to make me say I'll live in Oban and get out sometimes, but I'm being quite adamant about that as I hear the WRNS hostel which was meant to hold 15 already has 37 and isn't very savoury at all.

I had a killing interview. A rather efficient officer, I should guess someone's ex-private secretary, asked me if I had any training so I honestly confessed I had none at all. She raised her beautiful pencilled eyebrows and said, 'D'you mean absolutely none?' I saw my reputation slipping so I blushed prettily and said 'You see I married so soon after leaving school I had no time.' Reputation saved, except that the next question was 'Your little baby must be nearly old enough for school, isn't she?'

Anyhow I don't seem to have done too badly as I landed the job almost on the spot. It'll be the hell of a grind to start with, but I'm hoping I'll get into it alright and will probably rather enjoy it in the end.

Later, however, I reported one of my Wren friends from Lancashire saying: 'Don't know as 'ow you got married, you're not capable. You can't do a damn thing – but you've got all your teeth, suppose that 'elps catch 'em.'

My naval career is not among the 'spoils of time' with which I have any reason to be satisfied. I had never worked full time in a disciplined job and did not take to it with any humility. The job turned out to be making up and correcting the cipher books handed out to ships in a convoy. It was important to be accurate. I was put to work under an officer of the RNR, working with him in the same office. He was a precise and pernickety man, as indeed it was right that he should be. He had a chip on his shoulder, was a nationalised citizen with a foreign name, and therefore unpopular with the other officers.

I also put him in an invidious position. The Naval Station had been in operation since the beginning of the war. Its commander was a retired Naval officer who took a house and lived in Oban with his wife. Captain Stokes was an avid fisherman and had often fished Bobby's pool on the Awe with me, so we were already friends. He was also a friend of Molly's.

He was amused by my becoming a Wren – in particular my salute to him, which was a mixture of the military and the Girl Guides. He made it clear that this was not going to make him give up his fishing. The tidal pool had to be fished when the tide was out. So he watched the tides, rang me up when the tide was right and suggested I leave the office and come fishing. I often did and poor Mr P (the officer in command of me) could do nothing about it. Not surprisingly he took other opportunities to make life difficult for me.

Having signed up as an office worker, which the majority of the other Wrens had too, we were not pleased when ordered to drill after office hours. We had to gather on the Pier in Oban and were put through our paces by a petty officer forming fours, turning at an order right or left. In the heat of the moment, a number of us had difficulty working out which was which.

After I had been a Wren for a while, Captain Meikle came to work at the Naval Station. He was an RNR officer and had been captain of the CPR liner on which I had sailed to Canada. He was doing a rest job, having commanded convoys on the Northern Route to Russia under appalling conditions. This did not make life any easier for Mr P.

I exploited all these advantages to the maximum. My inelegant service in the Navy lasted just under two years and was recorded in my letters to Laura and my father. My work was a mixture of the terribly dull and the equally exciting in virtually equal measure. I told my family that I would come south in my uniform 'to show you all what an ex-female convict looks like!' I also reported:

Poor Mrs C-P had an awful week as our smallest evacuee fell in the fire and spilt a whole kettle of boiling water over itself – aged 14 months. Mrs C-P undoubtedly saved its life by covering it immediately in Tammic acid. The mother had hysterics on every possible occasion and the Granny who is terribly proud of having buried 8 of hers herself – never failed to intone Cath(olic) prayers at colossal speed while drawing breath to say 'Puir wee lamb, God be merciful she's gone – a weel I buried 8 before now'. It all got pretty nerve wracking so yesterday I drove the child into hospital where it is getting on alright.

I'm so bored at the office I could scream, but I guess someone has got to be bored so it might as well be me. Mr P doesn't dare lift a finger to me while my boyfriend the Commander is there – but he's on leave this week so I guess I'm in for a spell of narking. He started as the Commander's train drew out of the station! Why we let foreigners nationalize beats me!

On 15 July 1941 I wrote:

I am still doodling round this office with absolutely nothing to do but thank God 'P' [my RNR boss] is on leave this week so I can write to my family in peace. He had another row about me and complained to the Commander (with perfect justification as I went home without asking him) but the Commander just laughed at him and told him to boil his face. Well, I expect my fate is better than Patrick's although I wonder at times!

The Labour Exchange haven't deferred nanny's call up yet and I heard from them yesterday asking for further details of our household. I expect if they don't call her up this time, they probably will before the year is over.

147

In November I went to London and Laura and I gave a dinner party made memorable by 'a magnificent escort of esquires' at the Savoy paid for by a gift from my father. On my return from leave, 'P' had sent a petty officer to meet me at the station and I was almost put under arrest for overstaying my leave. As it turned out, I was home a day early rather than a day late. I was furious and by the time I had finished informing 'P' of this, all the others were furious with him too. One of them pronounced solemnly: 'If he'd been decently educated at Harrow he'd have been murdered for doing a thing like that!' I smiled sweetly and thought how much my father would have agreed. Finally the other officers told Meikle the story and he 'went up in blue smoke and had P on the mat all one morning'.

The naval duties of the Wrens were to deal with convoys which were loaded down on the Clyde and then distributed up the West Coast and hopefully 'hidden' up the different lochs, until ready to collect and meet at sea to cross the Atlantic. When these convoys returned they usually went back to the Clyde. They were often commanded by retired naval officers.

A family friend was Admiral the Hon Arthur Strutt, second son of the great scientist, Lord Rayleigh. He had been a frequent guest in my home and we had all known him and his family all our lives. He was known as Arka. He was overjoyed to be recruited to command convoys and loved finding himself on a merchant ship, in command of all the ships in line in a convoy. Very unexpectedly his command ship came into Oban instead of the Clyde.

Arka's arrival caused me some embarrassment as he walked into the operations room where I was standing, and seeing me in Wren uniform said, 'Frances, what on earth are you doing here dressed like that?' The generation to which both Arka and Captain Stokes belonged found it hard to accept that women could do a man's job responsibly and treated it as something of a joke. I am glad to say that my own parents did not take that view.

Arka swept me off to luncheon in the Station Hotel, where

other ranks were not allowed. For him there was no such thing as a female 'other rank', though that is precisely what I was. While we had a pre-luncheon drink in the lounge, Arka met Mrs Murray-Guthrie, over from Torosay Castle on Mull. She was a tall distinguished looking lady, a cousin of the Prime Minister on his mother's side. Quite oblivious to the other occupants of the lounge they began a conversation in strident tones, trying to decide where they had last met. It appeared to be a close choice between Downing Street and Buckingham Palace. I sat cringing:

I had great fun 2 days ago as who should turn up but old Arka. He's the first admiral to come here, and I got a free lunch out of him in to the bargain. He was in good form in spite of five sleepless nights and lots of bother from 'bad men'. He was very interesting and we had an amusing gossip. I hope he turns up again. They were so funny about him in the office as they were even more impressed with his honourable than his admiralty.

Meanwhile Patrick was still a prisoner in Germany. The first camp he had been in was Oflag V11C. This we traced eventually to a place in South Germany called Laufen. Patrick described looking through a window onto snow-capped hills in pretty country. It was a hutted camp. Just before Christmas 1940 the camp had been split and he had had to leave many of his Black Watch friends, whom he missed. Among these was an old friend, David Walker. He and David had been at Sandhurst together, had joined on the same day and served together in India. David had succeeded Patrick as ADC to John Tweedsmuir, and while in Canada, had married Willa McGee, also a friend.

Patrick wrote that he was still with his Ludgrove and Eton friends, the closest amongst whom was Charlie Hopetoun (from whom he claims to have a caught a flea, thus, he commented, at least socially acceptable) and Martin Gilliat. 'Martin is a great chap', he wrote. 'He has a marvellous sense of humour – you would love him.' They had formed a football team, Highland

Brigade versus Green Jackets. Martin broke a rib, and Patrick landed in bed with a swollen foot from a kick. The German doctors were very conscientious. General Victor Fortune, who had commanded the Highland Division, was in the camp and was allowed a two-bedded room which he shared with his lugubrious ADC aged 52!

The General had served under Patrick's father in the 1914-18 War. He was kind to them and allowed them to retire to his room occasionally – 'a great relief to get away from the maddening crowd'. The General got quite sentimental when he reminisced about the time he was ADC to my Lyttelton grandfather in Dublin and had ridden in Phoenix Park with my mother before she married. Nor was their news all bad. Fourteen prisoners had opened 72 tins at Christmas, resulting in a five course dinner. The Americans were generous with their food parcels and, as Patrick put it, as a result, they ate 'like fighting cocks'.

All this time Patrick and his fellow prisoners were working on their escape plans. The first effort was to be a tunnel. In television programmes made after the war, escape stories invariably consisted of half-an-hour of packed excitement, acted by fit young men. The truth was rather different. All attempts to escape took careful planning, and it might be a year before they could 'break'. The engineers had to work out meticulous plans, finding the safest place in respect of drains or electric cables, how to ensure that the noise of excavation would not be picked up by the guards, and numerous other considerations.

Getting rid of soil removed from the tunnel took endless time, since it was hardly possible to fill a bag and dump it by the rubbish bins. All the soil had to be removed in small handfuls. One method was to dribble it down their trouser legs as they exercised.

They formed committees or teams to work out their plan of action. All this was done by men whose energy had been sapped by poor rations and lack of facilities to exercise. It was also dangerous, one of them being killed in a tunnel. In spite of these difficulties the enterprise gave the non-scholastic among them a purpose.

Another hazard was that rather unsportingly, the Germans would suddenly move them to another camp and so all their work would be wasted.

Patrick wrote a postcard of two lines on 10 October: 'Tomorrow the whole camp moves to Oflag VIB love Patrick.' A few days later, on 1 November, I received a letter dated 28 October:

Still in the same camp, as Martin, Charlie and I had a shot at copying Hugh Durnford [a 1914 prisoner who had escaped]. *Unfortunately the plan failed so here we are shut up in a couple of cells, well treated and in good form if a little downhearted. You must not worry there was no risk. I can't tell you anything about it except that I had a beautiful beard after five days. Although restricted in space I have never felt better in all my life. We have had a good many laughs. Charlie looked like a beachcomber or a character out of a S. Maugham novel, as his shoes are worn out and he can't get his boots back, I am without some clothes too, but we hope to get them back before we move. Martin looks after us both, as usual and doles out the food and manages everything. Our jailers think we are quite mad which we probably are.*

A few days later he reported that he had spent another three days in the cells, but Charlie and Martin had gone to a new camp: 'Peter Greenwell [Reggie Colquhoun's brother-in-law] is in the next cell, a nice chap so everything is O.K.'

In November 1942 I gave my father Patrick's version as relayed to me:

I suppose Lolly has told you of the sad but inevitable ending to Patrick's bid for freedom. 5½ days on the loose is a pretty good effort don't you think? He wrote and told me that he promised he wouldn't take undue risk, but I must realise he must and would do things like that. I perfectly agree with him and I must admit I wasn't in the least surprised to hear he'd tried it.

I'm afraid I don't consider myself in the least entitled to write and ask him not to do it, as when one is free one can't have the least idea really of what it is like to be a captive. I'd be the first to be jolly pleased if he brought it off too! Anyhow they all three [Patrick, Martin and Charlie Hopetoun] seemed to have enjoyed the whole trip immensely and received very fair treatment on their recapture. I'm jolly proud of him for doing it!

Patrick escaped outside the camp twice. His and David Walker's last effort was from a camp at Warburg. Theirs was an elaborate plan and it took a large team to organise it. They built a bridge across two perimeter fences. The planks for the bridge were made from the shelves of the library, which also served as a music room when a pianist was available. If the guards were spotted about to come on a routine check, the shelves had to be replaced, often in seconds, while the pianist played to cover the noise. Everything was timed to the minute – the time it took to sling the bridge across – the time between sentries walking the perimeter – the time each person needed to cross the bridge.

On the chosen night, those selected by the committee to be the escapees all got out. Patrick and David were free for several days. But I think only one escapee got home. They were caught and, after being in detention for some time, they were both sent to Colditz, a castle closer to the Russian frontier. After Airey Neave's escape earlier in the war, it was made virtually impregnable and reluctantly they decided there were to be no more escape attempts. They also thought that the war would soon end.

In December a postcard arrived from Patrick. After that letters continued to meander their way back from him. This rather tortuous correspondence ploughed its way past the censors. These sometimes arrived heavily blacked out or with parts cut out by scissors. It was difficult to fathom the mind of the censor. One of Patrick's cousins wrote to him, and stuck for anything to say, mentioned that there was snow in his garden in England. The whole letter was censored. Apparently it was forbidden to write about the weather, which seemed strange since letters took at least a month to arrive and presumably by then, even the Germans must have known it had snowed in England.

At other times quite sensitive remarks arrived safely. Bobby wrote of his voyage and arrival, and of his spell in hospital after being wounded. That letter, and letters to Patrick from the Middle East describing battles, passed through uncensored.

There was an upsetting incident for Molly and me when we got a letter from a censor at a censorship office, who claimed to be a cousin, unknown to Molly, commenting on our letters. We were both worried by this.

By January 1941, regular letters were getting through. After the war Patrick and I discovered we had kept every letter we sent each other. I wrote a diary letter every evening and posted it once a week, so it served as a daily bulletin both of my life and of our family. The letters chronicled Mary Ann's babyish small talk.

By the end of the war we had been separated for five years, our married life together consisting of only nine months. We were never able to express deep feelings in our correspondence, and took the view that it would be unkind to give vent to feelings of sadness and depression, which could easily be long over by the time the other read about them, letters taking so long to arrive. So our understanding of what either of us had gone through was necessarily limited.

Pipe dreams were a large feature in our letters – charming scenarios of what we might do, or be, in the future. One idea was that we would set up in a farm in Argyll. When Patrick began an agricultural course in prison and urged me to do one too, my answer was, 'Can't you till the land while I make butter and have babies? I don't think anything else is quite my style.' My father also kept in touch with Patrick, filling his letters with references to 'melting ice creams', a coded reference to the Italians.

Life in London continued apace. In January 1941 Laura wrote:

Evelyn Baring [later Governor of Kenya] came to lunch on Tuesday. He must have thought us quite crazy, for Mummy was just off to Bristol, where she went for the night to attend the funeral of the Y.W. people who were killed there. You know what it is like just before Mummy goes off anywhere, a sort of in at one door and out of the other, business. I don't know why, but feeling was running rather high that day about roof spotters. Principally I think because Mummy threatened to go off and sit on a roof herself. Daddy and I were rather naturally upset at this, and so that subject caused rather a lot of argument and shouting, and talking to me under their breath while the other was bellowing. Poor Evelyn, he always seems to catch us on a particularly dotty day. I don't know really why I try and make out that one day is dottier than the other, because as a matter of fact it's about the one stable thing in this family, the amount of dottiness.

It was now nearly a year since the first bombings of the Blitz and we were getting used to this peculiar way of life. Vera described the Highway Clubs, in the East End, where boys and girls gathered, of bombs, the difficulties of evacuating, and of tiring negotiations with local organisations. By now a number of charities were pouring in help, but this led to rivalry between them and the Borough Council, and Vera found herself involved and caught up in their arguments – a trying addition to the normal stress.

The first feeling of excitement about war was wearing off. We were now entering the phase of endurance, and tiredness was beginning to show. In October 1941 Vera was involved in an attempt to get 100 tons of coal delivered in the name of the South African 'Coal Gift Scheme'. Once obtained this had to be distributed to each church or voluntary body, the cause of many arguments. Vera went round South Africa House and was impressed by the generous quantities of clothes and woollen comforts sent from South Africa, not to mention the large sums of money sent to the Red Cross, canteens and relief of Air Raid Distress. As ever there was a problem getting the supplies to their destinations.

Vera pressed on despite fires blazing across the river, and bombs flying around. Those at her centre dwindled from 800 to 170, and at last some of the old folk were sent away to safety. She and Irene Ravensdale battled gamely with the bureaucracy of government offices.

In May 1941, Rudolf Hess, one of Hitler's closest associates flew alone to Scotland and landed on Lord Clydesdale's[4] estate. My father wrote:

We are alright. Harry came down and has been with us here. He is very fit and well. V. had a nasty time, one direct hit on the house next door! She can't get it much closer than that – she looks drawn and personally I wish we could get her away from that job, and into some service job. Eliz Dawnay, who is warden in Chelsea, has been here once or twice and lunched with me today. She also had a very trying time on Saturday and Sunday. There was a very big smash around Harrods. H's windows were smashed but otherwise no harm done – but Basil Street, Hans Crescent are all absolutely smashed down – an awful mess up. 14 bodies so far recovered and poor Eliz D has to be on duty all day waiting in case they find some more. There are 5 or 6 still buried. The other two big smashes in our neighbourhood were a shelter in Eaton Square where the Mayor of Westminster and a good many others were killed and at the Alexandra Hotel, Knightsbridge – a direct hit right down the lift shaft and burst at the bottom, some of the people's clothes were flung across Knightsbridge and are now spread out high up in the trees in Hyde Park. 140 people were got out, about 15 bodies have been recovered and about 15 more still to be found. The smash round Hill Street, Green Street is bad and from Gower Street to St Pancras awful.

4. Marquess of Clydesdale – in fact 14th Duke of Hamilton & Brandon (1903-73).

I am told a map was found on Hess with Clydesdale's place marked – he apparently knew C as a skier and if this is true he made a deuced fine trip. It is an amazing thing. Surely he can only have come because he disagreed with something the Boche intends to do and disagreed so fundamentally that he came to inform us! If it was only to save his own skin, he must be a worm indeed. I would show him no mercy. Dope him, make him drunk, do almost anything to him until he disclosed his plans and the condition of Germany. There is nothing good in this blackguard but he must have given the whole German system a shock they won't get over easily.

Meanwhile my sister Mary was trying to settle in Canada. Soon after her arrival, she was joined there by our cousin Molly (Grey) from Howick. Molly married Evelyn Baring and they had three children. Her sister Elizabeth, always known as 'Nisset', had married Ronnie Dawnay and they had four children. Ronnie was a regular soldier who had been posted to Cairo before the war. Nisset had gone out to join him for a short visit and had been caught there by the war and also by sudden illness.

Molly took Nisset's children and her own from Howick, joining Mary in Canada, where Nisset then made her way from Cairo to join them. Their household consisted of twelve children under twelve. Since Mary had also brought a friend's child with her, by the time Mary's baby son arrived that December the total reached fourteen.

Although there were two governesses, Mary's cook from Chewton and two nannies, their workload was considerable and their financial situation difficult. Neither Molly nor Mary had ever cooked, washed clothes or ironed.

Nisset arrived from Cairo, very ill, and a tumour was diagnosed. Her death in February 1941 was an awful tragedy for all of them. Communications were fitful, all letters travelling by ship. With the war waging in the Atlantic, many never arrived. Molly and Mary were homesick, worried and felt completely exiled.

Mary had the consolation of her baby son, James, born in December 1940. But in her letters she expressed herself forcibly:

Your lovely letter reached me a few days ago and warmed the cockles of my heart. It has been fun getting your letters during this last week. Its been so very queer having James in such splendid isolation that I hardly really believed in him at all until I began to get your letters confirming his existence. I haven't now had one from Geoff which is rather mouldy, but when that comes I shall really and truly realise that he really and truly is there. Mails take at least five or six weeks now, which means it takes ten or twelve weeks at least to get an answer to anything, which is rather hard to get used to, and everything comes all jumbled up and hopelessly out of sequence.

She was irritated by the censor who cut Laura's letter into ribbons. Nor did she understand his methods, since he would cut a story in one letter and leave it intact in another.

I loved your account of your family tour and your thumbnail sketches of them all. Poor old Polly, it must be awfully trying for her and she really is a grand girl the way she keeps on such an even keel and is such a darling to everyone and keeps so sweet tempered and sensible through it all. I really do think she and Reggie are the two in our family who are what I consider genuine saints. The rest of us don't qualify to any extent, as we each in our own way answer back and retaliate with considerable acidity, where those two just scratch their heads and grin and proceed unruffled on their way.

You are quite right to remind me not to judge Canada by the Province of Quebec. It certainly is not an impressive province, but I don't think it can all be blamed on the French. Why when you buy a toothbrush do all the bristles fall out into your mouth? Why when you get a maid does she smell so nasty that you can't possibly have her in to any of the bedrooms, and even the French Canadian woman with whom she lodges says she can't endure it? Why when you wash a garment made of blue baby wool for which you have paid 30 cents an ounce, and wash it as tenderly as you do the baby itself, does the dye instantly swim out of it leaving it a pale and unattractive beige? etc etc.

I wonder if its true that quality exists practically only in England. I believe it very nearly is. Three things I give full marks to in Canada. The telephone, the cars and the toilet paper. All three are excellent but man cannot live on these alone.

Mary then went to Quebec, fell under the spell of the Citadel, and saw at once how it must have been the perfect way to meet Patrick. She continued to send us sweets and offered to send clothes. Her exile in Canada lasted till the beginning of 1943. At that point Molly's husband Evelyn Baring was appointed Governor of Southern Rhodesia (today's Zimbabwe) where Molly joined him. Mary returned to Britain, experiencing just as perilous a journey as on the way out.

THIRTEEN

My Mother's Journey

IN LONDON the fabric of family life was kept going by Minnie, who cooked, cleaned, washed, ironed and shopped. This was a major undertaking, as she would get up very early and go to whatever market was open to get whatever was available before others got there. She never admitted to fear of the bombs, only confessing they did keep her awake – sometimes. Laura and I worried about her and occasionally I was able to claim her to look after Mary Ann, to give her a break. It was ironical that, although our mother cared deeply about social justice and the fate of the human race, she never grasped the burdens she put on Minnie or any domestic. On top of all her work, my mother expected Minnie to mend her clothes and do her packing.

Following a visit to me in Scotland in August 1941, Laura returned to an empty house, where she had great fun looking after herself for the first time in her life:

I had no idea that life was so complicated though. I could never look more than one meal ahead, and then found that I had forgotten to buy the bread, or else, far more likely, that I had got too much of some commodity, and that unless it was all eaten within a few minutes it would be bad, and then what would Lord Woolton say? So I eat as I have never eaten before.

I was determined not to exist only on eggs (I bought masses down from Ardchattan with me) but to launch out onto more ambitious lines. One evening I had a sort of macaroni cheese, made out of stuff called vermicelli, which I found in the cupboard, and which was very eatable. Then I got my meat ration. A large and formidable lump of steak which haunted me from then on. I tried to get someone to come and help me eat it, but they all said oh no, wouldn't I go out with them instead. So the steak still remained in the larder. Then I cooked it and ate a strip. Rather underdone, but very succulent and juicy.

Although I was nearly bursting, I still found that there was a vast expanse of meat left on the dish. All the time that I was tackling these household cares, I was doing the most extraordinary job by day. Roger Makins' mother-in-law, Mrs Dwight Davis, who is woman number one in the American Red Cross, and her assistant Mrs Eustis, came over here on a visit, and I was told off to be secretary. With visions of American efficiency, and the way American executives rush their secretaries off their feet making telephone calls, typing letters, fixing up appointments etc, on the films, I was rather nervous but thought it would be fun, and braced myself up to meet what was before me.

I was taken up to Claridges to meet my new bosses, who looked slightly appalled, but hadn't really recovered enough to realise what was before them, after arriving at one in the morning by clipper. We fixed up their permits etc. that morning, and all went well. They lunched at the Ritz, and spent the afternoon at the American Red Cross Office here, ending up with a press conference. That afternoon I waited in their suite at Claridges, rather apprehensive that the press and everyone else might ring up, and then what should I say. However nothing happened, so I tucked my toes up on the sofa, with a newspaper, lolled among the flowers and had a very restful time, and then when they came in I had tea with them as though I lived in Claridges all my life! I quite thought that it would take them a day to settle down and get something for me to do.

Next morning I went up to them at a bright and early hour, to find one still in bed, and the other wandering around with her hair in curlers, in a dressing gown. I did one or two telephone calls, otherwise sat about with my hands and feet feeling, as they so often do, very unnecessarily large. I was slightly staggered to find that Mrs Dwight Davis having arrived over here with a more than adequate wardrobe (I knew it inside out because I'd been through their cupboards while they were out the day before), declared that she really couldn't exist without a new dressing gown, new bedroom slippers, 6 pairs of silk stockings, two blouses, two jumpers and several pairs of gloves! I said rather mildly that she couldn't buy anything without coupons, but that I would see what could be done. While I was playing around with the addresses of various offices of the Board of Trade, they discovered a much quicker way through the American Embassy, by which they could get anything they wanted off the export quota, and did. That attitude rather surprised me as I fancied they had come over to work their guts out, seeing how difficult it is to get a passage, and not to amuse themselves. However I was very much mistaken. Lady R had planned an elaborate programme for them to tour various London Boroughs, and see the work in progress, then to spend the night with her in Sussex, and go the next day on a tour of activities in the country.

By Monday morning they were on the verge of being complete wrecks. However, they and Mrs Winant [wife of the American Ambassador] were to spend a long day touring round our headquarters, so that they could see all the different branches of work on hand. They were supposed to go on till four o'clock, but by three they couldn't take anymore, and so faded away to have drinks with Quentin Reynolds and other journalists.

At 5.30 we all went to the Guildhall (yes, the one in the City), where about 600 WVS members were collected for the first public meeting since the 'second fire' and the first women's meeting ever to be held there. It really was quite impressive. An asbestos roof has been put over the hall. The walls are scraped very bare, and all that finery and detail have disappeared. Still the Guildhall does stand, and is capable of having meetings even now! There are some black charred patches on the walls which tell their tale. I've only been in the Guildhall once before.

When I got there, I was feeling rather baffled and angry with my two Americans. They were supposed to be the leading women in America, the counterpart of Lady R, and yet they gave everyone a *great deal of trouble to get over here, and to have things arranged for them, and then behaved as though it was just a good opportunity for them to see their friends here, buy a few trophies, and just be typical American visitors at their worst. I must say I suppose it is difficult to believe that we are a beleaguered fortress, fighting for our lives etc etc, especially in the Claridges-Ritz atmosphere, but even then, I expected them to have some imagination. I think they did just begin to realise that there was a war on at that meeting. One very good speaker was the head of a clothing store, who got up and gave a very telling account of the work she had done all through the Blitz, making it amusing and pathetic, courageous and tragic, and very simple all at once. She was so obviously sincere, and all her stories so true, that it carried a great deal of weight.*

The next day I had a telephone call to say that there really wasn't enough for me to do, so I wasn't to bother to go to them. In other words I was given a gentle sacking.

What a waste all these useless people buzzing about the Atlantic at will.

Harry was on leave and Laura found him in good form, going with him to a dinner party given by Reg and Joyce, and to another given by Howard Clegg, a Canadian from the Ministry of Information. There was lunch with everyone except our mother, who was 'lunching in fine but less enjoyable style at Downing Street.'

Despite snowy roads, my mother was back cycling, and enjoying the deep breaths this made her take and the wind in her face. She had the latest news on Arthur Strutt:

Arthur Strutt lunched today, furious because the Admiralty had given his convoy due to sail Thurs. to someone else as they'd heard he was not yet fit to go to sea again. He'd consistently told them he was (which he obviously isn't) and was livid at the interference. He looks very white and shaky still, and his broken arm prevents him cutting a loaf or pouring out his own coffee. But Thursday's convoy was to go South West, the direction he wanted to go to avoid Halifax, where he landed so knocked about last time. He is sure seagoing is the best of tonics for him – odd I call it, when convoy work must be one long continual strain.

All through the summer there was a family debate about the advisability of my mother making a hazardous journey to Canada for the YWCA. Laura looked on it as a choice between two evils, veering on the side that the bombing and domestic events were causing her great stress, while the hazards of the journey would be counterbalanced by a month free from sleepless nights.

My mother was determined to go, though she felt guilty leaving her husband and daughter in London. She always worried about us and both in peace and war, whenever we went away, she insisted that we let her know we had arrived safely. She and Susie Tweedsmuir shared a lively imagination, conjuring terrible fates for us when out of sight. 'No news is good news' was not her motto.

Eventually the counsel of various ministers and of Mrs Churchill herself prevailed and she set off for Canada. This left Laura with the care of our father, who was not always very well, but it meant they could lead their lives at their own pace for a while.

Before her departure in October 1941, my mother issued her instructions:

About Min, I think she'd best go to you after I go to Canada – as it is a bit imposs to spare her. Min aches to come to you I can see. Her stony comment on my going merely was 'Humph? You'll be in the war over there soon.' Cryptic but designed and depressing, funny old thing.

Before Hilda left, she visited an east coast naval base, sleeping in the commander's quarters and witnessed the 21st birthday party of a young Wren, who made all the arrangements herself:

I had to cross the estuary in a little pinnace (calling on a tanker, en route, to fetch off an engineer) in the early dawn to catch an early train on a lovely morning. We looked bang across the North Sea and they have alerts every night, but almost no one has been killed. Oh! And the drilling – they told me everyone hated it at first and then ended up by liking it. I wonder if you ever will.

Did you hear Cripps [our ex-butler] has been heard of as a Prisoner-of-War in transit camp in Crete? I think they must mean Greece. If only he could get as Batman to Patrick. The poor old Ruskeys! Oh can they hold out till winter comes? [The Germans had invaded Russia on June 22 1941].

My mother left for Lisbon and America on 26 October. The days preceding her departure were chaotic. She was only allowed 44 lbs of luggage. Laura had been amused by her farewell telephone call to me:

It was rather comic watching Mummy pouring her soul into the mouthpiece and sitting with an ecstatic expression on her face while you presumably poured yours, not one syllable of which could she hear!

My mother got stuck in Lisbon for ten days. She immediately made links with Mrs Ian Campbell and the depot from which she organised the prisoner-of-war parcels and the letters. Eventually she reached New York via Bermuda aboard S.S. *Exeter.*

I wrote you a PS to my letter posted at Bermuda to tell you a few more and comforting things about Prisoners-of-War that my nice friend Mr Key from the USA Embassy in Rome has told me. He's been a good deal in touch with their people in Berlin and says that the Army so jealously guard the right to have the say about P's of war and keep the Gestapo out. He said that under the Geneva Convention the Germans will be bound to give the exact whereabouts of the camps for transmission to us in England so that out Airmen may know. It is forbidden to put any Prison Camps within Military or Munitions areas.

It was his job in Rome to keep an eye on all our Prisoners' Camps there and he saw our four poor Generals there, who are almost too well treated in being given a good villa to live in, who beg to be sent to the camps where the bulk of Prisoners are. He said General Carton de Wiart had been trying to play up his 11 wounds of the last war as a reason for being exchanged as totally disabled. But the Italians pointed out he had been in 3 campaigns since in spite of them and so they refused. Gardening is the one solace our poor Generals can go in for.

My mother went to Quebec, feeling bereft of news from her family. But she found that those Canadians who were conscious of the war believed fervently that all Britons were heroes and heroines. While the evacuated children were generally beloved, their parents were not, and their nannies were without exception hated.

My mother stayed with Mary and insisted that we cable her every ten days or she would never get our news. From London in December, Laura wrote:

Maria and Mummy went to Montreal, Toronto and Ottawa, being lunched and photographed at every turn. Mary says Mummy is doing most frightfully well. She looks quite lovely, slightly tired and fragile and they are lapping it up. Her broadcast was a great success and Mary says her voice is rather like the Queen's. Maria says when Mummy goes into high emotional gear and gets a bit mystical neither Mary nor the Y.W. understand a word of it, but it goes down awfully well.

Although the bombing went on, it was less fierce and had settled into a curious occupational hazard of everyday life. Harry, Bobby and Tommy all went overseas, Harry to India, Bobby and

Tommy to the Middle East. For Molly at Ardchattan it was grim, and we all hungered for letters and news from wherever it came. At least the threat of invasion had diminished and people began to tell each other the news was good.

Laura was still working with Lady Reading in the summer of 1942, combining her office work with cooking and housework. The Eton and Harrow match was played again that year, which Eton won. She got caught in a violent thunderstorm and fell into conversation with a rather sad-looking American soldier:

> I was a bit staggered when he offered to escort me home, especially as he had asked me how to go back to the Eagle Club in the Charing Cross Road. However I thought we must all cement Anglo American relations, so off we set. Before we were half way here, I had the whole of his life story and on arriving on the doorstep he asked if he could write to me. In self protection I made it quite clear that I already had a boy friend (!) but that he could most certainly write if he wanted.
>
> About two days later I got the letter, signed Jimmy Honeyman, a corporal in the Canadian Army, which he's now trying to leave to join the American Air Force. As always happens in this house, wherever you put a letter it either finds its way onto the Allatini files, or the Y.W. files end that's what must have happened to the letter!

In August Laura went to the Proms at the Albert Hall:

> It was rather a sight to see, that enormous place really pretty full. I prommed down in the middle, and was astounded to find that at least half, if not more of my co-prommers were men, not aged or decrepit, I only counted 8 in uniform. I can't quite make out what they were, or why they managed to be there. At any rate they made that part of the show as normal as can be. Actually I was rather disappointed with the whole business. The Albert Hall is too big for that. At the Queen's Hall you really got the feeling that you and

Elizabeth Schumann were the only people in the room, and that you could relax and just listen to her singing because you liked it and so did she. But at the Albert Hall the artists had to concentrate on avoiding the echo, and on pitching their voices to the right place. I went principally to hear the Beethoven Choral Symphony, which didn't quite come off as the choir wasn't big enough and didn't make enough noise. Still after going there I defy anyone to say the English aren't lovers of music. There was a particularly sole-penetrating kind of carpeting, which couldn't have been more wearing to the feet, and yet the majority of people there were regular goers, and the seats were all packed right out.

In November my father reported what he called startling news:

I had told Minnie there might be exciting news on Sunday so she listened in at 7 am and came and told me. I have been so impatient as the days pass and us not occupying the N(orth) A(frican) coast but I do see now that it was vital for us to get the USA to take the sky. Mum and I met the USA C-in-C and were introduced to him by Mr Winant [the American Ambassador] in Lowndes Square just the other day and I discussed the improvements to the square and London now the railings were taken away!!! He then disappeared. The papers said to USA but I had my doubts and I expect he really went to Gib as I knew USA troops were landing there in thousands. What a dirty dog Rommel must be, leaving the Italians to starve and get cold feet while he saves his own skin. I never have believed in the tactical ability or real courage of the Boche and Rommel has confirmed my opinions. Well the 51st led one of the breakthroughs – poor Patrick how he must have longed to be there, but good for you perhaps that he wasn't, and good for Mary Ann. Harry will be tearing his hair out. Still he will get his chance, but I would sooner have twelve days shooting against masses of Boches than having to pick off dirty little monkeys from the trees. Dear old 9th. I hope they are leading the pursuit.

I was OC the leading squadron of British Cavalry at Loos,

straining at the rein to lead the pursuit and at one moment we thought we were off but it was only a moment, but such a moment, those are minutes when you live! I had got the 9th keyed up alright. If only we had been given the chance to show of what stuff we were made! Well darling we are off now, there's no going back in our plans, whatever they are. Of course we have first of all to get Rommel in the bag alive or dead. Dead for choice. A Sunday paper has a photo of Montgomery meeting the Boche general and shaking him by the hand. I don't think that is the temper of the British public, certainly not of our Allies.

We must at all costs drop any chivalrous feelings, these Boches aren't soldiers, not as we understand soldiers and gentlemen to be. They are real gangsters of the most cruel and unchivalrous type. No! there must be no shaking hands as if they were equal and unfortunates. Certainly not, if we want to lead the Russians and European people in the Peace. They all expect us to shake hands and forget what the Prussians are and the Prussians expect us to do it too! That's why Prussians and our allies are suspicious of us and why the Germans will still gamble on their being able to fool us again. No, 150 years is long enough for their innings, and we must teach them and destroy them like we would a plague. Mary Ann must be spared what you have been through. We must steel ourselves to it. Prussia and all it stands for must be destroyed or later on they will produce another Hitler.

FOURTEEN

Vera in Canada

VERA HAD endured nearly three years of bombing and was exhausted by her efforts. At that point her worried grandmother, Lady Grey, stepped in. Lord Athlone (Queen Mary's brother) had succeeded Lord Tweedsmuir as Governor General of Canada. His wife, Princess Alice, Countess of Athlone (a grand-daughter of Queen Victoria), had a lady's maid, Fernande, who had previously been Lady Grey's maid for many years. They had remained friends.

Fernande told Lady Grey that Princess Alice's lady-in-waiting was leaving and asked if she had any suggestions for a successor. Lady Grey proposed Vera for the post and she was accepted. It was a cultural and physical shock for Vera and she was only half pleased. She had many friends in the East End and worried about leaving them and us.

After she went, she was widely missed in Stepney, two letters bearing witness to this. In 1942 Rev. John R. Leigh, Vicar of St Mary's and St Michael's, in Commercial Road, wrote:

I can say truthfully and sincerely that you will be greatly and sadly missed. Your social work has made you almost a household word in this district, and your magnificent work during the 'Blitz' has entitled you to a place among the heroines of this War. I don't know what would have happened to the poor people of this locality if you hadn't been at hand to fill the breach during the many emergencies which occurred when the enemy was overhead.

In 1944 WPW H Harris, of 'Post 16' wrote to her:

I have no doubt that you will be more than surprised to hear from me but I felt that I had to write to you and I sincerely hope that you will forgive the liberty in me doing so. Things in Stepney have not changed much. We in the ARP still carry on with our work as best we can, as in the old days of the 'Blitzes', but I must confess that I myself and particularly the people of our little area miss the greatest friend one could ever have. More than once they speak about her, her understanding ways, her foresight, her goodness, her sympathy she expressed and felt with the various persons she came in contact with. Can anyone forget her kindness she used to show or could the people concerned ever forget those long dark dreary nights when 'Jerry' was giving them 'Hell' and into their lives came an angel who administered to them words of courage and hope and a nice cup of hot cocoa with a bun, always smiling whatever the conditions were outside. No 'Jerry' terror could keep her away. Always ready to serve others, not thinking of the danger she placed herself in and Miss Grenfell. I mean this sincerely, and personally I think I can say for all those people concerned that, that angel was none other but our good kind Miss V. Grenfell.

My girls – I mean my daughters – have asked me more than once when is that lady coming to see us again but when I told them that you had gone to Canada they felt very sorry. For though they had only seen you once they felt that they have missed a great friend.

Vera sailed to Canada in January 1943, another trans-Atlantic voyage that caused us all to worry. As she sailed, Vera was upset to hear on the short wave news that there had been a direct hit on a London school with the loss of fifty lives:

All we were told was that it was one of London's most populated boroughs, and needless to say my mind rushed to Shadwell, and was it one of our nearby schools? I know there are many other populated boroughs, but I have such a gnawing anxiety it may have been that part.

On 23 January she disembarked, amazed by the brilliant lights, though informed that they were dimmed:

After getting our reservations we went for about ½ hours walk in the town, lovely with bright sun, but very slippery underfoot. Strange to see shops filled with oranges, pears, lemons and grapes all at very reasonable prices. We lunched at the big Nova Scotia Hotel, and my eyes nearly popped out when I was served with ½ real grapefruit. A friend of Pat Gault's came to lunch and kept on as to how difficult it was getting food etc. Thinking of England and what we had not only just seen, but eaten, we both very nearly laughed, couldn't really commiserate over the new butter rationing of ½ lb a week.

It seems so strange to be travelling in well-lit train with no blinds down and to see lights outside in the towns. Just about to reach Montreal and you are all just lost in slumber or should be.

Vera suffered from homesickness throughout her service in Canada.

Back in London, Reg and Joyce were out every evening, while Joyce was filming, and thus started her day at 5.15 am. Laura listed Joyce's doings. One evening they dined with Sir John Kennedy and his wife, the latter being a great friend of Joyce's. Sir John has been in the entourage accompanying the Prime Minister to the summit with Roosevelt at Casablanca. Laura relayed a story of a tiff between Mr Churchill and his valet:

One morning on the plane he came into Winston's cabin, looked at him propped up in bed in his siren suit and said 'You're sitting on your hot bottle.' Winston looked down to see in fact he was but said 'Why shouldn't I?' to which the valet replied 'Well it's not a good idea.' Winston's answer was 'It's not an idea, it's a coincidence.'

My mother had tea with Clemmie Churchill, enjoying what she

called a 'nice warm gossipy visit' and observing Winston in his habitual zip-suit being charming to the Attlees and their five children and showing them round the house.

In June 1943 Mary came home from Canada after another difficult voyage, in the course of which they picked up 88 survivors from another ship, and ran into fearful equinox gales.

My time in the Wrens came to an end in 1943. This was partly for personal reasons, as Mary Ann's nanny wanted to get married. At the same time, the base at Oban was changing, and they found that the service needed to be more flexible. 'Immobile' Wrens who couldn't be posted elsewhere because of family commitments, such as me, were becoming an irritant, so the parting suited both sides.

Geoffrey had been posted to York, and Mary joined him there. As she had no help, I bustled off to join her. Laura came to visit, and reported that I was 'up every morning by 7.30 and on the go with such patience till 8.30 at night'. She recognised that I was homesick for Ardchattan, and that I was concerned about Patrick.

News had reached us that the Germans, who were now losing the war, were taking it out on the prisoners. The rumour was that they were shackling the prisoners in Colditz. Although Patrick did not mention this, Martin Gilliat did. I heard about it as I had made friends with Martin's parents when I was down south and they sent me a copy of his letter. At this point I had never met Martin, or I would have understood the situation better. He was a master at making the most of such stories.

To his parents he described in tear-jerking detail how they knelt for Communion with shackled wrists. Patrick never mentioned this and after the war made out it was a minor incident which lasted about a week and was stopped when the few prisoners selected, all thought of as 'bad boys' by their captors, let it be known that they were delighted they had irked the Germans and were honoured to have this treatment meted out to them.

My father immediately sent a copy of Martin's letter to

Churchill to point out the magnificent morale of the prisoners. Counter rumours began that we would retaliate on the eye-for-an-eye basis, which made me write a wonderfully pompous letter to Churchill remonstrating against us stooping to Nazi tactics. The heart-rending image of the knightly soldier kneeling at the altar for Communion . . . Patrick was highly amused by this story when he got back.

Meanwhile Patrick was bored in prison, but in good spirits, wishing time would go faster, and enjoying news of the air raids being reversed on the Germans. His American parcels had of course ceased. The prisoners depended entirely on the Red Cross.

Parcels were important in our lives too, not only for providing the odd luxury but often a much-needed essential. Having benefited from this, Vera became an outstanding provider, sending orange juice, sweets, macaroni and bananas. Once at Ardchattan Molly and I received a parcel containing tea. Never having encountered teabags before, we unpicked them with great care, and wrote to tell the sender that we had teaspoons and could measure our own tea. Only some time later did someone tell us that we could use the bags as they were. I gave Vera my news:

I firmly took three weeks holiday. I spent a week of it with Maria at the first cottage she had here, and worked harder than I ever did in His Majesty's Service. We washed up all day long, and never got any gossiping in at all. After a week of this I went firmly to London to have a spree. There I found the family in fairly good heart. Daddy looked particularly well, and was most cheerful with many plans for making £10,000 a year without much effort, and with a fascinating and marvellous scheme, which he is working on with a Persian architect, for rebuilding Belgravia after the war as the United Nations Centre. It is the most drastic, but perfectly lovely scheme, but I doubt if there is anyone with as much foresight and dash as Daddy has to get it carried out. It would take a lot of courage to put it into effect. To us, knowing Mummy and Daddy's capacity for rebuilding castles out of garages, it would not seem so drastic, but for the more conventional minded I think it would be rather a tough pill to swallow. I am sure he is absolutely right.

The main and most lovely feature of the plan is two perfectly lovely straight processional avenues, one from Eros right down to Hyde Park Corner, with a lovely conference building where St George's Hospital now is, and the other from Hyde Park Corner straight down to Victoria Station. The architect says that standing in Hyde Park Corner one should be able to see to the end of both roads. It would mean London beating Paris and the Champs Elysée into a cocked hat. I hope someone will sponsor it and get it done.

Mummy is in a perfectly terrific mood of making plans, morn, noon and night, and madly taking action about everything so that one finds ones most innocent remark come back at one like a boomerang with a whole lifetime of plans fixed onto its tale. Now that I have left the Wrens, I am fair game for any plan that is going. She is a wonderful woman, but goodness gracious, she is tiring.

After my fortnight free in London, I bounded up to Ardchattan for one weekend to fetch down Mary Ann. My in-laws are in good form, although we have been anxious rather about Tommy, who got very badly wounded in the bottom, during the Argylls last battle on Long Stop Hill in Tunisia (I wonder if you saw the account of it in the Times, about 3 weeks ago). But we heard last week that he was quite recovered. Ma-in-law is rather disappointed as she had high hopes that he might be sent home to get toughened up and get fit again.

They have had horrid casualties, heavier even than the Guards, and I think Tommy is about the only original one left. He has had bad luck, as he was very highly recommended by the Colonel for an MC because very early on in the fighting he went out alone and rescued three officers who were wounded, among them Alec Malcolm, only one stretcher bearer would volunteer to go with him. After rescuing them he went back again and brought in his two anti-tank guns, which he had to detach from their burning vehicles.

It seems almighty mean which he should be passed over just because there aren't enough medals to go round. You either are brave or you aren't, and I don't see why the number of medals should be limited, or it merely becomes a racket with no point to it at all.

I had a letter from Patrick yesterday dated May 20th. He sounded in grand form in this letter and was full of the salmon fishing which I am to take for him, and even gave me the names of the rivers, and says I had better find out about them soon and get cracking as he doesn't think it will be very long now before he is home.

After a spell I returned to Ardchattan. There I found Molly still entertaining all comers, but with no staff to help, and so Peggy and I took on the jobs of housemaids.

As our father got deafer, a hazard was that he would embark on a conversation which became a monologue – these monologues could cover a lot of ground and last, for most listeners, too long. The family were inured and carried on their conversations sotto voce as if to background music. We did, though, find them embarrassing at times. Laura described a typical experience in June 1943:

Daddy is very taken up with plans for rebuilding Belgravia. He is very taken up with it all, and it gives him a lot to think about, endless little walks to do. Lords still remains the great attraction, and yesterday Daddy had an absolute field day there. At teatime we sat up along where the President's box is, by the clock, and Daddy found himself next to a man called Sir Kenneth Barnes, who made the most perfect audience anybody could want. Daddy didn't miss his opportunity, and went straight off into Fowler's Year [a famous Eton and Harrow match played in 1910], which he has now made topical by claiming that Alexander [by now General Alexander, C-in-C North Africa], then Captain of the Harrow eleven learnt his tactics off Fowler [the Eton Captain who won the match], and therefore Tunis is an Eton and not an Harrovian victory! We then went straight through the finding of the Gainsborough, the Titian, how Daddy saved Rhodes from going bankrupt, his adventures in

Mexico and buying the Fields of Abraham [Quebec] which he had decided on when walking with this man and Lord Grey.

It was quite fascinating, but I got a bit embarrassed when he bellowed out at the top of his voice how he'd given £20,000 for this, and a million for that, and everyone within earshot was obviously wondering if he was J.P. Morgan or something of the kind. Luckily he ended up just as loudly that we hadn't a bean in the bank now, and I felt much happier, even though our audience was a bit disappointed.

Laura expanded her garden to keep hens and help with the egg rations. Although on a minute scale in a tiny basement garden, her agricultural and horticultural activities helped to keep her sane. After Hermione gave her some wire netting, three hens obliged by producing four eggs a day. She battled with the vegetable garden, spreading poultry manure everywhere, but there was too much coke for the soil. She had better luck with her tomatoes, beans and shallots. I wrote to Vera from Ardchattan, also in October:

Mummy has just sent us your lovely letter about Quebec, which was absolutely fascinating. Patrick got your letter. It was good of you to find time to write and he really did love it. He and David have now been moved to this new 'naughty boys' camp, which is a very high-class thing to be, but Patrick isn't over keen about it. It's a very small camp, so difficult to get entertainments and things going in, and Patrick says all the inmates are crazy and mad and a lot of them foreigners, but he doesn't think he'll be there for very long, and hopes to be out before next summer. He's most cheerful on the whole but it's hard on him having to sit back when both Tommy and Bobby are in the thick of it and he's wracked with anxiety about them, and of course knows so very little news about them.

We've all been tremendously thrilled here because Tommy has got the MC. My Ma-in-law is delighted of course, that her ewe lamb should be the first of all the family to win a medal. Bobby was in

Sicily too, and we presume is in Italy now. We had one ecstatic letter written in the midst of the Sicilian battle, in which as far as we could gather, in spite of being a gunner, he had somehow acquired a tank, and was charging about all over Sicily running the whole battle. He has the most extraordinary little Scotch bonnet with a red bobble on top which he wears all the time, and got cheered by all the Sicilians shouting 'Viva Marina' as they all thought he was the French navy come to their rescue. Both he and Tommy said they got tremendous receptions from the Sicilians, but for all that didn't think much of them as specimens of humanity. We've had no news from any of them for a long time now.

My Ma-in-law is wonderful and amazingly well and cheerful and good about it all, although it's not much fun for her. We've only got the old cook here now, and Peggy's nanny, so Peggy and I do the housework and Peg waits on the cook and nanny. We've been fairly busy lately with large portions of the Grenfell family coming and still larger portions of overseas officers whom we entertain for their leave. Reg and Joyce and Mum all came in one week and it was tremendous fun seeing them. Joyce couldn't have been nicer, quite her old self and so easy to entertain and not a bit theatrical minded. Reg divine as usual and really looking awfully well and they both looked so devoted and happy. Reg went out fishing every day and Joyce was as good as gold about it and kept saying of course he must do whatever he liked . . .

We had old [General Sir] Arthur Wauchope staying here the other day. You knew him in Palestine didn't you? I thought he was a most charming old boy, he's got a very bad heart now and can't do much, but he's Colonel of the Black Watch and takes an intense interest in all of them. I quite lost my heart to him and he was most interesting about Palestine. Before him we had the Red Duchess [of Atholl] and she told us all her inside information about the Spanish War, rather vieux jeu but interesting all the same. She was madly pro-Baldwin and we tried to argue that one with her, but didn't get far.

Sir Arthur Wauchope was also a friend of Lord Dowding, the

Air Chief Marshal in command of Fighter Command throughout the Battle of Britain. He described to us the traumas of high command and how near Hitler had got to wiping out our Air Force by bombing the airfields, and the relief when the German Air Force ceased this tactic and turned its ferocity on London and gave the RAF time to recoup.

I searched for a small cottage near London. Minnie was nearing a crisis as she was exhausted. Laura and I worried as it was difficult to envisage our parents coping without her, but the relationship between her and our mother had almost totally broken down. My mother mentioned that I had borrowed Minnie in order to be able to go south:

> I let Minnie go, Fuffs and Laura declaring they'd do the cooking, clean the rooms etc between them. That of course meant just muddle-issimus, for Fuffs isn't a born cook, and Laura started getting up earlier and earlier and going to bed later and later and looking more tired every day. For there is no doubt Min has been feeling the strain more and more, she has been growing such a martyr complex and has been taking it out of me so much and making Laura feel she must take on more and more to save Min the overwork.
>
> They really got into a vicious circle. Frances found a little cottage near Reading. At the moment she is having an extra strain through rumours which are flying around that Prisoners-of-War of over 3 years are to be sent to Sweden. So of course she sees herself going off there. It most likely isn't true but it makes her feel more and more that she must have Minnie for Mary Ann.

Laura explained the situation to Vera in November, writing from Avenue Cottage, in Bucklebury, near Reading:

> Frances has been down, with Min up in Scotland looking after Mary Ann, from where come almost regular bulletins that poor Mrs C-P has had a telegram saying Tommy's been wounded dangerously – for the third time – with a bullet extracted from his brain and the

probability of losing one of his fingers, and last night she rang to say she had a telegram that Bobby had been wounded too. I suppose you heard that both he and Tommy have won the MC. As both her sons in law, Raymond and Ian Fraser are in Italy too, it's not much of a picnic for her. Luckily she has had reassuring news from and about Tommy and they are hoping very much that he will now get sent home.

Darling, the most perfect parcel with a heavenly jersey, just the right colour and everything, the socks for Reg and the battery for Daddy – and wonderful pot scourers! It suddenly struck me the other day that practically every moment of night and day from when I get up in the morning to put on the underclothes stockings and jersey, talk to Daddy at breakfast through his battery, wash the pots with the scourer, take a picnic with the thermos and cake, make the soup for dinner in two ticks with the Lipton's noodles – wash pots again and sink gratefully into bed, my face smeared as it needs to be! You really are an angel . . .

Daddy keeps going because his other scheme, the re-planning of London. Joyce is due to go to the Middle East etc with ENSA by special arrangement with Noël Coward, though not actually touring with him in person, quite soon after Christmas! Two films in which she appears for a fleeting moment all showing here now, one called 'The Lamp Still Burns', the film of Monica Dickens's book 'One Pair of Feet', and the other one 'Semi Paradise'. It's awful I haven't seen either yet!

This is a minute little cottage half an hour bus ride from Reading. It's got two bedrooms upstairs, a sitting room and dining room, hall, bathroom and kitchen down with a nice patch of garden at the back. F. is coming to live here for a time, with Minnie to look after Mary Ann, while we have (we hope – she hasn't come yet!) an ex-maid of Lord Radstock's. F and I are down here for the first weekend, having rather a battle with the fire, the boiler and the dirt but we're winning through and we hope to do great things tomorrow in the cleaning way but its beautifully cheap and once cleaned up will be fine.

Letters to Vera went in a new form of letter called an airgraph, on which you wrote one page of a letter on a normal size form. This was then reduced by the Post Office and arrived as open mail the size of a postcard. Even those with good eyesight had to read it with a magnifying glass. In January 1944 I sent her one of these airgraphs:

Although I write from the cottage so that you can have the address I am actually staying at Ardchattan for a few days and arrived to find your perfectly lovely Christmas parcel waiting for me. A real live rubber hot bottle and the combs and the lovely paint box for Mary Ann and the knickers and the stockings. I can't tell you how much I want them all and only hope you aren't quite broke as a result, which I fear you must be.

The last few weeks in London have been far from peaceful. Mummy has been in one of her really terrific moods. She reaches such heights of energy in them that one has to remember hard not to be exasperated by her entire lack of practicalness and the way in which she drives us all relentlessly to do a million things which we don't know how to do and don't want to do. Anyhow she wore herself to a frazzle when to our horror she announced she was taking another garage and furnishing it and letting it. This sounds all very fine on paper because as Mummy says she has an enormous amount of tables, chairs, beds etc, but when you let a house furnished you also want the million and one things like saucepans, sieves, coffee cups and all the odds and ends which cost a fortune to buy now. Also it's all very well letting the flats we own but taking more is a little poopsy, especially when it's a pure spec. But still, Mummy of course achieved it, and let it, but at a cost, not only of cash but of energy on all our parts. It nearly killed her . . .

It hasn't been unfunny at Chesham Place, Mummy having procured an Irish maid whose previous reference was for 32 years. Mum was delighted with her – never ceased telling me how much nicer she was than Min, so active and willing and how she loved the unexpected. Well Mum setting out to be deliberately unexpected was something to cope with. She had six people to every meal and never told Annie the maid until five minutes before, quite deliberately in order to be delightfully unexpected and spring a big surprise. Annie walked out and God knows I don't blame her. So then I told Min I thought she ought to go back, but she absolutely refused.

Daddy is really in great form and on the whole awfully well, thrilled with his scheme for rebuilding the more possible it becomes, the more grandiose and colossal his plans become. Last week he thought of liquidating the Green Park, Waterloo Barracks, Horse Guards Parade and a few other well known landmarks in order to have a processional way straight from the Abbey to Buckingham Palace . . .

My ma-in-law is well. She was awfully pulled down at the beginning of the winter but has now got her second wind and is much better. Both Bobby and Tommy have recovered from their wounds, but we hope to see Tommy soon. Bobby is busy blasting the German out of Italy and writes and assures us that neither Raymond (who is out there now) or T are in the least necessary and that its only the gunners who are needed at all. Raymond writes by the same post to assure us neither T or Bobby are needed as he alone can end the war. T writes lovely lofty and superior letters saying he'll try and contact Bobby and Raymond and give them a few fighting tips. Ian Fraser is out there too so its quite a gathering of clans.

Patrick writes cheerfully on the whole. I gather his days of escaping are over, and he is now a tremendous cook and says we'd better have a hotel after the war. 3 days a week he cooks for 70 men on a very small stove. I don't look forward to housekeeping for a husband who knows so much! I hope to goodness this is his last year.

My mother got a letter from Patrick from his punishment camp near Leipzig, as she explained:

There are 300 or so of them there, and it's very cramped, but they have hot water laid on and indoor lavs so they make a lot of that. He's unhappy about Charlie Hopetoun who is singled out for v. harsh treatment and allowed no letters from home and is in solitary confinement. But they are all proud of being very naughty boys! Patrick has to do the cooking with v. inadequate cooking pots.

In October she reported from London:

Losses in Italy seem to have been so much among our friends lately, and now today comes news of Patrick Alington dying of wounds and of the Winants' son as 'missing'. Last month it was both Madeleine [Countess of] Midleton's sons being killed, Francis [Stewart Mackenzie] who married the Lyell girl, sister of Lord Lyell VC, who was killed in N. Africa, and now his younger brother Michael, Laura's contemporary and friend ever since Bernie and Flukey days. The news one gets given gets sparser and sparser as events get more and more important and the lack of detailed explanation is really serious from the point of view of keeping the workers edge on for production. But I suppose it can't be helped

It's been a bad month of anxiety and loss. The 2 Campbell-Prestons (Tommy wounded again but has gone back and has got his MC), Johnnie Tweedsmuir in it, and the fate of our Ps of War in Italy so uncertain. How could such a war with its horrors untold for people and peoples not hang heavy on all our hearts, and tempt us to continual cries of 'A quoi bon?' But such tremendous things are happening, victories in Russia, Italy and out in N. Guinea. The map of such huge events is being unrolled. All an invitation to thrilling and glorious speculation. But more and more and hourly and daily do I become convinced that it is in the lesser arena of our own personal lives that the real drama has to be played out and the WAR is the weather outside and not drama itself.

FIFTEEN

My Mother's Further Travels

DURING these weeks, another plan was forming. My mother was stirring again, this time with a plan to visit New Zealand and Australia. As usual, it was the subject of a great deal of discussion, the various pros and cons dominating much of 1943. Presently my father concluded it would be better if she went. Her work with the British YWCA was not leading anywhere, whereas the World's Council was prepared to give her the full red carpet treatment. She had worked herself into the ground over Mary's return and there had been further causes of stress and commotion.

My mother worried inordinately about the pros and cons. The means of travel was one concern. Flying or journeys by boat were equally dangerous. But danger was by now so endemic that it became an exercise in balancing one risk against another. We all threw our opinions around but we knew that once our mother had made her mind up, it was useless to disagree. I arranged to be near my father while she was away. Joyce was also going overseas, as I described:

I wish you could have seen Joyce and Mummy together, they were so funny about their respective journeys. Lolly swears she had them both almost nude in the drawing room one day displaying their various inoculation marks and vying with each other as to who had the most. Joyce had one for typhus so Mummy promptly got done for Yellow Fever. Of course poor old Joyce, who objected to having them done at first but ENSA said she couldn't go if she didn't agree to be done, all the time told the doctor she'd be done as a matter of form, but of course there weren't such diseases anyhow, went down like a ninepin with every one and was in bed for two days with her vaccination! Not quite C.S. as Reg said. I haven't heard yet if she's gone or not. How our family get about don't they?

At the end of December 1943 my mother was ready to set off to India on her way to Australia. She awaited her final summons. Meanwhile all her letters were censored except:

A last message from Nellie Graham's [Lady Helen Graham] *employer* [the Queen] *and some more of the M of Information stuff which I am to take. The former had to be altered from its original and very uninspiring form and now at last I am taking one after my own heart ending with a sentence saying I am to report to her on my return, which is the whole point.*

I'm determined to see Harry and go direct to Delhi with every kind of letter of recommendation to 'Archie W' [Field Marshal Earl Wavell, then Viceroy] *to be kind to me and get me on by Air on the last lap of my journey. The authorities here were so urgent I should go and have done everything (including finance) to smooth my path . . . Everything has strangely fallen into place to make it possible so off I go to Teheran – Baghdad, Basra, Karachi, Delhi and from there I must do all I can to get sent on in the way I plan, grasping a very useful letter. AW wrote me before he went saying all possible help would be given if I turned up. I am you see pursuing my real benefactress* [the Queen], *whose help is so potent and so freely offered if only I can tap it.*

The Indian visit became suddenly very urgent because of the tone and the political views of the senders of the invitation from there. So all hands were turned on to get me there.

My visits before I leave to leading personalities took me to Lambeth for a very nice talk with the Arch Bishop [Temple]. *I am so full to the muzzle with NCSS news and I am seeing Dorothy Elliot on the latest trade unions moves and aspirations, new head of the ATS and Violet Markham and so on and so forth for in the*

Dominions they do fall on one for information and interpretation of so much over the whole field of local govt and social service, as you know well.

My mother finally departed for her trip in January 1944, as Laura wrote:

She's going the loop way, not the quickest direct route, and so may not get to Harry [in India] until sometime in February. She got the OBE in New Year Honours list – pretty stingy considering what she's done! Joyce has also left on her trip – I do hope it's a success. I'm becoming quite an expert cook and its rather fun, but I hate sweeping and dusting!

Meanwhile Geoffrey and Reggie had both become Majors, while Joyce was touring hospitals in Algiers. Laura noted:

She seems to be working v very hard, as after doing 10 or more concerts a day and talking to all the patients individually, she gets called on to dine with the Duff Coopers and entertain them, which I should have thought would be the last straw! However, she seems to be thriving on it.

In April my mother was still away. I thought it hard on Laura to have to cope with my father on her own, not to mention her continued work with Lady Reading. But my father was still in fine form:

He's been having what he calls cheerfully a nasty go of lock jaw lately. It seemed to be an odd disease as he was only ill from Mon to Friday and was full of beans at the weekend. Lolly discovered he'd sacked Mrs Ker, Mum's German secretary, in a moment of valour, but didn't dare see her again in case he might relent, so stayed happily and securely in bed all week with lock jaw and so avoided her successfully.

On the first leg of her trip, my mother arrived in Cairo, where a car from the High Commission was waiting for her. This did not surprise her, but it surprised the High Commissioner, who thought the Mrs Grenfell who was arriving was his niece Joyce, not her mother-in-law. There were always delays between flights, often of weeks rather than days, so it was not until February that my mother reached India to stay with Sir Archie and Lady Wavell, he being the Viceroy. In the meantime she spent three weeks flying via West and Central Africa, Sudan, Egypt, Iraq, Persia, Saudi Arabia. Besides staying at the Embassy in Cairo, she stayed with the Consul General in Khartoum. Then she motored around the YWCA places in Egypt and Teheran, also staying in Baghdad and Basra. She found it all 'unbelievably thrilling'.

At length she arrived in Delhi. Thanks to Lady Helen Graham, the Queen's lady-in-waiting and my mother's colleague in the YWCA, she had with her a letter and message from the Queen. Suffering from mild dysentery, she delivered this from her sick bed, rather startling Sir Archie. He was reported to have said: 'Why can't that grey-haired old lady go back and cook for her husband?' Wavell was renowned for being no conversationalist. If he had nothing he thought worth saying he sat in silence. Harry, who had been asked to Viceroy House too, and my mother were baffled by his silences.

My mother found Harry looking well and jolly and satisfied with his lot. He met his new Commander-in-Chief, Lord Louis Mountbatten, and became interested in Indian politics. Confined to bed, my mother's only regret was not being able to see Mount Everest.

Back in London, my father wrote to *The Times* on the subject of London morale. This letter was reprinted in August 2004:

Sir, – During the recent counter-attack on South England by the Germans with their flying bombs, I have been close to two incidents. The first was near the Strand. I was on the scene within minutes.

Order reigned. The police had already readjusted the traffic routes. Firemen had taken all necessary measures to rescue people and prevent fire. First aid stations were established. Stretcher-bearers were enrolled by a lady warden not more than about 26 years old, but blue-jackets and British and United States soldiers fell in most willingly and carried casualties to the ambulances that had already arrived.

The approaches had been roped off and a boy, not more than 15 or 16, in battle dress uniform was posted as a guard at the rope. A Major-General with rows of ribbons pushed through the crowd, obviously intent on lending a hand. He lifted up the rope and advanced. The guard at first hesitated, but then said: 'I am supposed not to allow anyone to pass under the rope.' The general looked at him for a minute and then turned on his heel, lifted up the rope, and went the way he had come. I do not know who he was: I would have liked to tell him how great an effect his dignity and discipline had on the crowd.

A few days later a bomb fell in a park not too far from a bandstand where a military band was playing. The bomb uprooted small trees and took every leaf off the big trees. Two foreign friends of mine arrived and I pointed out what an extraordinary effect the blast had had on the trees. One turned to the other and said: 'What is more extraordinary is that the band has never stopped playing.'

With such examples it is not surprising that London morale is high.

From Delhi my mother eventually went down to Sri Lanka, from where there was considerable difficulty getting her a passage to Australia. After a great effort by Archie Wavell she was booked on a ship about to sail on a dangerous voyage across the Japanese lines of communication.

In the midst of some confusion, my mother boarded the wrong ship. The original one was then sunk with her name on the passenger list, but mercifully this news did not reach us until we knew she was safely in Australia. In April she sent an airgraph from the Karracatta Club, in Perth, Western Australia:

Well here I am and safe and with very much to be thankful for . . .
After all I am to complete a week here and 10 days at Adelaide and
Alice Springs before reaching Canberra. I've had a lovely welcome,
so genuine and un-gushing and warm hearted. I'm staying in the
Ladies Club. Domestic staff shortage, as acute here as at home, has
prevented Govt. House having me. Today has meant 2 speeches and
a broadcast, tomorrow 2 more, one broadcast, and much visiting of
WRAFF, WRAN and AWAS (ATS) places, gunsites etc. and the
University and of course Y.W. Civilian and Service Clubs. A luxe
Reception yesterday, a Public Meeting tomorrow and so it goes on.
Tiring very, but people are so kind and loving about getting me rest
times which I find I do need more than when I was in Canada. But
the journey here was exhausting, tho' my fellow passengers so nice.
We were only 11 people.

My mother enjoyed her visit:

I love Australia and Australians already, they are so utterly sincere
and warm hearted and direct and so British and amused and
amusing in British ways. A blessed absence of gentility and no gush
and this is a lovely place with divine climate. I'm in the posh Ladies
Club. Shall fly to Adelaide tomorrow and on up into the Centre to
Alice Springs and then back to Canberra and Melbourne and Sydney
before going to Queensland and I hope P. Moresby and New
Guinea. Its all less of an effort than my last tour in some ways,
people here so bone of one's bone, but much more critical and
discriminating as audiences and so humorous as speakers. Delicious
people.

After Australia my mother went to New Guinea, where the
famous American General Macarthur had his headquarters. She
secured an interview with him, something rarely given. Though
pleased by this, she was not impressed when one of his aides

informed her in awed tones: 'Now you've seen God'. In June she
wrote to Vera from Government House in Sydney:

*I have had a glorious tour of New Guinea. Am finishing here soon,
then N. Zealand. I feel pretty stale and hope I'll soon never have to
make a speech or broadcast again. But it has all been immensely
worthwhile and the kindness I've received from all authorities, Civil
and Military, limitless. I've only been in a train four times since I left
London Jan 10th. Invasion and Robot planes* [the first flying bombs
were falling on London] *keep one in a perpetual agony about home.
But after this tour I feel certain that those of us doing
Commonwealth Jobs are doing work of long-time value that are far
more important than we can see now in strengthening spiritual
links.*

My mother was in Christchurch, New Zealand, in July 1944,
longing to come home:

*General Mc A says 'No' to my flying home but 'yes' to a boat
passage. But I mean to fly somehow and mean not to be defeated.
For get home I must. One moves as in a dream doesn't one?
Everyone all over me here because of my Grandfather Lyttelton
being Chairman of the original Canterbury Settlers Assoc: and
everyone of 90 rings me up to say they knew him and Mayors in
Chains almost embrace me at Civic Receptions and the shell of me
is made much of – but the real ME is at home. I must fly everywhere
as I have consistently since I left England.*

*My beloved Host and Hostess played me exquisite Schumann song
records and Bach and Schumann's voice was more than I could bear
as it spoke of the world that one knew and loved. We mustn't crack
under it all but it is hard isn't it. One must just hold on to its
somehow being all meant.*

Despite General McArthur's decision, my mother wangled her
way onto an American or Australian Air Force plane to the USA,

the crew being rather surprised to find an elderly English lady as their freight. From the USA she got a BOAC flight and returned in August.

Her original intention had been to be home by spring. After a perfect Clipper crossing, she arrived home and came to stay, bringing my father with her. She was relieved to find my father looking well, though she was depressed by the filth of Chesham Place, which she proceeded to clean with vigour. She saw London with new eyes:

London looks much shabbier than before and heaps of places have 'got it' round about us. There were lots of Doodles over but not at the old rate but often enough it seemed to me. But every one is unconcerned and there are delicious Doodle stories. Reg had one of their chars saying, 'I don't like these Bombs nearly as much as I did the old ones'. The very word Doodle is so like us to use to belittle things. But oh! Quite a lot of friends have been killed: Rosamund Lynch, 2 Maxwells, Edward Hay and Ralph Cobbold. Dad's stenographers 2 friends and Hopey Buchan [wife of Alastair Buchan, the Tweedsmuirs' daughter-in-law], *so it shows how general the attacks are. Dad and I never hear the alert, but one can't but hear the thing it makes such a noise and the crumps are very loud. Two of our YW HQ staff are in hospital from bad wounds, but the office is untouched. So it's a bit like the old days – only fires are much less and actual HE is far less. Dad tells killing story of a very fat little Dutch man flinging himself flat on his face over Dad's very feet as one appeared to be coming straight at them and then when it passed over and crumped quite nearby he jumped up and almost hugged Dad in his joy at escaping while Dad roared with laughter at him. Of course Dad never lay down, he was far too interested to see what would happen. Oh! Dear Celia Coates' Anthony, Cecilia Fisher's 2nd boy gone (she's widow of the Great Admiral who died just before the war).*

The cost is going to be very great among friends, as it has been among my family, Gilbert T [Talbot], *Christopher Ford, Anthony*

Lyttelton, Jim Stephenson, John Hichens, Bobbitty's [Marquess of Salisbury] *second son and Pam Shuttleworth's second husband killed in accidents, such a waste! But the news is so tremendous I do hope even their stricken hearts can glow. I fear Canada's losses will be high. Joyce very pretty but too thin and a bit too preoccupied with self, but very proud of Reg. She hates the Doodles but pluckily sticks them.*

There's such gaiety and sobriety in the air. I do love my own people. Its as if they'd all proudly and gladly come to terms with discomfort, fear and death, patience of officials, as people stream out of London, and the general calm uncomplainingness is wonderful.

As soon as I moved to the cottage, I needed a job. I had made some friends in the village, particularly with one or two contemporaries of my own age. These had had babies and were now quite anxious to do their bit. We ended up packing biscuits in Huntley and Palmer's factory in Reading. This was a testing job physically if not for the brain. It meant standing all day lifting heavy trays and it was monotonous. But working in factory conditions was so outside any experience I had ever had that it had its fascination. Before the war the factory had been run on the 'Bedaux system'. He was an American, who had devised this system, and had got considerable publicity after the Abdication by lending his chateau at Candé to the Duke of Windsor for his wedding to Mrs Simpson.

Bedaux's method for increasing production was to time workers as to the speed with which they could pack biscuits within a given period. As soon as a worker reached this time they would ratchet the time up and the wages were paid in ratio to how a worker achieved the Bedaux time. This meant that you could never win a bonus because as soon as the capability to pack biscuits at a certain rate was achieved up went the rate. It was a system much resented by the workers and the trade unions. But unemployment was high before the war and resistance therefore fruitless.

This system had to be dropped during the war as labour was
short and even fumblers like us were employed. But to keep some
sort of control the Bedaux inspectors still came round, if a little
half-heartedly. Many of those working alongside us had worked
in the factory before the war and the odd one had been sacked for
failing to make this punishing grade. When the inspectors
appeared, they would deliberately stop work, sit back on their
stools and light a cigarette knowing they could not be sacked.

We used to grind our teeth when, after our hurried canteen
luncheon, for which only half an hour was allowed, the manager
would stroll round, as we immediately imagined, after a three
course meal with probably two or three glasses of wine, and I
even remember one who always had a buttonhole of the latest
flower. The tune 'Workers Playtime' is with me for life.

Bucklebury soon had an American camp where troops began to
be assembled before D-Day. There was a long wide avenue
leading out of the village and there they made camp. Their
commanding officer was a loose-limbed South American, very
attractive and keen on the local ladies. Passing the cottage he saw
Mary Ann playing in the garden and chatted her up. Mary Ann,
pleased with the attention, informed him her mother lived alone
as Daddy was a prisoner of war. I soon had a call. Minnie was
horrified. He became a friend of most of the grass widows, of
which there were many in the village. We enjoyed it, and we were
even more amused when we discovered that in peacetime he was
a travelling salesman specialising in ladies' corsets. Minnie had
picked up the village gossip, which she never passed on to me, but
knew of at least one pregnancy credited to him. I was, therefore,
never allowed to be alone with him. Whenever he appeared she
would move into the room with the mending basket and sit in
unbending disapproval. One day he asked me to a regimental
dance, but before I could answer, she said firmly: 'Mrs Campbell-
Preston does not dance'.

Once news came of the successful D-Day landings in Normandy
final victory seemed assured, despite the bombardment of

Bobby and Angela's wedding group at Blair Castle, 1950.

Patrick with Brigadier Russell in Berlin in 1950, on the occasion when he had all the Black Watch tin hats painted black.

Laura before her dance in 1946 (which was attended by Princess Elizabeth). A portrait by Lenare.

Hilda Grenfell during the war, 1943.

A family group: Robert, Patrick, Frances with Colin, Helen and Mary Ann.

Ardchattan Priory. Beneath the photograph, in Patrick's handwriting, is the following:
'God gave to man all earth to love
but since our hearts are small
ordained for each one sacred spot
Beloved over all.'

Patrick and Frances.

Bernard and Laura: when Bernard was
Governor-General of New Zealand.

Prince Charles's visit in 1967. The group includes Mary Ann and Alastair,
Henrietta Fitzroy, Frances, Helen and Colin.

Sir Martin Gilliat, the Queen Mother's Private Secretary, outside the Castle of Mey in 1992, accompanied by some of her Corgis.

Joyce, Frances and Robert in Scotland.

The Queen Mother with those members of her Household and staff who had been in the services, photographed at Clarence House after the D-Day anniversary celebrations in 1994. (*Left to right*) Reg Willcock, Sir Ralph Anstruther, The Queen Mother, Frances, Sir Alastair Aird and William Tallon.

The Queen Mother and Frances in an open landau outside Clarence House.

Frances and Laura on the Royal Yacht *Britannia* in New Zealand in 1967.

A royal duty. Frances following the Queen Mother on a visit to the
Princess Alice Hospital in Esher, 25 March 1996.

'Doodle bugs' and V2 rockets over the south of London.

From Canada Vera described the Quebec conference, news of which had been so secret that all notes about it passed between departments in at least three envelopes. Even the Governor-General's summer plans had to be changed as the Citadel was equipped with telephone lines, lighting for maps, and sitting rooms converted into bedrooms:

> Our Comptroller who stayed on there found the only place in which he could comfortably install himself was the 'Downstairs Gents!!' Security and transport arrangements to be seen to, special passes almost with finger prints, in fact a variety of things to do which sent everyone into a flutter and scurrying hither and thither, all which had to be carried out under a veil of secrecy and as if it was part of the ordinary day's routine.
>
> The veil of mystery was only lifted when the Churchills had arrived at the port of disembarkation. Our party, who had been sent to vegetate at a fishing camp in the wilds of Quebec Province during the days of preparation, returned to Quebec the morning of the arrival of the two great leaders. As there was no room at the Citadel we stayed in our railway coaches at the station. Down we drove in state with an escort of motorcycles, the Mounted Police gay in their scarlet coats; Mounties were lining all the road to the secret station of arrival, now revealed to have been Wolfe's Cove. Here we greeted the Churchills and Roosevelts, who arrived in their respective special trains almost at the same time. The only assembled crowd to witness this arrival were the highest ranking officials, our party and about 200 reporters and press photographers.
>
> My people [the Athlones] went aboard each train to personally greet the leaders and then came the moment when the two great leaders were to greet each other. This was the moment for which the press had been waiting, and so eager was each photographer to get the best 'Take' of this great historic event that they all swooped down like a pack of vultures onto a kill, and before we know where we were we found ourselves in the midst of a rugger scrum. In fact

it was only due to the timely intervention of Field Marshals, Admirals of the Fleet, Air Marshals etc who came to the assistance of the ADC and myself that the Governor General of Canada and a Princess of the Royal blood were not trampled underfoot; as it was we all felt like the smallest sardine at the bottom layer of a large box!!!!

The President certainly looked older and more thin and drawn in the face than last year, but his same charm of manner was there. Churchill looked better in every way than when I had last seen him and was like an exuberant schoolboy, simply bubbling over with good spirits and full of jokes. Later on we saw the models of the different kinds of boats, amphibious buildings etc which had gone to the making of the large 'Mulberry' or Harbour on the beaches of Normandy. They were quite amazing and it was thrilling to see their every detail. Everything had not only had to be constructed but towed into position from England, and there were certain parts of it which were equivalent in size and tonnage of one of London's big club buildings – just imagine, and all this had to be so scientifically constructed that it allowed for the rise and fall of tides, rough or smooth water and the full fury of an Atlantic gale.

Another very thrilling half hour was that spent in the P.M's Map Room. Here are wondrous maps of every kind and of every front. The President with Mackenzie King (as an also ran) gave their Press interview, all without a note of any kind. Churchill and the President were both masterful or rather masterly in the way they handled them, for of course they could tell them little if anything of what had been decided, but Churchill in particular was splendid in the way he got them, with a certain amount of friendly chaff, and anyhow for a brief while kidded them into thinking he had told them everything.

What amazed me was that here was this gathering of the picked reporters of Canada and America and that out of some 150 odd only about 6 (and they were English representatives and from External Affairs here) were doing short-hand. The rest all had stumpy short pencils which they licked feverishly as they frantically tried to get down in long-hand (such illegible long-hand too) the words of wisdom that dropped. Do you wonder that the best account of this meeting was that given over the BBC broadcast and in the English press! All the time cameras and movie cinemas were clicking and buzzing, which I should have thought was most disturbing to those speaking and also to those trying to get the speeches down.

One could sense a marked difference in the atmosphere this year, every one knew each other better and got down to business right away. There was a certain lessening of tension in the knowledge that the careful planning of last year had met with such success. One came away feeling inspired by their confident optimism and feeling that all were determined to achieve ultimate victory in the shortest possible time. It would involve maximum effort but every detail would be most carefully considered so that there should be the minimum of loss and suffering, and that the dawn of peace was beginning to streak the sky, and not too distant a sky at that.

As one listened to this and to that one was almost aghast. The amount of detail of thought, planning, construction and effort by an unbelievable variety of people, and assembling of every sort and kind of thing necessary before D-Day could even be contemplated was bewildering, and the thousands of different things that had to be taken into consideration and allowed for quite staggering. A Second Front – yes, one thing to shout for it, quite another to prepare for it and yet again another to put it into successful operation, a success which never could have been achieved had it not been for the combined efforts of all, men, women and even children.

The Roosevelt entourage all seemed confident of his re-election but with a diminished majority, but thought it would be a pretty tough fight and that the Republicans would gain extra seats in the Senate.

Quebec was at its loveliest all the week of the Conference, lovely sunshine and the views from the Citadel over the St. Lawrence to the hills beyond quite superb. Must admit it is a very excellent setting for such conferences and set away from the town as it is, there is nothing to disturb those who work there and they can have real peace and quiet. They were all at it morning, noon and night, the citizens of Quebec were bitterly disappointed as the only chance they had of seeing the President and Churchill was when they arrived or left, and as the hours of this were more or less secret only a few of them were lucky.

Vera was still generous with her gifts from Canada, as I acknowledged in October 1944:

I got a most superb box of chocolates from you from Quebec. I must admit I get almost as much pleasure looking at them, as eating them. Just to think there are still such things as luscious boxes of chocolates in the world. I don't think Mary Ann has ever seen so many sweets in one place at one time! Min promptly said I should put them in the bottom draw and save them for Patrick, but I just couldn't and I regret to say they are disappearing. Thank you so much darling, you are the world's best rememberer, and I really thought that when one reached the advanced age of 26 birthdays didn't count any more. But I am awfully glad they do. Unfortunately I am still as greedy as I was when I was six.

SIXTEEN

The Soldiers Return

THE OUTCOME of the war was looking more positive at last. The Allied armies were winning the war, yet whenever the Americans won a battle, my father declared that it was actually two British Tommies who did it single-handedly. He credited all victories to General Alexander rather than Montgomery, and declared that Marshal Tito had joined the Conservative Party. My father's recipe for post-war peace was to starve the French, since he said as long as there were Frenchmen, there would be wars.

There was bad news from my half-brother, Harry. He had been in action in Burma soon after he had seen our mother and news came through in June that he had been wounded. At first it was difficult to get an accurate account, but in the end we learnt that a mortar bomb had gone off near him. He had lost one leg and the other was badly damaged.

Although there was a considerable front opened in Burma, the invasion of Europe was on its way and a number of doctors, nurses and hospital ships had been withdrawn from India and relocated in Europe. As a result Harry suffered some grizzly doctoring and nursing and long waits till he could get a hospital ship home. Even when eventually he got to the Middle East he had to wait for another hospital ship.

Having lost his right leg, Harry was undergoing rehabilitation on the left leg. This caused inflammation and a high temperature and he was pronounced unfit to travel. Once his temperature had stayed normal for 72 hours, he was offered an ambulance drive to the port, and was on his way home.

At home, life was as confusing:

A fearful uproar over here in the ID Press, because someone in the M.E. [Middle East] gave out that if a man's wife was over 35, and he wanted to have a baby he would be given first priority for leave. The result was that this end, soldiers' wives were called on by strange well-meaning women who asked them if they wanted babes when their husbands came back or not. This was said by the press to be quite uncalled for interference with private people on the part of the War Office. They were full of indignant letters from women who said they were earning a packet in munitions and certainly didn't wish to be blackmailed into having a baby by the W.O.!

Lolly is very well on the whole, but I am afraid awfully tired. This summer has taken a lot out of even the most stout hearted in London, it has been an awful strain. They themselves don't realise how tired they seem to us outsiders when we go there. Peg down from Ard noticed it very much. I don't say they couldn't and wouldn't have taken it for twice as long if they had had to. But thank God they didn't. You never see Lolly sitting in a chair, she always seems to be on her feet doing something for someone. Of course she is an old goose in a way. When you have as much to do as she has, it seems to me a little unnecessary to break your back when you have five minutes to spare, gardening in that minute piece of garden. She has had quite a crop of tomatoes, I must say, and a meal or two of beans and peas, but they have cost rather a lot in effort, what with remembering to water them and one thing and another.

I am very excited as one of Patrick's greatest friends was among the repatriated who came home a fortnight ago, and I am seeing him this week. He wrote me a charming letter this morning to say Patrick was terribly well and had never had a day's illness in his life there, except for a slight chill last winter which lasted 2 days, and once a sore heel, which he got escaping, and made the most of with the Hun. He says he's a wonderful cook-housekeeper and that they have never had such good food or catering since Patrick took it on. In fact he was full of praises for him. So I have been feeling very pleased with myself all the morning. Two of Patrick's friends came back, but one poor man died most tragically after he'd been home only a week. It must be rather awful for his family.

Mrs C-P remains at Ardchattan, reorganising the Nursing Association, and doing all her various jobs, besides being a very bellicose County Councillor. Bobby is trying to get through the Gothic Line, and Tommy has disappeared again but they are both quite cheerful when last heard of. In fact Bobby enjoys every minute of this war, and makes no bones about it. He has been living in a luxurious Italian villa, living very literally off the fat of the land.

Harry's plans also preoccupied my mother, as he reached Egypt in a hospital ship from India:

Airgraph today from Harry says my cable to Lord Killearn produced a visit from his ADC and a stir-up out there, also Alan L-B [Lennox-Boyd] cabled and stirred up Grigg [Minister of War] to act, at last comes a cable saying they hope to start on the 9th. The Archbishop's death [William Temple], the most awful loss. Every one grief stricken about it. He was a delicious man, as well as a very great one. I went to represent the YW to the Abbey Memorial service. Sat opposite Gouser, the Russian ambassador, who sat next to 2 Orthodox priests, – was in friendly conflab with them and sang 'The strife is o'er' Alleluia hymn loudly, strange to see.

It's been confirmed that Harry started 9th, General Grover his General now top welfare here, who Harry took me to tea with in the jungle, is here and came to lunch and has got busy about those Burma wounded most usefully.

Laura also kept Vera posted about Harry:

We are all waiting for Harry to come now. It is maddening that he should be stuck halfway, but he may turn up any minute now. Mum and Dad went to Roehampton on Friday. It does mean warnings and doodlebugs but there must be a time limit on them you'd think.

We'll be able to get to see him at R.

F saw a man called Jack Fawcus, repatriated from Patrick's camp and is full of him! This man finds it extraordinarily shabby here – he's horrified at the independence of women, doing everything themselves, and he went out to dinner and dance in a black tie and was furious to find no one else changed! He thought them down right lazy. He has no sense of time and for this first fortnight or so couldn't face lunch at all – just breakfast and dinner. His wife saw he was apt to forget where he was and once she caught him walking down a hotel corridor without a stitch on! He was most reassuring about the future, which was very nice to hear.

The rest of us are ok! Mummy spoke frightfully well at the Royal Empire Society this week. It was a great success.

Harry ended up in Roehampton Hospital, the house where he, Reggie and Vera had spent their childhood with their ponies. He came home looking very thin, but his return to Britain caused his spirits to rise. He did not seem to mind the bad news that he had to lose his other leg as well. Harry was able to spend Christmas with my parents and on Boxing Day my mother wrote to Vera:

Harry was longing to tell us everything and got it all off his chest in the first 3 days, tho' its only here 2 days ago he's told us of the Hell of being carried through the paddy fields with drenching rain directly after he was hit. The mortar bombs kept coming and the natives who ought to have carried the stretchers bolted, so men from nearby units had to be found and it was so muddy they had to proceed by lifting the stretchers up on the terraces of the paddy fields and leave them while they clambered up themselves. One man died on the journey. Harry said his mind was perfectly clear and his legs quite numb, no pain and longing for food. At Casualty clearing he got his blood transfusion and his legs put in plaster, then two days in a paddle steamer down the Brahmaputra. Then a hospital train for 3 days with nurses, but unimaginative ones. At B. there were no fans, no penicillin, filthy food. It's a nightmare to look back to now, one can see.

    Poona was efficient and clean and cooler, tho' it's there they put the blood into him too hot. There was a gathering of the clan to see him, Mary, Katie, Reg and Frances all came up to see him. So it was a glorious family pie. As it was within a week of my inducing a very fierce but very clean and capable cook general to come to me I was nervous as to her reactions, but she stuck it with only a few outbursts and now Harry is here as the wounded hero she is all over him. . .

Marmaduke Hussey, who some years later married her granddaughter, Susan Waldegrave, was also at Roehampton and came with Harry for Christmas dinner:

    Young Hussey was a marvel of courage, he'd only once been on crutches for 2 mins, but he asked for Harry's and got up the 5 steps at the front door, putting real weight on his 'pylon' for the first time. Beads of sweat came out in his forehead from the effort which shows how great it is. Harry was most impressed and it'll help him make his first effort of the kind when the day comes.

    Goose, Xmas pud and mince pies all were there, plus brandy butter, grapes (filthy but seasonable). Then we all listened to the King's speech, jolly good wasn't it? and then got young Hussey away in the ambulance and then one and all we fell asleep till late tea which Harry had in bed.

    Next morn: Lolly took him to Harrods to buy books. Young Hussey hearing he'd shopped longs to too. So one day we must try that for him.

    Alan Lennox-Boyd came the day Harry left us, the same as ever. He had a nice story of Clemmy's spouse who when asked in Paris about the stabilisation of the Franc replied 'Je me suis tout a fait impuissant'.

Reggie came to see Harry and spent the morning shopping for him, purchasing an orange and yellow mustard dressing gown and salmon pink pyjamas, best observed through dark glasses. Reggie was most impressed with Harry's positive approach. He, himself, was feeling a bit lonely as Joyce was again on one of her tours, busily boosting the morale of the troops. Meanwhile my mother continued her relentless visits to Y.W. hostels and stately homes, frequently departing on the wrong train, and leaving a trail of spectacles and gloves behind her wherever she went. There was news of the Campbell-Preston brothers:

Bobby and Tommy are both floundering in the Italian mud with slight breaks when they get to Rome on leave. Bobby goes to the Opera and seems to go to an inordinate amount of audiences with the Pope but Tommy becomes more Anglican after each visit and his description of the Vatican was that it was very cumbersome. Poor old Raymond is in Greece and at one moment was mayor of a Greek town and giving banquets for the locals and making long speeches in Ancient Greek. The next day his guests were having pot shots at him. I must say his speeches were received very coldly apparently but if someone addressed us in High Old English I suppose we should be a bit cold too. My ma-in-law is alone at Ardchattan so I am going next week to be with her for a month or so.

The last days of the war approached. In March 1945 my mother wrote:

Harry was home for a lovely month which began by being a fortnight and then stretched. We are in cook trouble again too. And Harry wants to come back on Thursday and I am due to go to Katie that day, she coming up in her car with her lame Bailiff to buy a Bull at Reading! So it's a bad patch for us all. Poor little Fuffs is at great tension of course. But is so good. Fuffs had a letter from Patrick dated Jan 27th saying food situation good as HM's nephew [Viscount Lascelles – later Earl of Harewood] *had appeared in Camp with some food he'd hoarded. So Patrick as cook was a bit busier again and the general tone was a bit happier.*

These remained anxious times. Joyce came home, and I stayed with my parents to help them and to act as cook, nurse and companion to Harry. Doodlebugs still fell but 37 Chesham Place survived. Harry began to walk on his wooden legs, with the aid of two sticks. It was refreshing to watch him in his quest to regain his independence. Meanwhile my father observed:

He and Frances get on very well, he hustles and rather bullies her, which she thinks is great fun. F is becoming quite a good cook. I'm sure the fact that she is occupied all day and tired by the evening is really a great help to her these anxious days.

By the spring of 1945 we knew that at last the war was ending. Excitement mounted, but I was afraid. The month before Patrick got back was the most gruelling. The Allied armies were advancing across Europe but my eyes were fixed on a tiny spot, and anxious about the fate of one individual caught up in this huge drama. To my fevered imagination the armies appeared to zig-zag all over the place, which army, which General would reach Colditz first – mad rumours circulated. The Germans in a final gesture might shoot everyone? Russians might get there first and everyone disappear into a rambling mess? The prisoners might break out and stream home on their own.

My father's optimistic and fairly pragmatic foretellings were a steadying influence, along with Minnie at the Bucklebury Cottage who looked after Mary Ann while I flitted nervously between there and London, Mary Ann's routine going on quietly, and Minnie making me concentrate on calculating the points system in the ration book. Should we use the 2½ points left over at the end of the month, owing to a lower consumption of golden syrup than planned, on buying 2 ozs of raisins and currants or half a dozen prunes? When Minnie got absorbed by these calculations she pinned me down and I ended going in embarrassment to the village shop to get a spoonful of raisins or a few prunes, illogically feeling like Shylock.

On 3 May 1945 my father reported the news of the end of hostilities to Vera, still in Canada:

After dinner came the announcement of the unconditional surrender of an army of a million men to Alexander, so we wondered whether Lady Freyberg5 had heard of this. I expect she had as she seemed in very high spirits. Nothing could have been more startling and dramatic than this sudden announcement, and it does seem poetic justice that the first really big surrender should have been to Alexander, who is certainly the best General in the Field on any side, and who has certainly been the most generous and loyal of all the Commanders. I think everyone is delighted that it is he and his Command that have given the last push to the German wall which is now tottering so rapidly.

I should think Himmler's account of the death of Hitler is probably nearest to accuracy and that Hitler either had a bad fit or a real stroke, and that his end was then probably hastened by some of his gang. Why this idiotic sailor (Nazi Admiral?) [Admiral Karl Doenitz] should have tried to pretend to us that he was the new Fuehrer appointed by Hitler is difficult to understand. He must surely have known of the negotiations that had already taken place and agreed to surrender to Alexander. But as Lady Freyberg said, quite rightly, one almost forgets now to speak of Hitler or Mussolini. These men who have brought this tremendous suffering on the world and brought ruin to Europe, have never filled a smaller place in the world than they do today.

I think I am right in saying that the general feeling here is not one that would lead to great 'mafficking'. I think there is a deep feeling of anxiety whether it is going to be possible to exercise future wars and prevent the building up of new Dictators, and stop their trying to impose their political theories on other countries. Already most of

5. Barbara Jekyll (1887-1973), whose second husband was General Lord Freyberg, VC. A childhood friend of my mother's.

us realise that the British Commonwealth and the United States will
be forced to maintain tremendous Armed Forces, certainly on the
seas and in the air, not only to prevent the possibility of another war
with Germany but to prevent Europe being plunged into another
form of slavery. These are gloomy thoughts and have robbed our
great victory of its glory but, perhaps quite contrary to all the
examples we have in history, Jo Stalin may see the light and confine
his own ideologies to his own people and learn to leave others free
to practice theirs as the majority of people wish.

In the middle of April President Roosevelt died. My father
was much moved and his account of the President's death in
his letter to Vera accurately captures the feelings of many. This
was also the moment of Patrick's return. Even today it is hard
for me to remember that day properly, other than as one of
pulsating excitement but with the facts blurred:

Soon after your interesting letter of your visit to the White House
arrived, came the news of the President's sudden death. I am so glad
you had those days as his guest as the memory of it will live with
you always. The news quite stunned us all. Everyone from the
highest to the lowest felt they had lost a real friend – never has there
been such sincere and universal feeling on the death of a foreigner.

But in some ways it has made his splendid work stand out – to
have exhausted yourself and used up every ounce of your strength in
assisting your friend, is after all the greatest thing you can do – and
perhaps there is poetic justice in the thought that destiny will state
and make clear that Winston, our peoples, stood alone and saved
the world but we couldn't have defeated the Germans alone and so
looked westwards and the great American nation, thanks entirely to
Roosevelt, came forward and helped us, and he gave us all that he
could do and having done so, in sight of victory died and left
Churchill alone to finish the war he had begun! Mum went to St
Paul's as representing YW. She said poor Winston was in tears and
unashamed at showing his emotion – he looked really distressed.

There is no doubt he and Roosevelt had such complete confidence in each other that they played with each other like good polo players, and we depended tremendously on Roosevelt in the match with Stalin and in securing freedom and voting etc in small countries. His loss therefore is immense.

Frances has been going through a really difficult time, until one could hear Patrick's voice, one could not be sure that he was safe and well. With the stories of the rescued camps and especially his, one didn't feel too sure. So poor F. rushed to the phone whenever the bell rang. We hoped for his arrival today!

Last night at 1pm the phone next to Mum's bed rang. In two seconds Laura had woken up and was on her way to our room. Frances was still awake when I told her Patrick was on the telephone – poor little darling she hardly knew which to do – laugh or cry – there he was in Buckinghamshire. I believe the aerodrome is quite close to Beaconsfield. He should get through all necessary formalities this morning and be here this afternoon.

He sounds just the same and says he is well. That one horrible nightmare disappearing in the morning and it has been a long one. It seems only right that just as these men arrive, we are suddenly having such beautiful sunny days. The country has never looked better.

Laura confirmed the atmosphere in the house at that time:

Poor old Fuff was wonderful while she was waiting, but every telephone call was torture to her, and it never stops ringing in this house! She listened to every news bulletin in every language, of course the midnight bulletin that gave the news that the camp had been released caught me asleep, and I thought the house had had a direct hit when Frances let out a bellow like a mad bull. Then for a week, nothing. The only night F stumped off to bed before 1 a.m. of course the telephone rang at 1 a.m. and there Patrick was.

My father's letter continued:

There is chaos on a colossal scale in Germany and the U.S.A advance troops are so excited that they seem to add to it rather than at once establish calm and order. Luckily they have met with little or no resistance. The Boche had concentrated his best troops in the North and those opposite the Gauls had no stomach for war. What Lord French once said to me seems true, that in every army about a third like fighting, a third will go with the majority and a third don't like it, so when you had defeated the 1st third you find two thirds don't like it all and then comes the collapse.

Patrick has just walked in – he looks very well, a bit thinner which makes him very handsome – he is really very good looking – now and then like most men who have been through a great trial, a distant look comes into his eyes. When Patrick arrived at 12.30 Frances was wheeling Harry out for a walk as Patrick wasn't expected till after 3. However the formalities were hurried and he got here to be welcomed by Mum and self and then Mum ran out to find F and we have left them alone.

Molly C P came in the afternoon and his brother Tommy. I had almost forgotten how awfully nice Patrick was. What may interest H.E. is that 2 days before he was himself released, the Commandant told young Winant, who had only been brought into the camp a day or two before, that he and six others were to be moved. While they were all six 'prominentes'[6] as the Boche called them, they were all the inmates of one room. The other officers made a protest as they knew the USA troops would be up in a very short time. They tried to find a way of hiding them but that was impossible and at 1pm they were surrounded by German soldiers and marched off. The rest refused to move next day when ordered to get ready. The

6. The Prominentes were sons of eminent people, whom the Germans fleetingly thought they could use as bargaining counters. They were Viscount Lascelles, the King's nephew, John Elphinstone, the Queen's nephew, Charlie Hopetoun whose father, the Marquess of Linlithgow had been Viceroy of India, Giles Romilly, a nephew of Mrs Churchill, John Winant, son of the American Ambassador to Britain, and Michael Alexander, a maverick character who, when captured behind the lines and under threat of being shot as a spy, had the foresight to announce that he was a relation of General Alexander's, which he was not.

Commandant said they were orders direct from Himmler (that makes it look serious). They were taken to a camp near Dresden where high French political prisoners have been collected and they believe Stalin's son. The commandant seemed to acknowledge that there was a split between the SS and Wehrmacht but Himmler's orders prevailed. At first the Commandant and many of them thought the move was to get them out of the firing line as the village became a defensive post and they would have been in the front line. The extraordinary thing is the Yanks didn't seem to know there was any Officers POW camp there, even though Winant's own son was there! P. says the 'American Armoured forces do look tremendous, the quality, stupendous'.

Patrick stayed in London for two days, during which he went to visit John Elphinstone's parents to bring them news. He then went up to Ardchattan. My father wrote:

The more one sees of Patrick the more one realises that he has suffered very much and been through a tremendous ordeal. When he first arrived he was, of course, excited. One's first impressions were that he looked thinner, which rather improved his looks, but fairly well. But on second and third interviews one realised that he was not too strong and he is sure to have a reaction and will, I believe, require quite a period of rest, but provided he takes things quietly he will very soon be himself again.

I wrote my impressions to his Mother and she says she quite agrees with me. He has found that even a small walk very soon tires him. Luckily he and Mary Ann get on like a house on fire. She is extraordinarily like him and stands in front of him gazing on him with admiration, which is rather a good beginning; so I feel quite happy about him.

The first thing Patrick and I did on the day he arrived was to make for Mary Ann and the cottage. The first days were a rush of talk. This was the only time Patrick ever talked of his experiences. After that he never referred to them again. It was like lancing a colossal boil, after which the wound was sealed and healed.

I got the impression that the last two years had been the worst. When escape was impossible, when one or two friends had nervous breakdowns, Patrick worried that the younger officers captured at nineteen might find the constant disappointments almost too hard. (One of them had as good as committed suicide trying to make an impossible escape, and had been shot by the guards.) He suffered from the lack of news from home and the sense of being cut off from all our feelings, not only individually but nationally. This was further complicated by the arrival in the camp of Michael Burn and Giles Romilly, both of whom were Communists and who argued their case with skill. They made Patrick wonder what the national mood was, and where the future was heading.

His arrival back in the family home was a great surprise for him. He now had a five year old daughter, and this daughter faced by a proper father and not a virtual one. These were all hurdles to jump. Then times had changed dramatically since he left. In 1940 Ardchattan had been run with twelve indoor servants. On his return, his mother was there, running the house with Kate, the cook, and one daily lady with a small child, whom Molly was delighted to have persuaded to help her. Patrick asked me if his mother had gone a little mad.

Social changes were all around him. The seller's market baffled him. In quest of bedroom slippers, we went to Fortnum and Masons only to find they were out of stock. Patrick told them somewhat abruptly that if they continued to fail to sell him bedroom slippers he would remove his custom elsewhere. Embarrassed I led him out, all too aware of the sniggers behind us.

After we got back to Ardchattan he began to put on weight. His health improved rapidly and his strength returned. Minnie quietly helped Mary Ann, who found a strange man in her mother's bed frustrating and annoying – though she was fascinated by the acquisition of a father.

Vera was still in Canada. I related my news to her, which says something about how we coped with all this:

I am furious with whoever you left behind at G.H when you went West, as I cabled you at 8 o'clock in the morning before I did anyone else, about Patrick. I am so sorry you never heard. I sent it quick rate and everything. Anyhow, that is the past and thank you so much for your cable. It's quite unbelievable having him back, exactly the same, except a great deal thinner and very tired. They had the narrowest possible shave to being moved, but the American 1st Army advanced 45 miles in one day and caught the Germans napping. You may have seen the accounts in the Times of the 18th & 20th April, written by one of Patrick's fellow prisoners. Of course they were terribly upset by the removal of 7 'prominentes', and so far no news of their release.

Lascelles was in the same room as Patrick and he was rather fond of him, and made him make the toast and carry the coals. He said he behaved extremely well over the move, and appeared quite stolid and unmoved, which was pretty brave under the circumstances. Patrick said he was surprisingly unspoilt and worked quite hard in the mess. I do hope they get released soon, as they must be having a beastly time. I feel so sorry for poor Viv Hopetoun, as it was such a near thing their release.

We got up here about a week ago and Patrick looks better every day. Mary Ann is a bit astounded at her father. She took him on at once and behaved as if he'd never left the house, but on second thoughts she finds he occasionally gets in the way and has a habit of meaning 'no' when he says 'no'. She doesn't approve of him sleeping with her Mamma and has said several times that to her mind it would be far more practical if he slept with Minnie, and she and I slept together. She said to Min after the first 3 days of his return, 'Do you love Daddy?' so Min said 'Yes', 'Well, why don't you kiss him all the time like Mummy does?'

SEVENTEEN

Peacetime

AS THE war ended, all aspects of life began to return to normal. To my father his touchstone of cricket and Lord's took its place. While Patrick and I were recovering in Scotland he wrote excitedly to Vera:

Yesterday the first day of cricket at Lords. Australian RAF v an England side, a lovely very hot day, so I got Harry up there with his chair, he managed the few steps into the row of seats in the Pavilion. Charlie Lucan was in the President's box just behind us and so came up and had a long talk and gave Harry a warm welcome I am glad to say. We have got the Committee to allow wounded candidates, who in normal circumstances might have become members of MCC as playing members and be elected right away, and so I got a young Hussey who was in next bed to Harry elected yesterday.

The game was rather slow when a huge Australian came in and began to wake things up, but it was so hot I began nodding and was almost asleep when I heard voices – Look Out!! So I looked up and saw the cricket ball – which looked almost as big as a football coming straight at us, quite forgetting in the few seconds available that Harry was unable to move – I ducked and looked after myself. Harry sat as quiet as a mouse and quite calmly caught the ball!! Tremendous cheers from all the Members, very few of who knew he had no legs, but Charlie L was so thrilled, he rushed into the boardroom where a Committee was sitting and shouted Arthur's boy caught the catch and the Committee rushed out to shake Harry by the hand. One old man ran up and offered him a cigar!

It was only after he had caught it that one realised what a splendid example of calmness and control he had shown. It really was a good show. I had to push him back in his chair all the way home as there wasn't a taxi to be seen anywhere but I was so delighted at his performance that it was a pleasure. I'm not surprised – his battery all praised his calmness and courage under fire.

Mum asked L-M [Lady Mary Herbert] if she thought we could get Harry into the forecourt at BP on the night of VE day – and the Queen as usual at once asked us to go there, so we went through the Garden Entrance – sat in the forecourt saw nearly 100,000 people cheering and singing – it was a marvellous sight – I wonder if it makes a great impression on the Yanks. I rather doubt it – they know so little what it means. The illuminations consisted of flood lighting of Government Buildings, St Paul's and one or two of the bigger offices, there was not time and certainly no labour and probably no money for private people to light up their houses as in my young days. Still there were high spirits and not much damage. No taxis as the drivers were all afraid the Yanks would smash them up.

Winston had a tremendous reception from the balcony of Ministry of Health in Whitehall and made a good little speech, but somehow there is hanging over us a cloud which damps down one's joyousness. The reports coming in from Yugoslavia, Eastern Austria and especially Hungary of Russian behaviour are awful. Just the same as the Bosch secret police, looting wholesale and disappearing of whole classes of people. There is such an awful wide gulf between democracy as understood in Russia and by us and USA that one can't see how it is to be bridged. We have pledged our word to small states and if we keep it what and when is the next step to be taken? I have preached and preached and prayed we should have been 'en place' in Southern and Eastern Europe and now we are too late.

As Patrick got better, so did his desire to pick up the threads of his army career as quickly as he could. I knew that was a natural instinct for him, but it brought home the horrible truth to me that our times of separation were not over, and I wasn't sure how my strength would last out. While understanding, I found it hard to sympathise.

Our eventual fate was uncertain, although both of us thought a home posting of some sort most likely. This idea was rudely shattered after six weeks when Patrick was posted to the Black Watch in Greece. This was an overseas posting, with no wives, and might possibly last for a year. It was a bombshell. Patrick was torn by mixed feelings. Principally he was delighted to feel he could get into the swing of things, and join a battalion on a semi-war footing. I was shattered and felt quite unequal to a prolongation of our long separation.

Patrick went in August, leaving me aghast and totally miserable. Needless to say my mother whipped into action and started making plans. They were directed to getting me to Greece. It was not long before she came up with a solution. I was to sign on as a member of the YWCA and 'volunteer' to go to Athens to work in the existing YWCA centre there. This was not a totally straightforward plan, the YWCA had to be persuaded, even convinced that this was just what they wanted.

I had to be found a passage on a troopship to Cairo, the only means of transport available, not to mention visas for Egypt and Greece. Undaunted as ever, my mother achieved her goal and in January I sailed for Cairo in a troopship, suitably dressed in YWCA uniform. The troopship itself was quite an experience. To arrive in Cairo from a rationed and tired Britain was fun – with limitless food, bazaars where you could shop and a number of friends in the Army living a fairly relaxed life. The only snag was the almost daily outbreak of riots. A month passed as I fretted to get my passage on to Greece. At that point a nice Army officer friend broke the news to me that Patrick had been posted to the Staff College at Camberley and would shortly be leaving for home.

This was a considerable complication. Fortunately my mother's gene did not desert me. It was extremely difficult to get any kind of passage home as all bookings were dealt with on a priority basis, there being many families and people who had been marooned in the Middle East by the war. Any flight or ship had been booked for months. But I found that the exception was Air France, which had acquired some redundant troop carriers and were open for business. I bought a flight back to London, which involved a night of travelling and arriving in Paris after two days.

For this a French visa was required. The riots in Cairo were violent and anti-British and everyone in the YWCA was confined to barracks. I managed to smuggle myself out and join a queue at the French Consulate. I sat there in vain for a whole day, discovering that a French queue was different from a British one. Next day I went again. After a while the man next to me asked how long I had been waiting. He told me this process could go on for days – but there was a solution. The official who dealt with visas used to run through the room where we sat going from one office to another. My friend told me to put a sum of money in my passport. He also said the official would never admit he couldn't remember a lady and all I had to do was stand in front of him and, as he ran, give him my passport, shake him by the hand, smile sweetly and say words to the effect that I was 'enchantée' to 'voir' him once again. Unconvinced, I did this and soon had the necessary visa.

The airfare and visa had depleted my ready cash, but armed with traveller's cheques I arrived to catch the plane. It turned out to be an old troop carrier with about twenty passengers who sat on seats either side facing each other. There was a problem at the start as a couple turned up with a small baby. There was a discussion about what to do with the hammock they'd brought for the baby. The pilot decided the best way was to hang the hammock from various points in the cockpit, shrugging his shoulders and admitting he didn't know what half the knobs were for anyhow.

Next I was approached by a party of Chinese. They explained they were putting a lady on the plane who was going from Chunking to Paris and that her only phrase was 'I go Chunking –

Paris'. Would I look after her? Her belongings were in a large bandana handkerchief. I could hardly refuse and foresaw no difficulties. We all got on the plane, which started very much like a car and off we took. We flew all day without stopping.

It was a bumpy flight, as a result of which everyone was uninhibitedly sick. I imagined the pilot was making a real effort to spend the night on French soil. Eventually we landed at Tobruk, and the pilot was delighted as we had beaten the train from Cairo by twenty minutes. The airfield was an RAF base which, with considerable puzzlement, gathered us in. They gave us a welcoming dinner and put us up for the night, my poor Chinese lady utterly bewildered. I had a hard time extricating her from the lavatory, the ways of which were confusing to her.

The RAF officers asked me kindly what on earth I thought I was doing on this plane. They explained that it was quite unsafe for air travel, pointing to a pile of spillikins which had been the last Air France plane to land there. They were sympathetic when I told my story. They also said that if all went well, we would journey for four or five nights and that we would probably land next in the Western Desert wherever there was an RAF airfield.

Their predictions proved correct and we hopped from airfield to airfield for the next two days, sometimes having very short flights between meals. Finally we got to Morocco, where we were served questionable coffee before heading on to Marseilles. There the plane landed – but died. We were put on the night train to Paris.

This proved a wonderful journey, and during the night our fellow travellers displayed to us the things they had smuggled – diamonds and money, revealing the methods they had used. What struck me was how they had managed this, as they all looked so exactly like one's imagined prototype of a smuggler.

The only other Brit on the plane had been a totally silent little lady with a seven-year old child who was returning to Birmingham. After delivering the Chinese lady to the Chinese waiting party, this lady attached herself to me in the hope that I would know what to do next in Paris.

We needed money to finance the rest of the journey, including the ship home. Off we set to cash our traveller's cheques, only to find they were not endorsed for France and nowhere could we get any cash. My ready cash was exhausted and I had come to my wit's end. Remembering my mother's approach to such occasions, I started with the British ambassador, but this failed to work for me.

In despair we reached our last stop – a bank which totally refused to help us. To my surprise my new friend said that as we obviously had reached the end of the road, perhaps she could help. She took her child to a corner and proceeded to undress her. Under her clothes the child was covered in pound notes – a more acceptable currency than traveller's cheques. She peeled some off for me. I gave her an English cheque which was then affixed to the Viyella vest and we all got home on the Golden Arrow boat train. Whenever we had been stopped at customs on our journey from Cairo we had been rigorously searched for currency. But the child had usually been planted on the counter and fed sweets by the unsuspecting customs officers. The whole journey took four days, and I reached London two days before Patrick.

While I was away the family decided to celebrate the peace. During the war Chesham Place had shaken with bombs. It had been where our mother started her evacuee rescue, and our father planned and planned. Latterly Harry had recuperated there and begun to learn to walk. Now they set about adapting the rooms.

Our Aunt Lola's gift to Laura was a length of silk, of perfect quality and historical vintage, which saved a whip-round for clothes coupons. Harry then gave Laura the money to take the silk to a top dressmaker for an evening dress. It was lovely and quite different from any material procurable at the time. To everyone's heartbreak it was stolen the next year. The dress's importance was more symbolic than sartorial.

Harry returned to his pre-war job with the British South Africa Company, stationed in Lusaka. In February 1946 Laura wrote to him:

I am in the office again, but I just can't concentrate on anything until I have told you both about the dance. There is so much to tell, I am bubbling over – you've never seen anything, such perfection, in all your life from my frock, which is a dream – to the house, which had just that touch that Mummy always gives of making the flowers, the food and everything else look personal and not bought – (which in fact was the case – being personal I mean) I must try and find a beginning and start from there.

Princess Elizabeth accepted to come just after F. had left. That threw us into a tizzy. Daddy had very Victorian ideas about wearing decorations and arranging quiet corners where she could sit. Everyone we asked, from Searcy's the caterer to the Band, said the one thing about her was that 'She's no trouble at all'. We had P.E. and Jean Gibbs the lady-in-waiting to dinner (in Lady Reading's house – who couldn't have been nicer. Reggie came to act as host. P E is so absolutely natural – very dignified while you are doing presentations etc. and then she opens with a very easy and cosy joke or remark, and you find yourself talking more naturally than at any ordinary set piece dinner. She had everyone in fits talking about a sentry who lost his hat while presenting arms, and they were deciding what happened to the poor man the next day.

Reg started off dancing with her and from that moment, she didn't stop dancing, except for very brief and skimpy intervals when she ate merrily, until nearly 2.30. The band organised everything their way. They were right about having Paul Joneses – which I had had qualms about, and they broke into reels and the Palais Glide, Boomps a Daisy, the Lambeth Walk, and best of all, the Conga, several times. P.E. immediately took the lead, with her partner clinging to her waist, everyone lined up behind and she led a stream of us in and out of the doors, round behind the lift through the hall, made an arch like in ring-a-roses, through which the tail went, and then darted off again. Daddy managed to get all his pictures lit. Mary and Katie brought up armfuls of forsythia, daffodils, ribes, primroses, snowdrops, flowering rhododendrons and so forth, and the rooms looked quite lovely. The food was quite outstanding. The offers of help we had were incredible. Ivy Price found an expert who was willing to do something in every branch. A New Zealand friend came in on Friday and made cakes all day – quite delicious, and looking most attractive – out of a tin of butter, eggs from Katie and Mary, and sugar I don't quite know where from. Another cook made chocolate mousse and produced masses of stuff – the Milk Bar round the corner here produced ham and tongue sandwiches and ice cream, The Bedford Arms produced drink, so Searcy's men were thoroughly impressed. Cripps turned up at the last minute, having said he couldn't, and threw a slight spanner in the works by barging in and doing the announcing, totally inaudibly and inaccurately, but it didn't matter in the least.

Sally [Waldegrave] *came, with her hair up, in a frock made of muslin curtains, but looking a dream. She danced without stopping, and ate with the same energy. Geoff dealt with the press and is now convinced he originated the whole party, and organised it, so he is happy.*

Daddy walked about with a grin of ecstasy on his face. He went up to everyone and told them about the pictures, and of course they were enthralled, because you just don't have dances where there are pictures worth looking at now. He had so many admiring remarks made to him about them – he is bursting with pride and pleasure. Mum looked quite lovely. She wore that black frock with the big swirl on the bottom of the skirt, her hair looked quite exquisite and it is literally true that a number of young men were so bowled over by her, they went about gasping to their partners, that they thought she was the loveliest thing they had ever seen. You would never have believed that during the day she had not only spent hours at the American Embassy wangling passages for Y.W. secretaries, but had dealt with a crisis when the piano failed to turn up, another when the electrician, after being warmly congratulated by Daddy on his work in lighting all the pictures, went home without fixing any of the ordinary lamps that were needed for the rooms, and so on and so forth.

The final thing was that she had to dress in her room with all the lights fused, and with her mirror removed by someone rather over quick, as we had to put it up in the Ladies Cloaks. All at the last minute any how. She really is wonderful, and what she didn't do and achieve for this dance is just nobody's business. Through it all, if one went into tea there last week, she was on hands and knees playing igloos with Mary Ann, and getting so enthralled that she rigged up the most elaborate lighting inside the igloo made from the arm-chairs, rugs, cushions and what not else.

What really thrilled her beyond anything was that on the morning of the dance, an invitation arrived from Buck House, for me to go to a dance there – what you might call a quick dividend, so you see Harry your frock is moving solely in Royal Circles!

My father also described the evening:

The day of our dance approached. Mary Ann and all hands polished the floors, cleaned up the rooms and they did look most awfully pretty. The dinner party was well chosen. From the start the Princess gave the lead to a really happy evening. She soon went off on her own and danced every dance. Thoroughly enjoying herself, the young Guardsmen in uniform queued up to get a dance. The successes were the reels. The young Scots took the reels very seriously and danced very well, full of go and claps and 'hacks'.

For drinks we had light beer and cider cup made up by my new friend at the local pub. I told him to put in very little gin and make it very weak. I quite forgot to taste it but everyone said it was A1 and every drop was drunk. At 2.30 am I had to put in my last reserves – a few bottles of cider and lots of soda water. Half an hour after the Princess had been in the house everyone was at her feet. I am sure she is going to be a tremendous influence for good. She can throw herself right into the fun and yet if there is any sign of over stepping the mark she draws herself up with great and natural dignity – I hardly spoke to her, as I felt it was a mistake to bring in old age to such a youthful happy family party, but as she said

Goodbye she said she had enjoyed every minute of it.

Mum has received letter after letter saying that none of them had any idea such a jolly party could be given. Mum's hard work in arranging all rooms, flowers, and food and looking like a Queen, doing just the right amount of presenting and leaving the Princess absolutely free, made certain of success.

Of course when one thinks that very few of the young men under 27 years have ever had a chance of enjoyimg a dance of all their contemporaries and friends in a private house, it's not surprising that they found it so enjoyable – still the credit must go to Mum.

Laura then described the Buckingham Palace dance, which contains the first mention of Bernard Fergusson, the man she would eventually marry:

We went off and drove in to the forecourt, went in and gave up our coats and then collected in the Long Gallery. At a given moment they signalled and we turned to the right, and filed through a very narrow doorway, inside which stood the Royal Family. You shake hands and curtsey to each, and it's a bit like the three bears, only there are four of them, because they start small, but by the time you get to Princess Margaret Rose, you can hardly reach that low to get her hand.

We then passed on into the next room, which is a perfect room for dancing, as it has a bow window one end, and two sort of wings, one where the band sat and the other where you could sit or stand, and which opened onto another sitting out room, through which was the supper room, and out of which you could get back to the gallery, where a buffet was. At the fireplace in the ballroom stood a magnificent figure, slightly tubby, but so covered in medals that Reggie said he thought he just pinned on a quilt – [General] Alexander. I've never seen so many ribbons, what happens when he wears full decorations I just don't know. Incidentally, everyone wore black ties.

The dancing started off quite soon. Nothing could have been more

*friendly and natural, and altogether unstilted. Quite soon the
Princesses were buzzing round the room, and the King was dancing
away for all he was worth. He is reputed to be the best waltzer in
the world, and he certainly looked it. Mary Strachey was just
starting to waltz with Reg, when the King claimed her – she dances
frightfully well – and they whirled round the room at top speed for
ages. Reg went crash into them once, but luckily the Royal rage
didn't break out – as apparently it can do.*

*Both Princesses danced without a stop, and the young men don't
seem to have any inhibitions about asking them. The Queen was
loaded down with pearls much too big for her, and glittering with
sequins on a grey chiffon frock. Obviously the young men were a bit
nervous of approaching her solo, so they always went up in twos or
threes. She manages to look tremendously regal. She didn't dance
very much, usually just the first bit, and then sat out, bolt upright,
very queenly, but with such a kind smile on her face. She went into
supper surrounded by a bevy of little boys.*

*They served champagne at the buffet, as if it were lemonade, and
I must say, it does help one to get through without that dragging
feeling that usually comes when you notice it's about one o'clock.
Bernard was very much in evidence doing the reel, with his monocle
flashing, and his rear sticking out in a most comic way. He made me
laugh a lot, because he was determined to say casually that he had
been for his DSO the week before, but he couldn't find the opening,
so he had to blurt it out direct. He seems to be busy rushing up and
down the country, doing I don't know what – something to do with
establishing schools, and is very much in the Laycock set up.*

EIGHTEEN

Germany

MY PARENTS moved out of their wartime quarters at Chesham Place and, through my father's involvement in the Lowndes Estate Company, got rid of Chesham Place and took on a house in Cadogan Place. They proceeded to turn it into flats, my father having the ground floor as an office. The alterations needed were considerable and gave my mother a great deal of work. Getting curtains, carpets and soft furnishing just after the war took a great deal of ingenuity.

For many years we had wondered how she lived her life at such a pace and predicted a nervous breakdown. This work turned out to be the last straw. It finally happened. She was given electric shock treatment, which, in those days was administered without an anaesthetic. She took nearly a year to recover. After this, although she appeared physically cured with her energy unimpaired, her character changed. The truth became whatever she wanted, sidelined at times, and her interests became obsessive. She was like a vehicle with no brakes.

This altered all our lives, but the principal victim was my father. He found mental illness difficult to cope with and he was terrified of it ever recurring – to such a degree that he never seriously opposed my mother again.

For the six months after our return Patrick attended Staff College at Camberley. We were blissful again. No more separations loomed in the foreseeable future. The war, both in Europe and the Far East, was finally over and our subsequent postings would be either at home or in Germany and neither were 'without family'. Then we were posted to the Highland Brigade in

Scotland and took a house just outside Perth. At last we could begin to live a normal, adult, married life, and seven years after we were married, we were able to celebrate our anniversary together for the first time.

We were snowed up for nearly a month in our first winter in Perth. I spent most the day in the cellar stoking a huge coal-fired central heating system – the first time anything so exotic had come into our lives. We had managed to buy a load of something called 'sea-coal', which was exempt from coal rationing. It looked as black as coal but was pebbles from the shore smeared with coal dust, and it never burnt. Patrick said it was colder than he had ever experienced as a prisoner-of-war. Electricity was rationed to a few hours a day and we huddled in rugs and overcoats. All was well the next year when Robert was born – on the newly-formed National Health Service – so we had none of the bother of having to save money, as we had had to do at the time of Mary Ann's birth.

During this time we had an uninvited guest in the form of Giles Romilly, Lady Churchill's Communist nephew, who had been one of the 'Prominentes' at Colditz when Patrick was there. Patrick was pleased to see him as he was extremely good company. Minnie remembered him as a small boy with his brother Esmond at the children's parties to which she had taken Laura and me.

Giles dropped names with generosity. We were told intimate details of life with the Churchills. Lord Beaverbrook was 'a dear friend' and we learnt a great deal about him. Trade Union barons figured often in the conversation, but they all seemed curiously reluctant to have Giles to stay. Giles committed one unforgivable sin in Minnie's eyes: he had no ration book. I was expecting a baby and in her view he was taking the bread out of my (and the baby's mouth). After a week or two she suggested to Patrick he should either produce a ration book or go. Patrick explained to her that, as a Communist, Giles's motto was 'What is mine is mine and what is yours is mine too.' Finally Minnie confronted Giles himself with an ultimatum. So ended a friendship, not wholly without relief on our part.

After two years Patrick was posted to the Black Watch battalion stationed in Duisberg, Germany. He went ahead in the spring and before joining him I attended one last party:

> *Just before I came out here I went and stayed at Carbury with the Elphinstones and had a royal dance with Princess Margaret – a very amusing party and she really is a poppet and so much prettier than last year and enjoying very much having the show to herself and not sharing it with Princess E. Bobby came with me in lieu of Patrick and when he danced with Princess M they got onto Joyce (who was on tour in Edinburgh that week), and she said the sketch of Joyce's she enjoyed the most was the people thanking the pianist for their complimentary tickets, 'Just like Mummy and Daddy all the time'.*

Our next few years in Duisberg were interesting. Bernard Fergusson took command, with Patrick as his second-in-command. Bernard had been one of Patrick's oldest friends at Eton, Sandhurst and the Black Watch. Their paths had divided before the war. The Black Watch, then two battalions, had one battalion in India and Patrick had opted to go there, while Bernard stayed in the home battalion. His experiences included the Staff College, and an appointment on General Wavell's staff – Archie Wavell claimed to have encouraged Bernard early on to be an unorthodox soldier, having seen a tendency that way. They remained friends until Wavell's death, with Bernard filling different jobs at various times on his staff.

Bernard also served in Palestine after the war. During it, he had a distinguished career in the Middle East and in Combined Operations. Then he went to India, ending up as a young brigadier. He commanded one of the two Chindit columns fighting behind the Japanese lines in Burma, one of the most dangerous and unpleasant engagements of the war. For these he was awarded the DSO about which he was so keen that Laura should be aware.

Bernard was tall and heavy, with a regular army moustache, but his eyesight was not good. He was told that wearing spectacles would put him at a disadvantage in the army, so he adopted a monocle, which was unusual in the forces. This gave him panache and led to some war-time newspapers claiming that he had had eyeglasses parachuted to him in the jungle.

Bernard had another side to his character. He was a gifted writer and poet and had supplemented his army pay by his writing, contributing to various periodicals including *Punch*. After the war his two best-known books about the Chindit campaigns, *Beyond the Chindwin* and *The Wild Green Earth* were both bestsellers.

The army families were housed in requisitioned houses, and as Bernard was then a bachelor, Patrick and I found ourselves sharing our house with him. It stood at the end of a crescent and had belonged to a prosperous industrialist, into whose fate we did not enquire too closely. It was spacious with a garden, quite large for a town house. What astounded us most was its modernity. It had clearly been built in the 1930s, at a time when we thought of Germany as an impoverished industrial country, bankrupted by reparations after the 1914-18 war. Yet we found ourselves with gadgetry we imagined only obtainable in America.

The main bedrooms were en suite, and the central heating electric (shades of the Perthshire boiler!). The large room on the ground floor, half sitting-room and half dining-room, stretched across the house. At the garden end was a huge plate glass window from floor to ceiling – a glass wall. At the press of a button this descended into the floor and you stepped into the garden. For us this was a mixed blessing as the electric supply, as happens after wars, often suffered power cuts and the house, if caught with the windows down, was chilly. But above all there was an electric fuse box. If there was a fuse you pressed a button to mend it. I caught up with this technology over fifty years later when I re-wired my London flat!

Minnie finally retired and went to look after Laura, and we

acquired Nanny Sinclair from Argyll who came with us. My first impressions went to Laura:

Mummy then drove down to Dover with me and saw me off on the Ostend boat. Patrick met me after considerable difficulty at Dunkirk and we started off for here. The car broke something awfully vital just after we got past Brussels. I think the reason was that we had the biggest lunch in Brussels either of us had had since 1939 and the avoir dupois was just too much for the car. Anyhow we had an amusing night in the little place where we broke down – found the mechanic in the garage came from Huddersfield and got a royal reception wherever we went. So we arrived here a day late – having had an amusing time in Belgium when Patrick tried to ring up here to say what had happened and asked them to find the telephone number of the 1st Black Watch – chaos ensued until a little Belgian helpfully translated it as la Montre Noire.

We arrived here to the house, which slightly embarrassingly belongs at present to both us and Bernard, to find Wavell, and Eric Linklater and Geordie Gordon-Lennox all staying. Quite a stiff party to hostess. Actually they couldn't have been easier. Wavell was absolutely charming, never drew breath and was quite fascinating – gave us a dissertation on Kipling of whom he is an enormous admirer and produced a never-ending flood of funny stories. Almost the nicest was of a naval officer in a company of men discussing the subject of love who silenced them all by saying 'Love? What the devil do you know about love? When I was in the North Sea last week a whale tried to make love to my submarine.'

He told us several very amusing ones about his days as a subaltern, and was quite thrilling about his air journeys during the war, especially when he was landing in India, Singapore, Java etc. With it all he was so charmingly humble and rarely used the word 'I' at all. Our CO (!!) of course worships him but he's not past seeing through it. Bernard was shooting a tremendous line about poetry one night (it is really quite genuinely the big thing to him) and was ever so slightly drunk and very emotioné reciting some

poem about Arras and dead pipers in the 1914 war – when Wavell
– who was sitting with his blind eye to me, turned his whole face
round in order to give me one of the most attractive grins I've ever
seen.

At the end of the dinner with Lord Wavell the conversation
turned to India, where everyone had served at some time or
another. Discussion got into full flow and began to include
examining what they thought had gone wrong. 'Of course what
the Viceroy should . . .' At this point Wavell got up saying politely
to me as it had been a long day he thought he would go to bed,
and left. As he closed the door behind him, Eric leapt up in horror
and said 'My God HE was the Viceroy'.

Eric Linklater looks surprisingly like Robertson Hare and a vicar
and was a dear little man – amusing and clever and excellent with
the old Field Marshal whom he tried to stir into committing himself
on various subjects – without any avail. Geordie Gordon-Lennox, a
beautiful gilded guardsman – but very nice and of course a friend of
Pat and Katie.

We had a tremendous weekend – with Highland games – drums
and pipes and whatnot playing on every conceivable occasion
including under my window at 7 a.m. one morning, which I took a
dim view of. I gather it's an old Scotch habit. We even had a dance
which lasted till 5.30 a.m. and was so Scotch we might well have
been in Inverness.

Oh my God this place! The only hope is to laugh at everything.
Our house is a spacious hideous villa with a garden going up behind
in which grow a lot of green things and a few dusty roses. Imagine
a villa on the outskirts of Reading – with trees up to the window and
then knock Reading down, starve what remains of the inhabitants
and make life for them a business of makeshifts with no hope. The
ruins of course shatter one – I think principally because it looks as
if nothing has been cleared up and as if it all happened last night.
There aren't really very many people about and what there are are

all dressed in black – or seem to be – and they kind of slink about.
The ugliness of everything is unbelievable.

But still things have and obviously are improving. For one thing
the Black Market has been completely eliminated by the new mark.
Coffee, cigarettes and chocolate have gone out as currency – which
means one can trade with the Germans with money, quite
legitimately, which you can't imagine what a difference it makes. It
makes the whole business much more dignified from our point of
view as one isn't perpetually breaking the law with people one is by
way of educating to respect the law. For me it removes a nice little
question of morals – as I arrived swearing nothing would make me
go on the Black Market – and I think I might have gone fairly
hungry. Now I can justifiably claim that we have ample and there's
no need to go bargaining about to get more.

Everyone of course grumbles madly and no doubt I will soon too.
They all say gloomily one can't ever get anything but meat for lunch
and dinner!

Before the new mark was approved as currency it was forbidden
for any of us to buy anything, especially food in a German shop.
This was reasonable as goods in these shops were being
subsidised by the Marshall Plan. Of course this led to a Black
Market as a lot of goods which were available to us through the
NAAFI, our forces shop, were as gold to the Germans. One
commodity, coffee, was priceless on the Black Market. Our
rations were allotted to us every week. They were delivered from
the regiment and were the basics – meat, sugar, flour, eggs and
such (choice was not the word). So when the Black Market
flourished it was tempting to swap a jar of coffee for chicken or
eggs or whatever the Germans were willing to part with. Apart
from food such things as coffee could buy almost anything.
Rumours were that enough accumulated coffee could buy a car.

When the mark was stabilized, the currency rate was 40 marks
to £1. This meant that living for us, in the German market, was
derisively cheap, including wages. If you had a married quarter,

usually a requisitioned German house, you had a fixed establishment of domestic staff allotted on the basis of rank, paid for by the Army. There was no reason why you should not employ extra staff at your own expense. The more people you employed the better for the local German community. This meant that at one moment my staff consisted of a governess for Mary Ann, several dailies, a dressmaker, a laundry maid, extra housemaids, kitchen maids and gardeners. It was a return to an Edwardian style of life. I further reported:

Bernard as CO is wonderful. Pomposity personified – but in many ways damn good. He's first class on paper though and mad keen on the job. The worst thing so far in this life is having damn all to do all day. I spent most the afternoon sitting on the banisters discussing the love life of Bernard and Patrick's drivers. In fact my house crawls with soldiery with even less to do than me.

To the other people the ugliness, the destruction, the Germans, have no effect at all on them and they are usually in a high state of indignation because a German has been uppish to them. I have so far been busy engaging the Germans they sack

Of course the servant situation seems fantastic, and I am amazed how nice and smiling they are. The stories of them spying and stealing don't so far seem to be true, and the two here are nice – not particularly clean, but efficient and able to do any job – the housemaid will cook and vice versa. Well this place is our fate for the next few years so we must make the best of it. Patrick thank heaven enjoys it.

Initially we found it strange to be living in a semi-friendly situation with a previously much-hated enemy. The dire living conditions of our German neighbours did not raise satisfied reactions of revenge at all. There were exceptions, as when there was a request for officers to volunteer to attend the Nuremburg trials. There were no takers, except one young officer who as a prisoner-of-war had escaped and ended up in Warsaw working with the Polish underground. He had been recaptured, and tortured terribly by the Gestapo. He volunteered with relish.

We were officially the army of occupation but we found it did not seem to work as we might have imagined. The next door villa to ours was still inhabited by a German family. They had a daughter of Mary Ann's age and friends were made over the garden wall. They had foreseen trouble as soon as the Nazis came to power and had transferred most their money to a Swiss bank account so were financially safe. They had servants and a smart car and seemed extraordinarily unmoved by the plight of their fellow citizens. A number of these citizens appeared to be living in sheds. We remarked that their ample garden shed was conspicuously empty.

The day came when they asked us to dinner. To our embarrassment, and probably resentment, we ate off gold plates, a scrumptious dinner of wild game unknown to us, and fresh vegetables (in short supply) with fresh cream in our coffee (on our rations we only had Carnation milk). We agonised about asking them back – army issue china and furniture, beef stew, if we were lucky with parsnips, and possibly biscuits and cheese and a butter ration. We decided to wait and consult my parents when they arrived to stay.

They told us to rise above such difficulties and act as if we faintly despised their affluence amongst so much destruction – not something Patrick and I would have managed to put across on our own. My parents oozed patronising kindness. It ended by Frau Blank asking if we could help with their seventeen-year-old son for whom they wished to arrange a holiday exchange in England. My mother told them, with apparent enormous kindness: 'I'm afraid that is a very dangerous plan. You see he might be cruelly received. A lot of the English still loathed the Germans'. Fortunately we moved shortly afterwards to Berlin.

Just before we left for Germany, Laura left to visit Harry in Lusaka – then Northern Rhodesia. She had given up her job with Lady Reading and went for her first good break since 1939.

While Laura was with Harry, Lady Reading remained in London, serving the Labour Government – the WVS (like the Civil Service) having been established as an apolitical service.

The WVS was soon asked to provide help in setting up the Government's scheme for a ground-nuts industry in Tanganyika and to encourage the unemployed to go out and work there. Every sort of infrastructure was needed – houses, schools, hospitals etc. The work on the ground was falling seriously behind, although people were already being recruited to go and work in what propaganda encouraged them to think was to be Shangri-La.

Lady Reading cabled Laura to go immediately and organise a team to hurry all these procedures up. There was considerable controversy about the wisdom of Laura doing this. Our parents were suspicious that it would end in disaster and Laura made into a scapegoat. But Harry advised her to give it a go and she went.

Laura arrived to find considerable chaos with very little of the infrastructure completed and the site a sea of mud. She sent an urgent wire to Lady Reading to get the imminent proposed embarkation of recruited families rescinded. Lady Reading's reply was couched in terms of 'Yours but to do or die – not to question why'.

Laura was equally displeased – even appalled. Our cousin, Alastair Buchan, was Assistant Editor of *The Economist*. Laura wrote to him saying something must be done. He asked her for an article which he would publish anonymously. This article became the basis for a debate in the House of Commons and soon after that the project faltered anyway.

After her return from Africa, Laura moved into her flat at 30 Cadogan Place. Minnie moved in with her and Laura got a job with the publisher Collins. They had started a magazine for children called *The Young Elizabethan* and Laura was appointed as editor. She was so happy that she said the importance of getting married did not seem so compelling, as she doubted if she would ever be so comfortable again.

We were in Duisberg for nearly two years. Bernard was determined that the Black Watch would not retire into being an introverted regimental clique, and that, besides soldiering duties, we should get involved in other affairs going on round us. Bernard used his many contacts to get people to visit us. There was a certain stand-off between the military and the civilian arms of the occupation forces, which Bernard refused to countenance. One of the charming friends Bernard found was Harry Collins and his wife. He was working to help the Germans with their Trade Unions, and to reconstruct the coal and steel industries in the Ruhr.

One of Patrick's friends from his prisoner-of-war days was Terence Prittie, a bilingual English-German speaker who had been the *Manchester Guardian's* German correspondent since demobilization. Terence had started on the *Manchester Guardian* as cricket correspondent on the retirement of the famous Neville Cardus. He was one of a group of ex-prisoners, who, on hearing that one of their prison guards was in danger in the East (Russian) Zone, managed to smuggle him out and establish him in the Western zone.

While we were in Duisberg the Russians set out to challenge the right of the Allies to remain in Berlin. The city was divided into four zones – American, British, Russian and French. The Russians tried to blockade the land communications in the hope of starving the other occupying powers and the inhabitants, thus initiating what became known as the Berlin Airlift.

The Black Watch was moved to Berlin immediately the Airlift ended. Berlin presented a totally different more cosmopolitan atmosphere to the Ruhr, thanks to the presence of the occupying American and French forces. Even the German attitude was different. Under allied occupation, the Berliners in West Berlin had stood beside us during the Airlift, and compared to the Ruhr, their self-respect was much restored. It was a pleasant change of atmosphere and we felt more light hearted.

All the time that Patrick and I were in Germany, Laura would come to visit and she and Bernard became closer friends. Patrick and I were certainly not innocent of match-making but we felt we were quite unsuccessful. Hoping to encourage matters one August, I used the excuse of my pearls needing to be restrung to consign these to Bernard when he went on leave. I asked him to deliver them to Laura.

I got a short note from her saying she had got them and that Bernard had asked her out, but rather characteristically she remarked that it was Bank Holiday weekend and London was empty.

Shortly after this, Bernard collapsed on a bus in Stranraer from a heart attack. Patrick went to see him and rang me in stupefaction to say that as he sat by Bernard's bedside, Bernard had said: 'I suppose this means I can't propose to Laura?' But when news of Bernard's heart attack reached London, Billy Collins sent Laura up to Scotland for an unnecessary meeting as a ruse to help the courtship along. Bernard's recovery was complete. He and Laura became engaged whilst he was convalescing, and in November 1950 they were married in St Michael's, Chester Square.

Patrick was due to take over command from Bernard shortly after returning from London, so when we went back to Berlin for a short time, Laura was our Colonel's wife. Berlin was a very interesting place in which to live, and we were lucky to have a charming house on the banks of the Havelsee, just outside the city.

To command the Black Watch fulfilled Patrick's highest ambition, and he was blissful, enjoying making his own imprint. It was an edgy situation as militarily one step wrong could mushroom into a major incident. One unfortunate day two young Black Watch officers, coming back from an exercise with unused hand-grenades, saw a German in a boat on the lake and in a wild moment threw a grenade. This was meant as a kind of prank since the grenade would only explode with a bang, nothing more.

But with the bang, the boat overturned and they had to alert the emergency services and rescue the boatman. Realising at once the stupidity of their action they raced back to confess to Patrick. He reached for his King's Regulations, the Army rulebook, read them a colossal lecture and imposed some punishment. He had hardly completed this before a furious general, having got the news almost as quickly, rang up demanding the immediate arrest of these officers and their possible court martial. Patrick said he had already dealt with them and he was sure the general would be aware that King's Regulations laid down that it was illegal to deal with the same crime twice.

So pleased was Patrick to find himself in command that he said to me the best thing about the job was that you could do whatever you liked. I challenged him, pointing out that he was always under superior orders. He undertook to show me and we had a bet on it. The brigadier was due to attend a parade and to address the battalion.

Patrick ordered everyone to wear a tin helmet and paint it shiny black. A puzzled regiment did so and on a boiling sunny day the brigadier was a little taken aback to find an extremely smart parade with black tin hats with their Red Hackle looking purposeful in the sun. Patrick looked on in smug, and not entirely unamused, pleasure. The brigadier thought it very smart and proceeded to make a speech saying it was the Army's role to put the word 'Great' back into Great Britain, seeming to imply that the Black Watch's black tin hats were a good preliminary move.

Terence Prittie came to stay with us when he was covering a Communist Youth Conference being held in East Berlin. Although it was forbidden for German citizens to go into the East Zone, Allied Forces were allowed in, although no Army personnel were permitted to attend this particular event. East Berlin was full to bursting point, every nook and cranny filled with eager young Communists. Terence had a press pass and took me with him. The only big shop in East Berlin was a huge state-run emporium. Terence wanted to see how this worked.

Going round the various departments we realised the gloom

and poverty of the clientele. Almost every commodity had a patient, defeated queue waiting to be served. We saw a pile of hearth rugs, costing £1 each and a good buy, and we joined the queue. Terence was a small impatient Irishman, who soon tired of queuing. He started to sell the rugs, as no salesman was in sight. After he had done rapid trade, a furious purple-faced manager stormed towards us. Terence had not endured five years as a prisoner-of-war for nothing. Before the salesman could open his mouth, Terence rounded on him and in immaculate German told him that he, Terence, was a government inspector and how dare they keep these German comrades waiting in this monstrous way and he would immediately report the matter.

As the next comrade waiting was an elderly lady, he ordered the salesman to carry the comrade's purchases down to the door for her – just to ice the cake. By now the salesman was grovelling. The rugs are still, in shabby condition, at the house in Scotland.

We were sorry when we were posted from Berlin to Buxtehude, a dismal barracks on the Luneberg Heath, not far from Hamburg, bleak and cold. Patrick became ill, but refused to admit to his condition of extreme breathlessness and tiredness. Then the battalion was ordered to get ready to go home and re-allocate for service in Korea. This threw a tremendous amount of work onto Patrick.

I knew his illness was serious. We had to go back to London for Patrick to attend a conference at the War Office. I had enlisted the help of the family doctor in London. He recognised the symptoms I described at once and arranged for us to see a cardiologist. The cardiologist took one look at my poor husband, and broke the news to him that there would be no Korea and it was hospital that afternoon.

It was a terrible moment for Patrick. In an instant, he had to face the reality that his Army career was over, and that he would miss the chance to wipe out the frustration and humiliation of the war by commanding his battalion in battle.

As Colonel-in-Chief of the Black Watch, the Queen Mother

attended the Farewell Parade. Afterwards she caused Jean Rankin to write a condoling and sympathetic letter to Patrick in hospital. I had had experience of what such a gesture means to someone when faced with a grim situation. I felt guilty that for the moment having Patrick in hospital was nicer for me than him being in Korea.

At this time we also had to realise that Ardchattan would no longer be our home and that we and our children could not just turn up there automatically when on leave. This was because in 1950 Bobby had married Angela Murray. She was already among my closest friends and had become Patrick's too, so we felt very lucky. We decided to buy our own house.

While in Berlin we saw an advertisement in *The Oban Times* for a house called Polfearn at the mouth of the River Awe in the village of Taynuilt that was for sale. It was on the opposite side of Loch Etive to Ardchattan and in a favourite place just beyond Bobby's sea trout pool. We rang Bobby and Angela and asked them to buy it for us. This they did. We arrived back to find we owned a small villa with a nice garden, five bedrooms and wide views across the loch. And so it was that when Patrick was released from Millbank Hospital after two months, very much better, we went to Polfearn, where we set up our first permanent home.

NINETEEN

A Time of Difficulty and Sadness

PATRICK'S health swung from hope to worry for the next eight years. At the time of Robert's birth in 1948, Patrick had a check-up and was told in a cheerful way that he had high blood pressure but it was nothing to worry about at his age. In fact, when he had his army check-up before being discharged, he was classified as P.8, which meant that technically he was dead. His heart was found to be enlarged, but it was considered that all should be well, and the situation might gradually improve. At that time people were only just beginning to understand the problems of high blood pressure. It was known to exist, but why it might be harmful was still unclear. Nor did we have any blood pressure pills. They did not exist.

It did mean the end of Patrick's army career. It was a relief when his discharge came through in 1952, as it enabled us to plan a new life. He had been restless, while he considered new jobs, mostly managing estates or in farming in some form. He undertook a farming course at Edinburgh University, which helped fill in the winter.

We spent our first Christmas at Polfearn and then found a flat in Edinburgh. Meanwhile Bernard had been appointed to the Joint Allied Command, SHAPE, so he and Laura were based in Paris. I reported on Christmas:

Your lovely parcel of sweets and paté and 'bouttons' arrived and are luscious and delicious. Daddy has retired to bed suffering from over-eating and Mummy has him on a diet of castor oil, Bovril, brandy, Xmas pudding and paté de f. So thank you an awful lot.

The parents are in great form. Mummy is crazy on manure – having just discovered (or invented) that the stuff is on the fields. Somehow it's all madly holy and Patrick has to listen for hours to a few facts of life about muck which he's known a long long time. We refer tenderly and reverentially to the compost heap and sprinkle magical powder – (sold by Boots, the C.G.A and Woolworth) which has been lately invented before breakfast by the vicar's wife at Betteshanger and about which (or whom) nobody knows.

Soon after my mother's recovery from her breakdown she had insisted that she and my father must move to the country as she could no longer stand the pace of London. This was not a move my poor father wanted. He had retired happily into the Cadogan Place flat, working a little in the office with Reggie, and making regular trips to watch cricket at Lord's and to art exhibitions. But he was too frightened of any recurrence of her illness to oppose her and went rather dolefully to live in the Old Rectory at Betteshanger, rented from Lord Northbourne.

Life was not noticeably more peaceful. My mother was a governor of the local prep school, managed to get seriously involved with the local mental hospital, and took up violent sides if any of the neighbours got divorced. They found that with neither of them able to drive, their transport problems became dramatic, ending in my mother buying a Rolls Royce which we were all forced to drive. It was broad and slow.

Joyce described a supper party on one of these expeditions to London:

They had driven up in a 1925 Rolls Royce driven by an Italian who has never been to London and speaks no English. Ye Gods. We brought the meat for dinner and Hilda had 'salad from the garden' and packet soup. We found the Italian, a big jolly outdoor countryman, in the kitchen trying to sort out this menu. The food was remarkably horrible.

My mother took up nature, treating it much as a lame dog. Ringing up one winter's evening when a blizzard was blowing my father reported she was out: 'I think saving the snowdrops'.

A lot of my father's zest for life deserted him. The one cause which kept him going was a long argument with the Foreign Office and any one else he could think of, against what he saw as a gross injustice that the chrome mines in Albania should be, as he saw it, pinched by the 'Communist Dictator' Tito without compensation to the previous owners. This battle was, of course fruitless.

After the reign of Professor Plesch ended, my parents turned with just as much conviction to Homeopathy. Staying at their flat in London we were delighted to find a small round pillbox and on the top of it written in Dr. Margery Blackie's neat handwriting: 'anti Tito pills'. My father pronounced Tito 'Tie-to'.

My parents also kept a small flat in London, and my father could still come up occasionally but, as his endeavors got more and more blighted, he grew disheartened, and the journeys became tedious. My father was much more of a countryman than my mother and so he got a measure of satisfaction living at Betteshanger. He died there peacefully in 1958. His battles were over.

Almost at once my mother left Betteshanger and began life in a series of London flats with attendant domestic dilemmas.

But all that lay in the future when disaster struck us in February 1953. Patrick suffered a heart attack in Edinburgh. At the time I described it thus:

He retired (hardly the word, he went goaded, insulted and implored) to bed last week with a pain in his chest. I got the doctor who got the shock of his life to find P with a blood pressure almost off the map. We were about to call in the heart specialist next day but the B.P. dropped and the pain went and the doctor decided after telephoning the specialist to take Patrick within a day or two to the specialists consulting rooms. So after four days in bed and no more

*pain, Patrick was allowed up for two hours and promptly got the
pain again – this time at 1 a.m.*

*He drank gallons of bicarb and announced fiercely and stoutly
that it was only indigestion. The next day I got the doctor promptly,
who got Gilchrist the heart specialist promptly, who got the
ambulance promptly and had P in bed in the infirmary and
confirmed shortly afterwards from his cardiograph that P had had a
coronary thrombosis. I never dreamt you sat up rather pink in bed
bawling for Macleans stomach powder and suggesting it was time
your wife took a cookery course at Atholl Crescent. But there it is:
you never know. Anyhow there the poor old pet is on his back for
4-6 weeks in a public ward in the Edinburgh Infirmary nursed by a
Miss Houston from Maybole, with an ex-moderator of the Church
of Scotland in the next bed. I hope this letter doesn't sound flippant,
I have actually just emerged from the worst 48 hours of my life –
only to be matched by June 1940.*

*The doctor put it on so thick and with so many hints about what
might and what might not be wrong with Patrick etc etc. I got quite
panic stricken and decided he was trying to tell me that Patrick had
cancer and everything.*

*When I got Bobby he rushed up here at once and saw all the
doctors for me, who swore they weren't keeping anything from me
and that all Patrick had was a thrombosis, that they are giving him
a so-called new drug, and that he must rest and rest for a long time
and with any luck he'll be cured. So after cancer, angina, a few other
things, I was relieved for it to boil down to a cosy old thrombosis.*

*It is serious because his heart isn't in too good a state before it,
although the thrombosis was in a minor artery.*

As with so many illnesses, there were positive and negative
swings. A few days later, I felt I had been overly alarmed by the
doctor. I regained my optimism, and only cared that Patrick
should not suffer mentally or physically. When he was allowed
out of the nursing home, we went to stay with my mother-in-law
at Polfearn for a comfortable week away from our rather

crowded flat in Edinburgh, not to mention the prognostications of the various doctors.

By the early summer Patrick was recuperating at Polfearn. While there he was reunited with his old friend, Ian Campbell, who had been a prisoner-of-war with him. He was now the Duke of Argyll, and married to Margaret Sweeny, who, as Margaret Whigham, had been a 'Deb of the Year' before the war. She was of course a celebrated figure on the social scene, whose marriage to Ian was to end in great acrimony and considerable publicity a few years later. It was a curious occasion:

We went out to luncheon and met Our Chief the other day. Patrick had a tremendous success with the Dumb Belle – although the conversation nearly made me do the nose trick with my mutton as they discussed sweet little rabbits and fetching little snails and things.

She has some of the most fascinating clichés, delivered in a bogus American accent, I've ever heard. 'I know nature is just one thing killing another. I know that, but really I can't agree with it can you?' 'My dear I don't read – I like living life myself not reading about it, don't you?'

We were then bidden to lunch at the Castle and went hot foot despite the lumbago and she cooed at Patrick and helped him in and out of chairs until he was totally soothed. They have done it up quite beautifully – even if perhaps the coats of armour picked out on a light blue ground and twined in the initials I & M is a bit over done (it immediately reminds one of M & B for some reason). But all the pictures have been re-done, and the really lovely Adams decorations restored. We came on the other side of the Duchess – the rather tough shrewd Glasgow business woman – which won't do the material side to say the least, any harm.

We had an amusing afternoon fishing at Inveraray the other day with Bobby – Bobby of course fell in the river in his excitement the minute he got a fish (an almost impossible thing to do as a lovely shallow shingle bank was almost level to the water). The weather

*was pouring so apart from that we were all soaked to the skin. We
were bidden in after for a Ducal drink and Margaret was sitting petit
pointing in the latest Dior, plus hat. Personally I rather suspect the
p.p.ing as the light at Inveraray is nocturnal and I don't believe one
could see to put the needle in. It's even too dark to see across the
room, but I rather think she's just going thro' the motions and her
beautifully manicured hands certainly look awfully fetching as an
occasional beam of daylight catches them.*

*But she and Bobby were well worth seeing – as he squelched into
the room, minus socks in an enormous boat-like pair of shoes – his
hair on end, his hands filthy and not very faintly fishy, and a
primeval pair of bright white corduroy trousers. Her opening
remark to the effect that she couldn't think how he could be so cruel
and beastly to the poor little fishes as their gasps on the bank just
broke her heart, stopped him dead in his tracks and he looked at her
as if she ought to be certified. Her beautiful black eyes were flashing
like a cat's in the dark, but Bobby made it painfully obvious he
thought they were merely rolling like a dangerous lunatic's.*

With the winter approaching, the doctors suggested that Patrick
should get into a warmer clime. My brothers leapt into the breach
and paid for us to go out and stay with Harry, and then to visit
Reggie at the Messina Copper mine in South Africa, where he
would be would be paying his annual visit.

We started our trip by going to Kenya to stay with Molly and
Evelyn Baring. Evelyn was Governor of Kenya, at a critical time
with the Mau Mau rebellion at its height. The Black Watch had
been sent from Korea to Kenya, which added point to our visit.
We arrived in January 1954.

In Kenya we were able to enjoy the 'red carpet' life of
Government House and travel about in large limousines. We met
MPs, bishops, generals, lawyers, officers of the Black Watch, and
we saw giraffes wandering about. As Governor, Evelyn was
charming, always dignified, yet never pompous. He was also
harassed and tired. They had turned Government House into an

exotic version of Howick.

My niece, Sally Waldegrave, was on Molly's staff. Amongst the guests were Molly's father, Charlie Grey (Earl Grey – my father's brother-in-law), and Lord William Percy, brother of the Duke of Northumberland, he and his wife being friends and neighbours of the Greys. Lord William was an ornithologist (amongst many other interests), and he spent his winters hopping from Governor to Governor-General, basing himself with them, and mounting extensive bird safaris. He had an enquiring mind and enjoyed tackling experts about their particular fields of interest.

But life was so busy with delegations of MPs wandering in and out that Molly and Evelyn were hardly ever at the same table – one starting lunch early, the other eating late.

We were keen to see the Black Watch, David Rose having succeeded Patrick as Colonel. His wife, Jean, had been at Duisberg with us. Patrick visited the only company then in Nairobi, and found them having a difficult time, the rather tricky white population seldom missing an opportunity to taunt the Scotch soldiers whenever they appeared in cafés. Fisticuffs frequently followed. A solution to this was found by sending the company up country. While most people thought the army was doing a good job, the officers felt they had failed and the Black Watch were hardly speaking to GHQ.

We found that the wives in the regiment were having target practice and carried various sizes of pistols and revolvers. We saw one wife with a vast gun neatly wrapped in a Jaqmar scarf in her handbag.

Patrick was offered a revolver, but the penalty for mislaying your gun was a stiff fine. When we went to restaurants, we often saw people with their gun holsters slung on the back of their chairs. Patrick felt that the chance of forgetting the gun was greater than that of encountering gunfire.

Shortly before we arrived, in December 1953, Archie John Wavell, the Field Marshal's only son, had been killed. He had been serving in the Black Watch, despite having lost a hand fighting during the war. It appeared that he had died as a result of a disagreement between himself, the police and the locals about what should be done about a group of Mau-Mau. Archie John and the policeman were killed, while the Mau-Mau gang got off Scot-free.

Towards the end of our stay David Rose arrived on leave. Patrick and he had a good talk about the situation with the Mau Mau:

David was in tremendous form and is obviously doing very very well. He has organised all the units of police, Home Guard, and Loyal Kikuyu in his area into one group under his command, stopped them all fighting and now they are fighting the Mau Mau.

He sets on gossiping settlers in the hotel bars and threatens them with libel actions if they walk about accusing troops of cowardice without being able to substantiate their facts. There is a great deal of this in the bars of Nairobi and Nyeri; and the gossip and stories about Archie John's death – even to the local newspapers who aren't past hinting that no-one has told the true story – are quite horrifying.

It's all quite malicious gossip and David suspects that there may be some nicely planted little traitors and fellow travellers leading the poor sillies by the nose. The settlers in Nairobi are all quite mad, mostly bad and a great thorn in the flesh of everyone. But David really is one of the few chaps we've seen who are confident in themselves and quite determined to put his plan into operation and not the least afraid of what anyone will say. He is a match for the 'smart' settler, the Lord Portsmouths and co, who have refused to deal with the soldiery up to now and only communicate with the GOC or Evelyn and are maddening. In fact he was bursting with confidence and simply delighted not to be in the Canal Zone. He said Archie John was doing very well and it was in no way his fault that he was killed and that it might quite as well have happened to anyone, it was a stray sniper. There was a row between the Black Watch and the police, but it was after Archie John had been killed, and in no way affected his death.

Patrick and I had our own experience of what seemed a curious attitude of the white farmer to the Army. We went to stay in the Aberdare Mountains. Evelyn's instructions to us were never to go out in the gloaming as it was then that you were liable to be attacked.

The first evening our hosts took us a lovely walk round the farm, both of us feeling it was cowardly to mention Evelyn's admonishment. I jumped every time there was the slightest noise of a twig snapping. We did find that a Black Watch patrol was camped in canvas there to protect the farm and its inmates. We also noticed a huge fire outside the house which was the boiler for the house's hot water. Africans stood by to stoke it all day. It rained tropically, and Patrick asked if the soldiers could come in for a hot bath as they were slithering about in mud and would give their eyes for a warm bath.

Our hostess was horrified and said you never knew what might happen if you allowed the soldiery into the house. We did point out the army had changed since Thackeray wrote *Vanity Fair*. The next evening our host, having taken us a drive, again came home in the gloaming. Our car broke down hopelessly stuck in mud. The Black Watch patrol saw us in trouble, came to help and escorted us home. As we got to the door, Patrick without reference to our host asked them in for a drink. Our flabbergasted hostess took it in good grace, and found the soldiers charming and civilised. They were almost all National Servicemen and came from every background; one was the son of an eminent Aberdonian academic. They were offered baths whenever they wanted them. We flew on to stay with Harry in Lusaka, in Northern Rhodesia.

The eminent plastic surgeon, Sir Archibald McIndoe, was staying with Harry. Sir Archie assured Patrick that he had rarely seen anyone looking healthier than him and described all heart specialists as 'professional crêpe hangers'.

Patrick felt stronger after this holiday, and dined out on Archie

McIndoe's definition of cardiologists. Bobby gave him a part-time job in his local seaweed firm, and Patrick stood for and got into the Argyll County Council, joining his mother, Molly. Local Government before Regionalisation was different from its modern equivalent. Patrick had to win his seat at his first election, but thereafter he was returned unopposed and most of our neighbours were only too thankful that he was prepared to serve on the Council.

Early in his new career Molly was approached by one of her cronies who told her that she must tell Patrick not to laugh at meetings. This resulted from their interviewing prospective headmasters for a school when members of the Education Committee. One of the CC members, whom Patrick had not met, was Naomi Mitchison, who had been born a Haldane, sister of the celebrated scientist J.B.S. Haldane. She was married to George Mitchison, who was a Labour MP and landowner in Carradale in South Argyll. The consensus of opinion on the CC was that Naomi was a Communist, to be viewed with suspicion.

Therefore her chosen headmaster was automatically turned down. Suddenly when her nominee was rejected, Patrick heard a voice giving vent to some of the best swear words he had ever heard in his army life. He turned round to see this respectable middle-aged lady in a Russian hat, and could not help laughing at something so incongruous.

Naomi was already a friend of Molly's and became one of ours. She and George were immensely hospitable at Carradale and Molly often stayed with them. Naomi's housekeeping could be eccentric. On one occasion Molly's fellow guest was Aneurin Bevan, the cook was a holidaying biology teacher, the food atrocious.

Before telephones became as widely used as they are now, the traditional ruse employed if you wished to leave a house party was to have a telegram sent to you to say that a near relation was on the point of death and you must leave at once. Molly met Mr Bevan stumping off to the village to send himself a telegram, telling Molly he thought one more meal might kill him.

Polfearn was often full of visiting family and friends. As Robert grew up, Nanny Sinclair turned herself from nanny into cook, sometimes keenly, sometimes not. This caused an interesting situation when some eccentric friends came to stay:

Nanny and Patrick who spar continually when not otherwise diverted, become like a couple of museum curators when an outsider appears and spend their entire time straightening bath mats, adjusting sofa cushions and getting in a frenzy if anything in the house is used at all. Our guests swan happily in, totally unaware of the crises they were perpetuating – sponge bags lay merrily about the hall, sofa cushions became chaotic, beds were left not only unmade, but frequently full of everything from boots to rolls of bacon, and the only thing in the house which remained virgin pure was the bath – although I must admit the only time it was used it looked like the wreck of the Hesperus afterwards.

But the best thing was the gorgeous wandering into meals which often left Patrick and Nanny standing stunned at the kitchen door, their stop watches buzzing away happily for hours. Poor Nanny, very much aware that Alone she is supporting the entire Domestic Weight of Maison C-P, was preparing to be removed on a stretcher when she found surprisingly that life still went on even when breakfast was at eleven, and that if one remained quite calm it almost became enjoyable. The only thing she will not forgive them for is letting the drawing room fire go out three times while they sat quite unmoving beside it.

In 1955 I was expecting a baby, as was Laura a short while after. Helen was born in August, and Laura's son George, called Geordie, arrived soon afterwards. Like her elder brother, Helen was delivered by our G.P. in the house. When Colin put in an appearance in 1958 I decided to join the fashion and go to the newly opened Maternity Hospital in Oban.

During 1959 Mary Ann got engaged to Alastair Campbell and

plans for their wedding were begun towards the end of the year. But Patrick's health deteriorated throughout the winter of 1959. With Mary Ann due to be married in April, our lives, our hopes and our plans did not always match reality – as so often.

Patrick never accepted that he was dying, and I tried not to. My mother and Dorothy Kerrin, a well-known healer, were 'on the case'. Finally he had a head-on motor crash and was so badly hurt that he never fully recovered. He died on 14 March 1960.

One of the hardest thing to cope with after a death is how to tell it and explain it to small children. I have always feared that I did not make an intelligent effort. Laura explained this to our mother:

Frances is rather naturally battling still – but very much to herself, with her part of this readjustment. The wonderful thing is that she is so sure all is well with Patrick and that he is happy, that she managed to answer Helen's questions where they came with simplicity – saying 'Daddy has gone to Jesus and is absolutely well with him, and able to do all the things like shooting and fishing and playing golf, that he couldn't do here.'

Helen thought a moment and then said 'Don't be silly you can't fish up there!'

Then, after asking how he went, Helen said 'I know Mummy, an aeroplane landed on that field out there, and Daddy just got in and flew away.' – adding that it was rather rude of him not to say goodbye.

Six weeks later Mary Ann married Alastair Campbell, a regular soldier in The Argyll and Sutherland Highlanders. In 1961, just before they were posted to Nigeria, my first grandchild, John Patrick, was born.

In September that year Joyce and Reggie came to stay at Polfearn on the occasion of John Patrick's christening. Joyce wrote a descriptive letter to Virginia Thesiger. They seemed to have arrived on a fine day – although Joyce remarks 'I have little faith in its durability.' Nonetheless she enthused about 'a pale sun turning the loch blue and the distant hills are faintly plum and green'.

Frances is such a remarkable and dear creature. She & Patrick were really happy. Perhaps because of this she goes on being so warm, relaxed, cosy and easy. She talks about him absolutely naturally & roars with laughter about things they did and laughed at. She has no feeling of separation at all. Her ma and bro-in-law are full of monuments and memorials and she can't handle it. They insist on a stone so it is being done with a space left for her later! She is very funny about all this. I imagine she is very lonely but this house is obviously cheerful somehow and there are the children, Robert 14, Helen 6, and Colin 3, so it buzzes.

Polfearn is an ugly little house with gables and eyebrows, but remarkably roomy and pleasant. Frances has made it light with pretty curtains, a pale green stair carpet and white walls. A small garden is bursting with dahlias, gladioli, sweet peas and roses. Besides the children, Mary Ann, Alastair, & their baby, there is Nanny and Minnie who at 87 is cooking scrumptious food. Evelyn Howick and Anne Dawnay come at night and Anne Waldegrave is here. How we all get in I don't know but we do.

Joyce described the next few days with picnics, expeditions in a small motor boat chugging up the loch and seeing seals, and birds, curlews and oyster catchers. One day she, Reggie and I walked for miles up the loch 'through bog, rock, grassy places and beaches' to rendezvous for a picnic. 'Cold steak and kidney pie was like nectar, eaten on a grassy mound in bright sun'.

One day my son-in-law Alastair went up the hill on a long walk to an inaccessible loch. Coming back he came upon a stalking party who were Bobby and Angela's guests at Ardchattan. They were struggling to get a pony out of a bog where it had sunk laden with dead deer.

Joyce wrote:

In driving rain they had crawled up hills on their stomachs all day and had been returning triumphant. Man's idea of fun is so interesting.

I took her and Reggie over to Ardchattan to play tennis – Angela was an old friend of theirs. The tennis rivalry was intense. Joyce always changed into 'whites' for tennis but noted that Bobby wore an old tweed cap and Angela appeared in 'heather-mixture pants'. At the Christening party 'Angela came in a hat she'd had for 32 years! Bottle green felt and from Scotts I fancy. She unchanged'.

After this visit to me in the early months of my widowhood, Joyce was inspired to write a poem. It is often read at funerals:

If I should go before the rest of you
Break not a flower or inscribe a stone
Nor, when I'm gone speak in a Sunday voice
But be the usual selves I have known
Weep, if you must
Parting is Hell
But life goes on
So sing as well.

TWENTY

Laura in New Zealand

A FTER PATRICK'S death I had to devise a new life style. Robert was twelve, Helen four, Colin exactly two, Mary Ann newly married. I was doubtful about facing winter alone in Polfearn. My mother rushed into action and she found a flat in London and conjured up furniture for it. There then started a complicated life, with summers at Polfearn and winters in London.

I also went, unelected and unopposed, onto the Argyll County Council in succession to Patrick. There I joined Molly and Naomi Mitchison. The Mitchisons were very kind to me and we also met in London. They invited me to their political parties and I met Labour luminaries, which I found fascinating. On one occasion Naomi introduced me to an extremely good-looking young man, Tony Benn, hissing in my ear that he was the hope of the future. Politics had always been high on the agenda of family discussions all my life, so my political interest was titillated. My brother-in-law, Pat Lort Phillips, had joined the Labour Party and I introduced him and Katie to the Mitchisons, who were a little surprised to find themselves on the same side as an ex-Grenadier Guards Colonel, although both George Mitchison and his Haldane brother-in-law had to admit to being Old Etonians.

In 1961 Bernard was appointed Governor-General of New Zealand, and knighted at Balmoral just before he took up the appointment. He served in New Zealand from 1962 to 1967. This gave us all great pleasure, and excitement. It was an especially happy surprise for Bernard as both his grandfathers, his paternal grandfather, Sir James Fergusson, and his maternal grandfather, the Earl of Glasgow, as well as his own father Sir

Charles Fergusson, had been Governor-Generals there. Bernard had spent holidays from school in New Zealand, and many people remembered his parents, Sir Charles and Lady Alice. He still had relations there, so to return to New Zealand was almost a homecoming.

Nevertheless, during the five years that he and Laura were there, he was conscious of the shadows cast by his forbears, and worried lest anything he did or might do should fall below their standards. He succeeded our Lyttelton cousin, Charles [Viscount] Cobham. This caused an elderly Lyttelton cousin, who took the particular view of many of her generation that the Lytteltons were unarguably the best, was heard to say how difficult it would be for a Fergusson to follow someone so successful. It was pointed out to her that Bernard had married Laura. 'Oh I quite forgot!' she replied, 'That will be all right.'

The year was taken up collecting a number of things needed for Bernard's life as Governor-General. Friends and relations were generous. Iain Atholl and my sister-in-law (his mother) lent silver from Blair Atholl, Molly Baring lent Laura her tiara, while Harry and Reggie provided financial help. They were going to a new way of life which demanded a household and staff, Bernard having two ADCs, Laura a lady-in-waiting, and Geordie a keeper. Laura also had a lady's maid, and there was to be a cook, a butler, and footmen and housemaids – not many native New Zealanders apparently being readily available for such jobs.

Laura was not known for her cooking. When at Auchairne she once telephoned me with the exciting news that there was a deep freeze shop in Glasgow where you could buy 'Arctic Roll' by the yard so all you had to do was lop off a few inches when you needed a pudding.

Since leaving the army, Bernard had been living by his pen, as a journalist and by writing books. including a biography of Lord Wavell, a history of the Black Watch, and his autobiography, *The Trumpet in the Hall*. Laura helped him with his research as well as looking after Geordie. She was both daunted and amused by the prospect of this new official life.

Joyce stepped in and took over Laura's wardrobe. Both Laura and I were well attuned to accepting Joyce's help with clothes, though Laura found it tiring standing for long hours while Joyce and her dressmakers attended to the fittings. Joyce's most generous gift was an evening dress from Victor Stiebel (then one of the most fashionable designers) and Laura said ruefully that she thought she had stood for two hours whilst they discussed the line of the right hip. Joyce kept up this role for their whole term in office.

Australia and New Zealand were still thought of in terms of 'the other side of the world'. Gap years for students had not yet come and there was no sense of nearly commuting as there is now. Mostly, travellers of a certain age followed the practice of emigrating families and went there by boat. Even air travellers tended to break the journey for a night somewhere on the way. Communications had not advanced spectacularly since the war. To telephone was expensive and letters took a week or ten days to arrive. The quickest means of communication was the cable.

Bernard and Laura finally left by boat with their entourage and several cars, their pictures, including the family Gainsborough landscape – a 'discovery' bought by our father in the 1920's – which measured 10ft by 9ft.

Like all soldiers, Bernard enjoyed ceremonies and insisted that the ritual be rehearsed and flawless. Laura was not adverse to things going a little awry. Bernard wanted to make a point of once again getting to know the Maori element of the population: he had done Maori lessons as a boy. He took this up again and derived much pleasure from their culture, music and history.

Laura found she could exercise some influence on various welfare schemes. If Bernard felt overshadowed by his ancestors, Laura was overshadowed by our mother and Lady Reading. Her lasting influence was to stimulate the setting up of a scheme to care for the disabled and elderly in sheltered housing, where they could go into flats with their own belongings, and be cared for by a warden. This was an innovative idea, preferable to being consigned to hospital before it was necessary. To this day the Laura Fergusson Trust still operates in New Zealand. Both of them encouraged music, and held musical evenings at Government House, where Kiri Te Kanawa sang. She became a friend.

In September 1962 they went to Balmoral to see the Queen, staying with the Private Secretary, Sir Michael Adeane at Craigowan, a house on the estate. Craigowan was by no means luxurious, both Fergussons having to sleep in what Laura called a large single bed, of brass and black enamel. It was on this visit that Bernard was knighted, being appointed GCMG. Laura described this:

We had a slightly frantic evening, as we all went to a cocktail party given by the Argylls (who are on guard this year). We'd been told to get to dinner early, but the Queen and her party showed no sign of leaving the party. We sneaked out after the Queen Mother, then back here to change in less than 10 minutes, instead of the hour we'd promised ourselves. We tore to the castle – to be told the Queen wasn't back yet! In a few minutes, her delicious beaming face came round the drawing room door, apologising like mad for being so late and diving off again to change.

The rest of the company assembled and I suddenly realised Bernard had vanished, and he reappeared a few minutes later in her company, the deed having been done! I found myself sitting on Prince Philip's right with Snowdon on the other side, and a footman breathing into my ear 'claret or hock my lady?' – Small wonder I felt slightly transported to another sphere – but actually the most astonishing thing about it all is that it was so easy, so normally enjoyable that you don't feel strange at all. After dinner we played racing demon – even after the men joined us – it might have been Nannau or anywhere!

It pelted with rain all yesterday, and is doing exactly the same again today – very miserable for those lined up to shoot, fish and kill things.

They left for New Zealand at the end of the year, while I settled into a flat at Rossetti Garden Mansions, in Flood Street. Helen was happy at school, and Colin and I caught the 49 bus every afternoon, crossed Kensington Gardens and then all walked home together.

My cosy existence contrasted with Laura's, as she took over Government House, giving white tie dinners, where the occasional hazard was a slow eater, and where protocol demanded that no one began to eat until Laura did. They flew to Auckland in the Governor-General's plane, which had a wonderful 'powder room', containing a dressing table, double looking glass, all trimmed with draped furnishing material, and beside it a bijou Elsan, with a ruffled skirt of the furnishing material, and a neat little upholstered cushion on top. This had been commissioned for the Queen.

Laura was amused by people curtseying to her: 'It's rather like watching a Fougasse *Punch* page come alive. There are the creepy crawlies, who don't get right up between Bernard and me, there are some who do their first curtsey with such élan, they get carried beyond me, and catch up with a bob. My favourites are the boomps a daisies, who can't co-ordinate with their husband's bows and collide, both think they'll do it the other way to me, and collide again.'

I wondered if Laura would be able to find it all funny for the whole five years of their appointment. She was amused by their first diplomatic reception at which the six couples of the American Mission achieved good curtseys, while the Russian minister said he had no white tie, and would come in lounge suit with medals. He proved a great dispenser of compliments while the Taiwan Chinese Minister told her that his elder two children had been born before he had the benefit of Moral Re-Armament, whereas his eight-year old son had benefited from their guidance in playing the violin.

She enjoyed inspecting a sea elephant called Blossom that had made its home on a beach almost in the city – while it changed its coat:

> *It is an extraordinarily ugly lump of sandcoated grey fat, and it lies quite still until it opens one round bloodshot eye, and sneezes down one nostril at you. There has been some suggestion that it might smell a bit offensive. The American ambassadress came along to look while we were there, and a small crowd collected. 'I can't smell anything badly offensive, can you?' Bernard asked. As the good lady is one of those who empties a bottle of Chanel No 5, or its modern equivalent, every time she goes out – and you can tell she's coming long before she rounds the corner – we were all rather hard put to know how to answer that one. B. of course quite unaware, as he can't smell anything anyway ever.*

In February 1963 the Fergussons had an official visit from the Queen and the Duke of Edinburgh. Laura wrote us an extensive and detailed account of *Britannia* sailing in looking lovely. When they went on board, they were inhibited by having precisely four minutes thirty seconds of conversation before disembarking to the jetty to receive the royal visitors more formally. Meanwhile the press photographers formed a kind of football scrum, cursing and swearing and shoving each other almost to the Queen's feet.

Indeed a feature of the Queen's visit was that there were so many cameras that the Queen and Bernard could hardly see any faces in the crowds, only cameras pointing at them. After lunch on board *Britannia*, the royal party disembarked. Laura reported:

> *The Duke is very funny. He walked up behind a woman journalist who was writing something in longhand in her note book just after the Queen had passed her in the hall of the house. We could see what he was doing but she was quite unaware that he was reading what she wrote. He then passed her saying 'I am sorry we disturbed you' and as we went down the path he roared with laughter, because what he had read was, 'I had to move out of the Queen's way so that*

she could see a picture.' She was left looking very startled.

A dinner party was held on board *Britannia*, at which the Prime Minister, Keith Holyoake, and his wife were the only guests not staying on board. The royal party did not return from the Maori welcome until 8.30 and the yacht was due to sail at 10.00. The Duke suddenly asked the Admiral 'When did you say we were sailing?'

'In eight minutes, Sir.'

They therefore had coffees and liqueurs very briskly, and they were about to say their goodbyes, when a harassed courtier nipped in and shoved a little box into the Queen's hand. It transpired that the Prime Minister was due to receive his C.H. that evening.

In June the Opening of Parliament took place, with the Governor-General and Laura seated on thrones. She wrote later: 'As I sat on my throne I couldn't help thinking how often as children one plays at Kings and Queens, and dash it there we were!'

In the same month, they dined with the American ambassador and his wife. Apparently, just before dinner, a crisis was averted:

Among our fellow guests there was the artist called Peter McIntyre, who is the best-known N.Z. artist and who incidentally has been doing portraits of Liz [Waldegrave, Laura's niece and lady-in-waiting] latterly. He told Liz that about five minutes before we were due to arrive at the dinner, the American ambassador arrived down in his own drawing room clutching his white tie and appealing for help.

His wife rushed to put it round his neck and didn't remember until too late that she had only just painted her nails bright carmine. Of course it came off not only on his collar and tie but all down his white waistcoat.

No time to change – consternation and a good deal of swearing, until Peter McIntyre had the inspiration to call for a paint box, and

*whitewash the ambassador! He just dried off in time. No wonder
they were a bit tied up with themselves by the time we got there. I
did notice that his collar was a bit blotched and thought that he
must have cut himself shaving. It must have been very worrying
wondering whether your starched front might suddenly shed its
white coating and reveal awful red blotches through the evening. I
do find it very comforting to know that that sort of thing can and
does happen, even in such sophisticated circles.*

In October, Hayato Ikeda, the Liberal Democrat Prime Minister
of Japan, and his wife visited New Zealand. They came to stay at
Government House and there was a dinner, at which interpreters
were needed. The couple proved to be polite, friendly and were
forever beaming with smiles. Laura was impressed that when the
Japanese ladies came out of dinner, they executed a beautiful little
bow to the photographs of the Queen and the Duke of
Edinburgh.

A number of New Zealanders invited to a white tie dinner and
reception for the couple declined, an indication that feelings
against the Japanese were still prevalent. Laura felt that if Bernard
could do it, having served behind Japanese lines in Burma during
the war, then others should have given them a chance.

A curious example of the deference shown to the Governor-
General and his wife occurred when Laura and Virginia Lucas,
who had succeeded Liz as lady-in-waiting, were driving along
some rough back roads and were met by another car which
almost ditched itself. The driver leapt out, gasping: 'Oh what an
honour to be put in the ditch by you!'

During their five years in New Zealand every member of the
Grenfell family visited them, as well as Fergusson friends and
relations. For many of them it was nostalgic, as they remembered
visiting Bernard's parents. Reggie and Joyce went twice, Joyce
giving performances in both Australia and New Zealand. They
were accompanied by Bill Blezard, Joyce's pianist.

My mother was among the first to go. She went by boat

accompanied by a granddaughter, Bronwen Lort Phillips, taking her own inimitable collection of luggage. Her trip soon became a mission. She wanted to proselytize the notion that new entirely ecumenical churches should be built. Thus one church would fulfil the needs of all the denominations, and when not being used as a church, it could be a community hall with leisure facilities. She had tried to get bombed churches rebuilt in this way, but with little success. Nevertheless she thought her idea might fare better in the New World, which would be more open to new ideas, as it expanded and developed.

To get her point across, she brought with her a model of a chapel with a miniature altar suitable for R.C. services, with small saints and other tiny models. It also had an Anglican altar, with minute altar fronts, and a Presbyterian table. Then a curtain could be drawn, and the church could be furnished with ping-pong tables, deck chairs for meetings etc. No doll's house was better equipped. Somewhere she had made friends with a man who loved making models – who, illogically, she said, was delighted to be thus occupied because he had haemophilia. All this fitted into a large packing case.

Before she left, my mother sent Mary off to buy her some electric bulbs for the model chapel. I bought her some glue, but without quite realising all this was going to travel to New Zealand, accompanied by several primus stoves, six pairs of combs, lots of transistor batteries of various sizes, all the family photographs since 1906, a great many letters and documents and much else besides, including almost the entire library of English poets.

Just after my mother left, Vera sent Laura a cryptic telegram: 'Don't let housemaid unpack, Mummy's underclothes in chapel. Good luck love V'. This puzzled Laura to say the least. My mother arrived in New Zealand in time for Christmas. In January Laura reported on her visit:

Everything has gone wonderfully well. In spite of not very good weather, they all seem to have enjoyed the journey hugely. The Merchant Navy ranks with the Church now – if not sometimes a bit higher, for producing Young Men with High Intellect . . .

As usual one could write a volume about darling HMG. The chapel plays quite a considerable part in all this, and was last seen being loaded on to the private aeroplane of the American admiral, who had been visiting us with his family, as a pay back for the hospitality he offered in Antarctica. He was heading for Christchurch, which is where Mummy now is – I told him I'd never speak to an American again if I found Mummy was the first woman to go to Antarctica officially. But I'm half waiting for the message to say that's where she is.

We had a very funny moment when we had her and 'Tubby' Clayton[7] as co-guests. For the first two days, Mummy retired quite sensibly to bed. She had done Christmas all out, and a good many gatherings involving the inevitable standing etc. (I always sit almost on getting into a room, so that she can follow suit, but she is very meticulous about doing the right thing.)

So Tubby had the floor to himself, which was quite a business in itself for the staff, with cars whizzing every which way, and telephone messages in all directions, and Tubby himself extremely likely to turn up late, without a collar on, and doing his best to tag along some acquaintance he'd scooped up somewhere. However, for the last two days of his visit it was a delicious mad house anyway. Funnily enough Mummy and he didn't click at all – they both wanted to sell the other their own wares and not listen to the other's story, and were both competing for the ears anyway, so it was just as well that didn't last too long.

In between plans for everything; John Gielgud was here doing three nights – rather ill-chosen ones bang over the New Year, but still. We went in tremendous force one night, Mummy, Tubby Clayton and all. The Great Man did a terrific evening of

---

7. Rev. P.T.B. Clayton, who ran the Toc H movement

Shakespeare excerpts, which is a great tour de force and the King Lear mad scene at the end is nothing short of brilliant. He came to meet us in the manager's office afterwards, and was duly gracious, and said he'd met Joyce somewhere where their routes crossed in Australia and so on. When it came time to go and we started to do the normal withdrawal, we were forestalled by a Shakespearianly regal hand being 'extended' at about shoulder level and we were quite definitely dismissed and almost crept out of the room. A magnificent gesture.

Our mother joined Laura during a holiday they took in February, tackled everything that cropped up, and apparently leapt elegantly on and off dinghies and launches, invariably clutching a most elegant Dolly Varden style shady hat, her string bag of books, three inflatable rubber cushions, a huge bag of toffees, blocks of chocolate which were apt to melt in the sun, and her mohair scarf. To these she clung firmly through thick and thin. Whenever possible, she held court with her model chapel.

Back home this news greatly entertained us: 'We are all rather wickedly laughing at the change in tone to real harassment which has crept into your letters since our female parent arrived. We are having such a lovely holiday! It's really so funny how that frail and handicapped figure can so certainly produce an atmosphere of tornado so easily!'

The Queen Mother was due to visit Australia and New Zealand, during the course of which Laura was destined to entertain both her and Queen Salote of Tonga to tea. She thought a trial run might not go amiss. They all fell for her because she was so friendly, especially to Geordie, telling him all about the ancient tortoise that Captain Cook had left in Tonga in 1777, and which was still going strong.

Reg and Harry had arranged for me to visit Laura shortly after my mother's visit. My visit to New Zealand was due to coincide with the Queen Mother's, and therefore Patrick's old friend from Colditz, Martin Gilliat, the Queen Mother's Private Secretary, put some of my luggage in the Royal Yacht *Britannia*. The Queen Mother cancelled her visit due to an emergency operation, but the yacht with my luggage arrived without her.

Meanwhile I went by air with conservative luggage – the clothes approved by Joyce. En route I paused in Canada, paying a visit to David and Willa Walker. There David read me a lecture on the decadence of the Old Country, demonstrated by the fact that our best selling gramophone record at that time was by a 'Singing Nun'. During my six weeks in New Zealand the Beatles toured America and took the place by storm, which was very satisfactory!

I arrived in New Zealand, and was at once swept into a huge luncheon party. Next day we drove to Rotorua, taking Geordie to school on the way. We saw the geysers and mud pools, and then a well-known Maori called Guide Rangi recognised Laura, and rushed up and rubbed noses.

We then went on to Palmerston North to stay in a hotel. Laura had no idea how to pay the bill, since normally an ADC attended to this, but we simply signed the bill and swept out without paying. We then attended a Country Show, which had been meant for the Queen Mother's benefit. We fished rather disappointingly in places chosen for the Queen Mother, and I got badly sunburnt. Laura joked that she sometimes enjoyed introducing me as 'Councillor Mrs Campbell-Preston', at which point a local mayoress immediately whisked me round some school.

After I left, the Fergussons set off on a much anticipated tour of the South Sea Islands in a party that included Peter Fleming and Geordie, then aged nine.

The person they most enjoyed meeting again was Queen Salote of Tonga. She had become a well-known figure in London at the Coronation, as it had been a wet day and the carriages and cars in the procession all had their hoods closed. Only Queen Salote, a very ample figure, had kept her carriage open. Sitting beside her had been a small, huddled, patently chilled little man. When asked who this figure was, Noël Coward had made his famous

joke: 'Her lunch'. This is how Laura described her visit to Queen
Salote:

*We've just left Tonga and it's been wonderful. Mainly entirely from
the presence of the Queen, who is all that she appeared to be at the
Coronation and more. We stepped off the Admiral's barge on to a
jetty, to be met by a monumental figure dressed in a blue nightshirt
with a folded rush mat tied round his middle. This was her son and
heir, who is also Prime Minister. He's a Royal Highness, so I
curtseyed. We were shown into a large car and with two motorcycle
outriders, and him in a car behind, we wound our way to the
Residency. (The motorbike's numbers were 1 and 2!)*

*We buffed up to go to our audience. B. was in full white uniform
and cocked hat. We went off again in the large Cadillac to the
Palace, a delicious 'Celesteville' sort of building with a little
bandstand in front. The Police Band and a Royal guard were on the
lawn. We stepped out and the officer in command saluted. He and
the guard were dressed in old type Scout hats turned up at one side,
white tunics, and a very neat white skirt.*

*National Anthem (ours) and B. inspected the guard. We were then
ushered in to the house, and into a rather deliciously Victorian
drawing room, with chairs ranged along each side, and a sofa across
the bow window at the end. There was the Queen, looking friendly.
B. was shown to a chair on her right, and I was to her left, and the
others took their places on chairs down the room, her ADC standing
respectfully outside the open double door.*

*Conversation was a bit stilted after the first exchanges, because it's
very difficult to talk easily to someone sitting in the middle of a large
sofa, from a large armchair placed some way away, and with a silent
audience lining the walls! After 20 minutes we withdrew. Back to
the Residency to doff uniform etc. and then go a short drive with the
Resident – mostly looking at boats along the shore and having
landmarks pointed out – and we met the famous tortoise.*

*Then off to the big 'green' where the feast was all laid out. It's just
like the photographs, heaps of food and fruit piled on suckling pigs*

*etc. First we sat in a line on chairs, the Queen between us – then we
were led to cushions on the floor – quite widely separated. Our bit
of the spread was laid out on a slightly raised table so we could put
our legs under it. B sat next to the Queen, and Geordie just beyond.
We ate either from beautifully carved bowls (with plastic teaspoons)
or nibbled in our fingers.*

*On my other side I had Tungi (the heir and PM). He is very
modern minded, adores travel – has just sent his oldest son (15) to
a school at Lausanne, and is said to incline to Japan and the US
rather to the exclusion of Britain. Bernard said you'd love to have
the son for a holiday in Scotland!*

*Then we changed for dinner at the Residency – it is a great honour
for the Queen to dine out at all – and a great honour for the two
sons and their wives to accept too, and in fact you can't be sure until
they arrive that they are coming! B. wore a strange get up of black
tie, sash and stars because they can't run to white ties in such places,
but the Queen likes the excuse to wear her sash! [the GBE]. I had no
sash (!), but popped on Molly's tiara for good measure – a rather
solo effort, but a gesture, for what it was worth!*

*The Queen arrived – the Band struck up the National Anthem –
and off we set. Jolly well done it was too, excellent food, well served
and table lavishly decorated with flowers.*

*When it came to the toasts, Queen Salote rose and just said 'The
Queen' and the band struck up our anthem. Then the Resident
toasted 'The Queen of Tonga', followed by the Tongan National
Anthem which is tuneful but long. Then we withdrew and went on
to the wide verandah, and I sat next to the Queen who couldn't have
been easier or more cosy. There's going to be a huge conference of
Pan Pacific Women's organisations in Tonga in August. The Queen
and Mrs Coode were swapping information etc. (the Queen is of
course absolutely au fait with all the arrangements). She turned to
me with deliciously rolling eyes, and said, roaring with laughter 'Do
you know – I received a letter asking me what people should bring,
and asking particularly if they should bring their own toilet paper!'*

After dinner the band played enthusiastically on the lawn, including some music composed by Queen Salote. When the Fergussons left at 8.30 the next morning, Queen Salote came out onto her verandah, waved and blew them a kiss.

Meanwhile, after my visit to New Zealand, I went to Australia, where my mother joined me after her visit to Papua New Guinea, having stayed with every state Governor. She gave numerous press conferences in a style reminiscent of Winston Churchill's 'we shall fight on the beaches' speech and the American President's State of the Union address. This was March 1964.

Hardly was my mother home than she headed off to France, another remarkable journey, even by her standards. None of us were quite sure the purpose of this trip, but it seemed to be a zigzag quest for Teilhard de Chardin. She stayed in monasteries, or hotels which cost 5 francs a night, and hostels. There were two occasions when she still did not know where she was going to stay at midnight. With her went four cases of books, and we felt that any teenage jaunt paled beside her achievement. She took in Geneva and Paris, and returned full of odd bits of information, such as the Prime Minister of Senegal being a poet. She made us all feel very parochial.

My life was saddened by the death of my mother-in-law, Molly, who died suddenly at Ardchattan in September 1964. This was a bewildering time, as I described:

It's one of those weeks when time as humanly measured really doesn't make sense – it's not yet a week since Molly died and yet life has really fundamentally changed course and whole areas of one's life and habits and time have somehow rushed from one. I don't really feel quite the same person – the babies remain just the same and Nanny's gloom is so constant that whether it's the fish that's gone bad or one's mother-in-law who's died the disaster is exactly the same. So just now one feels floored and jolly tired.

Sudden death is a bit grim for survivors as there is no nurse about or anything. Goodness, it must be absolute hell living without a faith. It's the most heart-rending sight, far more frightening than death I find. I think they are the really brave people in the world. I don't believe I'd try and live if I thought there was no future and no love in it, death would be such a despair one would go mad.

My mother-in-law's house was packed up, and we returned to London for the winter.

In January 1965 Sir Winston Churchill died, and I could not help thinking that Harold Wilson and Alec Douglas-Home looked like puppets when commenting between extracts from Churchill's speeches. Joyce and I bemoaned the lack of a real leader for Britain.

My mother went from strength to strength, incarcerating herself in a Bristol convent while she translated Chardin. She succeeded in persuading the wife of the publisher, Billy Collins, that he must publish five Chardin books, leaving him complaining that he would soon go bankrupt. Reg and Harry were impressed with the quality of my mother's translations, Reg wondering about some of the long English words that she used, and how she had understood them in French.

In New Zealand Bernard and Laura continued to work hard, with streams of guests, and a lot of travelling. I had to find her cooks and even more complicatedly, ladies-in-waiting. They had Lord Mountbatten in New Zealand, fishing on one of the north islands, when his sister, Queen Louise of Sweden, died. It was too complicated for him to get to Sweden for the funeral, so he cancelled his fishing, and remained doing nothing on the island. Being rather lonely, he rang Bernard quite often.

The Archbishop of Canterbury lunched with them, causing problems over the seating protocol. Laura found herself with the Archbishop on her right and the Speaker of the House on her left. Neither were 'dashing conversationalists'. At one moment the Speaker lent across the table and said: 'Your Grace, one thing I must ask you, as all New Zealanders will like to know. How did you leave our dear Queen?'

Gracie Fields then came to tea, with snow-white hair instead of her earlier brassy blonde. She was rather nervous, gentler than one might have supposed, though every now and again, 'good rich ringing tones with strong Lancashire bellowed out'.

Another visitor was Princess Alice, Countess of Athlone, granddaughter of Queen Victoria, then in her 80s. Vera had served as her lady-in-waiting in Canada. She invariably travelled by banana boat. On this occasion the boat was delayed due to a seaman being taken sick, and the boat having to return to Panama. Laura enjoyed her visit, finding her very funny, and enjoying her maid, 'Mademoiselle', who protested all the time at what Princess Alice was doing or was about to do.

All this gave me a good impression of Laura's life in New Zealand, which continued until 1967. I had no idea of the circumstances in which I would next visit her.

TWENTY-ONE

Lady-in-Waiting

IN MARCH 1965 an unexpected event happened to me when Martin Gilliat asked me to a drinks party in his apartment at St James's Palace. Before I could quite take in what was happening, I had been offered the job of lady-in-waiting to the Queen Mother. It was like a bombshell and I was left gasping.

As ever I turned to Reg and Joyce for advice. She said in no uncertain terms that it would be hell, very boring, tiring – an old-fashioned armchair job, and impossible to escape from if I did not like it. Joyce then left for the theatre and Reg telephoned to say the opposite – that it would be the perfect job for me. My niece, Sue Hussey, suggested I should play a bit hard to get and dictate some terms, and Ruth Fermoy, another of the Queen Mother's ladies-in-waiting, said the same.

My dilemma also involved the necessary absences from home and my young family, as being 'in-waiting' meant sleeping at Clarence House. So I dithered and pondered. The main trouble was Lady Jean Rankin, who was in charge and could be bossy, rude and interfering. When I got to know her, the Queen Mother said that what she really wanted was to be loved, and that if you remembered that, she was not difficult to handle. I had lunch with Jean Rankin, who announced that the salary was only £480 a year, which barely covered the cost of clothes. I resisted replying that I had never spent more than £50 a year on clothes in my life. Sue Hussey then recommended Nora Bradley in the King's Road, Chelsea, who was willing to provide outfits for 20 to 30 guineas, a substantial discount. In due course Joyce spun into action, helping by handing over couture rejects from her wardrobe; but when I did have to go to the dress-maker, I found the fittings rather irksome.

I wrote to Robert at Eton to tell him I had been offered a job, without saying what it was. He replied that either I was to be a lady-in-waiting or had been put on a Royal Commission on Birth Control by the Labour Government – *not* by the Pope.

Decision time loomed, Martin Gilliat invited me to dinner to talk it over, and the situation was not made easier when Joyce announced: 'Gosh, they must be scraping the barrel!' In spite of Joyce's prognostication it was really always a certainty that I would accept gratefully, and I did.

Fate took a strange turn when Niall Rankin, Jean's husband, suddenly died of leukaemia after a two-day illness in Bechuanaland. I had gone north, and she was on Mull, and feeling desperate. She suddenly telephoned and asked me to come and stay with her. So I found myself in the unlikely position of comforting her in her bereavement.

I went out of kindness, but inadvertently it proved a shrewd move. At that vulnerable time, I saw through her bossiness, and felt I had the measure of it. One afternoon a tactless person reduced her to tears with a stray remark on the boat to Oban, and I said to her, 'You know, Jean, after six months the shock heals and the sheer physical impact goes. It's quite an exhilarating challenge to find one can manage a lot one had never attempted before, and even running a show rather well. You'll love organizing Treshnish – even if you have to change course.' She pulled herself together in an instant and with a glint in her eye said, 'I know that's true – and I'm awfully bossy.'

Jean relished court gossip and possessed what one might call a 'banana skin' sense of humour. I did wonder what she and the Queen Mother talked about, and formed a dread that my new life might involve oceans of Dry Martinis (which I hated), being perpetually in my best clothes, and country house games, such as sliding down stairs on tin trays.

Clarence House, Birkhall, the Castle of Mey and Royal Lodge

were pleasant places to find oneself in. I stepped back into a world which had died for me in 1939 – a world of butlers, chefs, housekeepers, housemaids, footmen, kitchen maids, chauffeurs and gardeners.

It was easy to relax into luxury. I was called by a housemaid with a pretty tray of matching china – teapot, sugar bowl and milk – and then, as ladies were expected to have breakfast in bed, a heavy tray with fruit, cereal, toast, butter and marmalade, and grapefruit or slice of melon – all on another delectable matching china service – was brought to my bedroom door by a footman, and handed to a housemaid who staggered in with it.

It was necessary to arrive 'in-waiting' with your own lady's maid, and never having had one in my life, I tried to persuade Minnie, but she firmly refused to come. There was a pool of ladies' maids, who had retired from several Royal staffs, and these could be booked in advance for the fortnights during which each of the four permanent ladies-in-waiting was on duty. Minnie knew that not only were outfits for royal occasions important, but that of equal importance were underclothes to impress the lady's maid. Marks and Spencer's was all right as long as the labels were removed. This frightening and exalted being washed your clothes, packed and unpacked for you, laid out your clothes, and sometimes sewed on a missing button. Hats were required for daytime engagements and once, in Canada, I was rather proud of a new creation bought specially for the occasion. I returned from a long afternoon with the Queen Mother, only to be greeted by William Tallon, her page, a man with a good eye for all things, including matters sartorial. 'But you're wearing it back to front!' he exclaimed in horror.

At night the bed was turned down by the housemaid, but the lady's maid drew your bath, both before dinner and in the morning, regardless of whether you wanted it or not. They also spread the toothpaste on the toothbrush.

During the day the green baize doors swung open on a very regular basis. Breakfast was followed by an elevenses tray, tea or coffee, and biscuits. The ladies-in-waiting spent the morning in the office dealing with the Queen Mother's mail, as they were responsible for answering personal mail, requests for gifts, fan mail, or letters sent with information which the writers felt the Queen Mother should or would like to know. We also wrote to thank for gifts, unless they were from personal friends. The number of letters varied from day to day, but this activity usually took till lunchtime. In the afternoon tea was brought, followed by a drinks tray. At dusk the footman drew the curtains.

Early on the Queen Mother gave me a resumé on some of my colleagues, and sensed that I was somewhat daunted by the Treasurer, Ralph Anstruther. She explained that he was an only child, his father had died when he was a few months old. Schooling was Eton and Cambridge, with holidays often spent with a governess on the Continent. He spoke French fluently and passably in Italian and German. She said he was seen by some colleagues as being foreign 'because he chases his gravy round his plate with bread, like the French'. He was also Hereditary Carver to the Queen in Scotland.

One of the tasks that fell to him was to select and buy the household's birthday and Christmas presents for the Queen Mother. I came to look forward to his proposals for these. His choices were singular, as was his accounting. I can't resist giving a selection of these over a number of years. He wrote:

I have been reliably informed that Queen Elizabeth is in need of ice buckets and a biro pen and have accordingly bought these objects. Two buckets and a pen, plus the Page's bus fare to the shop work out at 76 pence for each of us. This is, I am afraid, a tiresome sum for those who like to pay in cash but as one of our colleagues here suspects that I make a profit on these transactions, I have calculated the contributions to four places of decimals and I shall in fact make a loss of .0299 of a penny.

In 1986 came another such letter:

I have long thought, as I fished sticky spoons from the honey at the Castle of Mey, that Queen Elizabeth might welcome one of those with a hook on the back to prevent it sinking. Now I have found one in the Silver Vaults and feel it might be an acceptable Christmas present to Her Majesty.

There is a small credit over from the Birthday present so, if you are able could you let me have £1.35 for another year.

Another time he proposed:

The usual source suggested yet another early morning tea set – but I thought enough was enough and have got a large and handsome cut glass vase in the Army and Navy Stores sale. It works out at £2.0119047 each – but I will happily settle for £2.

And again:

I have consulted the usual source and have been assured a breakfast service for those who have it upstairs would be welcome. It may indeed benefit some members of the Household.

The General Trading Company had run out of such things except in the antique department at £250.00 and I could find nowhere to park near Goode's. However I secured one at the Army and Navy Stores at £66.92 which works out at £3.186p each. I will settle for £3.18.

I have been assured by the Page that Queen Elizabeth is in need of an early morning tea-set and he has found one – two cups with a chaste pattern of roses, gentians and pansies.

In 1989, Ralph's choice failed to impress Jean Rankin: 'Rather late, I fear, inspiration has come for a Christmas present, and I have got a thermos jug to replace the one someone put on a hot stove in the Birkhall hut.' To this suggestion, Jean appended her view: 'Very poor gift'.

Conversation in the Queen Mother's Household was never less

than surprising. The prize was taken by a guest at Birkhall who made the complaint that the housemaid who brought her her early morning tray, on a cold day in Aberdeenshire, was wearing a *coloured* cardigan. Housemaids should only wear navy or black or, if frisky – possibly grey.

Curtseying was another routine. At Clarence House ladies-in-waiting curtseyed on seeing the Queen Mother in the morning, again at luncheon time, and on saying goodbye or goodnight. Men bowed from the neck, never from the waist. Early on in my waiting life when we awaited some German Royal guests, I asked her if I should curtsey to them (we did to other foreign Royalty). 'Curtsey?' she said indignantly. 'Of course not, they're Germans!' But as they clearly expected it, my nerve gave and I did curtsey, only to see the Queen Mother, with her eye on me, giving me the nearest thing to a wink I ever saw.

One soon realised the limitations that this apparently interesting and comfortable life imposed. The Queen Mother could never go out without informing a number of the staff – for instance, chauffeur, detective or dressers, let alone telling the people at her destination that she was coming, which involved private secretaries and ladies-in-waiting. All her shopping was brought to her. It was a rigid life.

Martin Gilliat was the Queen Mother's Private Secretary and the most influential person in the Household. Having spent five years as a prisoner-of-war with Patrick, he was an old friend and the reason for my introduction. He gave forthright advice to the Queen Mother, had served in several overseas posts on the staff of High Commissions, and his previous job had been working for Lord Slim when he was Governor-General of Australia.

Martin had a worldwide circle of friends. His gift for breaking the ice at the stiffest parties was legendary. A story was told of him when he was in Malaysia during a visit from a shy and nervous young King of Thailand. Martin had been told that King Bhumibol had a particular and unlikely skill. As they all stood round nervously before lunch, Martin said to the King: 'Your

Majesty, I understand that you are expert at standing on your head! Do please show us!' The King obliged and after that the party 'went like wedding bells'.

My first 'in-waiting' took place in November 1965. I described this to my sister, Laura, at the time:

I am almost through my first week and feel rather curiously as if I'd been at it all my life. The first day was a bit knee-knocking – but everyone was so ready to catch me and help that I got through nearly unscarred (I made 2 boobs, one of which was dropping and emptying my evening bag all over the pavement as we arrived at the Royal Society – about four O.M's retrieved it for me – most of them had the Nobel Prize too – as far as I was concerned they were nearly kissed as well).

After that all went well and I had a fascinating first evening being taught elementary science by the Top Brains – had a marvellous nonsense conversation with Harold Macmillan out of the side of both our mouths. He said (when we were barely half way through our programme):

'You goin' now?'

Me: 'No – got to see a film.'

'You goin' to the Lothians' party after this?'

Me: 'Good God no!' – not actually knowing the Lothians from Adam.

Macmillan: 'Seen Patrick Plunket to-day?'

Me, not knowing P.P. from Adam either: 'No not today.'

'You sure?' he said rather suspiciously and then ambled off.

I then found myself faced with a conversation over coffee with Julian Huxley – so said 'I've always heard about you from my Mamma.' It was open sesame and we were off about Mummy and Hermione so that was all right. Bless our family – you can usually find a link with the most unexpected people, from Julian Huxley to a hospital matron.

At that point David McMicking, the equerry, walked in with the news that the Queen Mother had flu and all engagements were cancelled for three days. Thus ended my first 'in-waiting'.

Racing was another feature of the Queen Mother's life, and early on I accompanied her to Windsor and Royal Ascot, finding myself in the Royal Box with just her, the Queen and Martin. We lunched with the Duke of Norfolk, but I found the walks to the paddock terrifying, with the great horses lashing about. The Queen Mother's jockey rode one race with a broken nose, having ridden the week before with two broken ribs. This did not augur well for any injury that might be sustained by the lady-in-waiting.

Even before my first 'in-waiting' I was aware that plans were afoot for the Queen Mother to go on tour to Australia and New Zealand in the Spring of 1966, to replace the tour she had had to cancel two years before. I was, of course, thrilled that, despite my inexperience, I was to be taken.

The Australian part of the tour was well settled, the New Zealand one less so. When the Queen Mother was shown the programme, she said: 'Goodness how dreary!' I therefore suggested to my sister in New Zealand that perhaps a visit to the odd farm or stud might balance the endless official welcomes. Christchurch seemed to provide an opportunity as there was a little spare time in the packed schedule. The tour manager said there were no studs nearby, and I could not resist saying: 'How terribly sad! What's happened to Long Beach?'

The problem with such tours was that the politicians were only interested in the Queen Mother being seen with them in as many places as possible.

For me the problem was once again my clothes. I shopped frantically, at a frightening cost, despite a fair allowance. I was in a quandary about what clothes would be suitable for the differing climates of Australia and New Zealand, and the formality and relative informality of the various occasions. A silk frock and a thick coat was usually suitable for a duty with the Queen Mother, but the rest was more complicated.

At Clarence House there were other concerns, as I explained to

Laura:

Entre nous this is a rather sad household as Queen Elizabeth is definitely not herself and seems so tired and fagged out. I find myself jumping in all the time to try and save her effort – and therefore chatter much too much and will probably shortly get the sack. Unless things look up a great deal the tour is going to be quite a grind. I think at the moment I'm about the only one looking forward to it. So I hope you'll be feeling very gay when we get there.

Jean and I had to give an interview to an immensely funny lady from the press who was very 'sincere' and humourless and arrived in what appeared to be a white flannel night shirt and black leather boots. We were trying to describe our duties – fortnight living in and then the tour and the dear lady said 'Your husbands must be angels'. I saw Jean going slightly dewy eyed and simply couldn't resist saying brightly 'As a matter of fact they are.' Solemnly the lady said 'What a sweet thing for two women to say.' I am glad to say Jean collapsed into a really good girlish fit of giggles, and we ended the interview rather hilariously. But I must admit the article was said to be for N.Z. papers and so dear knows what will appear – but to head off embarrassing questions on Q.E. I gave her some riveting stories of your private life. I hope you'll enjoy them – Crawfie won't be in it. John Griffin saw the article and said it was absorbing – about you.

And so we set off, myself and Jean Rankin as ladies-in-waiting, Martin Gilliat as Private Secretary, with the advantage of the many friends and contacts he had made from his days with Lord Slim in Australia, and with David McMicking as the equerry.

The purpose of the Queen Mother's visit was to attend the Adelaide Festival of Arts and open the new Flinders University, also in Adelaide. After two weeks in Australia, she would then undertake another fortnight in New Zealand.

We embarked in *Britannia*, after flying via Vancouver to Fiji. While in Fiji I sat next to a charming Fijian who, having seen the name Campbell in my name said we had a blood relationship.

When I asked how, he said amiably that his great grandfather had once eaten a Campbell.

I had looked forward to sailing calmly across the South Pacific in *Britannia*, and on Easter Sunday I told my sister that it was 'sheer Heaven'. I had envisaged a laze on deck in a suitable bathing suit as we glided over transparent waters. No one had thought to mention the South Sea swell. I was soon unremittingly sea-sick, and lay on the bed in my luxurious cabin, feeling as if I were on a trampoline.

In Australia we started in Adelaide, where the Queen Mother was Patron of the Festival. We saw the Australian ballet and met Robert Helpmann, attended concerts with the Australian Youth Orchestra, and went to the races. The flower displays for the festival included a floral carpet made entirely of rose petals. Millions of flowers must have been torn apart and it was a memorable sight.

The tour was incessant hard work but rewarding. The Queen Mother was in great form one day, then exhausted the next. We stayed at Government House, Adelaide, where the Governor and his wife were invariably to be found standing at the bottom of the stairs waiting for the Queen Mother on every occasion, which encouraged her to be quite naughty with them. She hated too rigid formality and in particular finding people waiting for her in a room, all lined up.

The Queen Mother excelled at making the atmosphere relaxed. She was tolerant about long or short evening dresses, and stayed longer than was expected on virtually every engagement. Martin assured me that nothing pleased 'People' (as he called her) more than if Jean or I did something wrong or arrived in the wrong place at the wrong time. All this astonished Lady Bastyan, the Governor's wife. As for Adelaide itself, it seemed like home to me. My grandfather Pascoe Grenfell had been one of its founders, there was a photograph of Joyce Grenfell in the foyer of the theatre, and a vast portrait of Queen Adelaide in the dining room of Government House, presented by Sir James Fergusson in 1870.

We visited Perth, Sydney and Canberra. Our visit to Sydney included a two-day tour of the Snowy Mountain hydroelectric scheme. This meant endless drives all day round curling roads in large cars. Prince Charles was then at school at Geelong Grammar School. The Queen Mother was the only member of his family who visited him out there and he joined us. Every now and again the royal car seemed to drive inside a mountain. It could have been the last scene in a Wagnerian opera.

Motorcades were a feature of these overseas tours – not something usual in the United Kingdom. The royal car was usually open and in the middle of the procession. On one occasion in Australia we were driving on the outskirts of the town, the crowds had thinned and it was a windy day. The cars began to speed instead of crawling, the normal pace of a motorcade. The Queen Mother had a diaphanous coat which she wore over a matching dress. She took it off in the car and handed it to me in order to stop it blowing away. I looked round and could see no safe place to put it and as it seemed to fold into the size of a handkerchief, I began pushing it into my bag. 'Don't do that!' she said. 'That's my best coat.' Ever afterwards the Queen Mother warned people not to entrust their coats to me. 'She'll put it in her handbag!'

We sailed from Australia to New Zealand in the *Britannia*, seeing an albatross just before we landed. As we left the Royal Yacht the Queen Mother was televised with her Household walking down the gangplank. Waiting to receive her was my brother-in-law, Bernard Fergusson and my sister Laura.

We drove off in a motorcade to the first of many civic lunches. At luncheon I told my neighbour by way of making conversation that Laura Fergusson was my sister. I was startled when her answer was: 'Oh I am so glad you told me, because when I saw you all coming off the yacht I said to my husband – "Oh dear! Something terrible has happened to Lady Fergusson"!' and she added happily 'It must have been you!'

The pattern of Royal Visits have an element of monotony. The almost daily routine of receptions at Town Halls, civic luncheons, displays by children, and parades, was followed by evening receptions, quick changes for a banquet, long evenings of dinners with many filling courses, followed by speeches and seldom bed before midnight. These were certainly redeemed by meeting a great many interesting individuals.

Laura's account to the family, seen from her vantage point as wife of the Governor-General, gives a vivid picture of the New Zealand part of the tour:

We went down to Invercargill to meet the Yacht. It was a beastly grey day that all too rapidly turned to rain. We went off in the barge to go on board to greet the Queen Mother. Met by the Admiral, shown in through a doorway and there was Frances all dressed up. Just time for a smacking kiss, a how do you do all round, and on in to meet the Queen Mother. We only had a few minutes, and then had to leave to be back on shore to meet her on the jetty. Frances had to be on duty as well as Jean that day (unnecessarily as it turned out) so we had the rather ridiculous situation of meeting them on shore, handing the Queen Mother over to the Prime Minister for the day's functions, and we went back again in the barge, to spend the day in the Yacht while she refuelled.

About teatime they all came back, absolutely soaking. There wasn't much time to see Frances then, as they had a Reception for the Press and tour personnel – which took place on the deck under a double awning which leaked like a sieve! Then we had to rush down and change for dinner – a party of 60 at the stupendous long tables beautifully set out – and it wasn't till the guests went and final goodnights had been said that F. and I even had a chance to speak – and of course we went on until about 2.30 am.

She looks in tremendous form, and is obviously enjoying it all madly. They make up a very happy party and a very giggly one too. Everyone teases Frances in good old familiar style and she loves it, and they seem to laugh their way through everything. The Queen Mother is quite marvellous. At first one is haunted by her tiny little lonely figure and it does seem such a burden to put onto one person alone. But having seen her in action at close quarters she really is endowed with something that others haven't got. It's a gift of communication from her to each individual in each crowd – and the most unflagging energy too. Dinner is seldom before 8.45 and we played games afterwards until about midnight. My heart sank when I first heard about the games, but they were such deliciously silly ones and make it so easy to have an evening of everyone joining in the fun and no-one getting left out, that it's well worth it and she is such enormous fun playing them. It's gloriously childish and very restful as a result.

We sailed that night to Dunedin, where we were greeted by a beautiful sunny morning. It looked quite lovely sailing up the long narrow harbour. B and I went up on deck quite early and got very soppy sailing past the house we lived in in February. Little powerboats came out to accompany us – a lovely sight. We went to church and drove through marvellous crowds – you could almost feel the affection welling out towards her. B. travelled with her, and I gather they had a deliciously giggly time while she was waving, smiling graciously as they could hear the comments being made. Frances and I travelled in great style in the car behind. That afternoon we took them on a picnic to a quiet beach where we strolled about for an hour and then had a picnic tea on the garden of some friends. He is a half Maori – Brigadier Honi Parata, whose son has just been commissioned into the Black Watch. They took it very calmly and sensibly.

Next day they went to fulfil various engagements. Then another Reception on Board, this time dry but chilly. It was great fun for us as we knew so many of the people.

Gosh the yacht is comfortable. We had a cabin and bathroom each and sitting room of our own between and B. was superbly valeted while I was beautifully looked after by Frances' (or rather Harry's) Elisabeth [Harry's housekeeper, who came as my maid].

The Admiral – Pat Morgan – is most awfully nice and joins in all the ragging (in fact he is very much apt to lead it all). I was taken round the ship and signed the various visitor's books in the different ward rooms. It was all most impressive.

On Tuesday we went a separated way up to the hotel and Wanaka, while the QM worked her way up through Alexandra to reach us about 4 pm. The autumn there is everything it is cracked up to be and more. Wonderful golden poplars, blue lake water etc. The whole of the new Tourist Board hotel had been taken over for all of us and the detectives, and millions of people who all do something but I'm not sure what. We had one or two things that weren't arranged as they might have been, but it all sorted out. Our next two days really were glorious – probably the best of the whole tour and what the Queen Mother will remember when the sea of receptions and so on are forgotten.

She climbed into the most delicious fishing clothes of waders, jacket, green felt hat and with huge pearls glittering set off into the water with her rod. She was very diffident about being photographed casting as she was sure she'd catch the back of her neck. Nothing like that happened and after a rather beastly ten minutes with the horde of photographers who looked as though they were going to swallow her, they all took themselves off completely. A caravan had been moved to the place where we were and everyone dispersed and fished or walked or got in one of the jet boats, and she was left happily on her own with an extremely nice local ranger. We assembled for a perhaps rather too simple picnic lunch, but she looked as though she was thoroughly enjoying eating chicken in her fingers. We all dispersed again after lunch – she fished some more, and then stretched out comfortably on a lilo until we started coming back for tea which we brewed up in the caravan. It was hot – much too clear for fishing, but highly enjoyable and quite lovely.

We went back to the hotel in the jet boats – she and I in one, and B in the one accompanying us, and it was all too cosy and delicious for words. Some of the ships officers and the man in charge of the Queen's Flight, who had been to NZ on the High Commission staff before, went off fishing elsewhere, a long way off, and starting earlier and going on later, and they came back with the limit bag *each. It made a wonderful sight when they brought in their catch on a tarpaulin and laid it at the QM's feet, she being dressed in a full skirted evening crinoline dress.*

Next morning it was back to the job again for her. Before leaving the hotel there was a line up of the staff and a large number of them went individually to say goodbye and be given a present – cooks, waitresses, maids and anyone who had played an individual part in looking after her.

The QM's party moved northwards through varying weather, which came to an appalling head in Wellington with a full scale gale and freezing cold wind, a great shame. They had been to Timaru, Christchurch – oh and Queenstown and Arrowtown on the way up. They went on to Wanganui via Palmerston North, and then we rejoined them at the big Wairakei Hotel. They didn't join us until about 4.30 or 5 (they always ran late to their schedule) and I imagined they would all long to put their toes up.

Not a bit, within minutes the QM was out fishing. She felt desperate about not getting anything as so much hope and care had gone into it all. This time she triumphed and caught one which was just big enough to keep – and was much photographed and celebrated. We had another gay but late night. Next day it teemed with rain, but in search of this elusive catch of fish it was ordained that she should drive for over an hour to a particular reach of the river, and the picnic etc, should happen there. So off we all went and I've never been so wet in all my life. Most embarrassingly I caught one fish, and the ghillie with us hooked another on Bernard's line while he was lighting a cigarette and no one else caught anything. We had a long very damp and slightly chilly procession of cars back to the hotel. Hepe Te Heu Heu (the paramount chief) and his wife, came to call, and had quite a successful half hour or so.

While the Queen Mother was fishing in the rain, the river suddenly rose and became quite dangerous, as it became a spate. She turned to come out as water was starting to swirl round her. She was rather taken aback when the ranger acting as her guide said, 'You coming out? I must say you were braver in the war.'

The next day they left for Hamilton and Rotorua. They flew in on Sunday afternoon when it was pelting. We had a big do at the Town Hall with over 2,000 girls of the Life Brigade and B. addressing them. He insisted they should all disperse in time to go and join the throng in the streets. Jenny[8], Andrew[9] and I slipped back here, got out of our finery and went and stood under our umbrellas in the street and waved like mad things as the Queen Mother and Frances drove by. Unfortunately – or perhaps fortunately, they didn't spot us. It really was very moving to find the crowd made up of all ages and with plenty of tight-trousered long-haired youths, happily standing a couple of hours in the rain, for yet again the crowds had been greater than had been allowed for and so they were very late in getting back on board.

For the next couple of days there was a constant coming and going and telephoning between us and the Yacht. Angelically it had been arranged that Geordie and two pals should go on board and be taken over by an officer and shown round and off they went. Frances and I went back to the Yacht for tea in the ADCs' room with the boys, when who should walk in but the Queen Mother, on her way to a cabin that had been fitted up with a microphone for her to record her farewell broadcast.

Our Reception went off very well. She and Frances arrived in a very giggly state and we never looked back. She stayed until well after 11 pm and it was a warm moonlight night and quite lovely.

She had had a tremendous triumph in the morning with 26,000 children yelling their heads off quite uninhibitedly; had spent the afternoon visiting a stud farm, and so I think had had one of the best days of all. The following day she went to the University and on to the Races, to which we had gone ahead. I don't think racing here can be much fun if you haven't heard any of the horses' names or

8. Jenny Gibbs (now Jenny Gordon-Lennox), Lady-in-Waiting.
9. Captain (later Brigadier) Andrew Parker Bowles, ADC.

anything, but she had the great gift of looking interested, and any way being able to talk technicalities.

That evening we dined on board with about six other couples, and after there was a Reception on board for about 200. They are a bit disappointing looking really, the big Receptions on board, as they are held on a deck, covered with an awning which leaks badly. There is nothing very splendiferous or royal looking about it. Unfortunately a sudden very strong downpour came on and suddenly cold water was dripping down our backs quite unexpectedly. After this we went back to the drawing room and just as we were preparing to come home we were told the Queen Mother had accepted to go to the Ward Room to say goodbye, so off we all trooped, and rather surprisingly it turned into a very wardroom-ish party. We got back here at 1.15 – not at all our usual bedtime. How they all kept their eyes open I can't think – and they had to be ready for off by 10 the next morning.

We went back and B. drove out to the International Airport with her (their two standards flying side by side) and Frances and I very cosily chatting away in the car just behind. It's a terrific long route to Mangere, and it was lined throughout. A lovely day luckily – and it really was astounding that so many people could be all along such a long way.

At the end of the tour we left the Royal Yacht at Wellington to sail home without us and caught a Qantas flight from which I wrote to Laura:

As we shut the doors of the aircraft we all said in one breath, 'That was the best farewelling ever,' added to by saying it knocked Australia into a cocked hat. It was so gay I hope you didn't feel too pangy – I shall never forget Martin crying when we said goodbye to the Yacht, when I kissed you good-bye I nearly blubbed. Jean and I are so proud of Bernard kissing us in that hat, that winning group of your household farewelling last of all at the steps of the aircraft. Tell Fred[10] there's something about his bow which makes one howl.

It was all such fun and you and Bernard did superbly and gave NZ
a neat aura for all of us – but particularly for 'People'. They got in
better and better form as we journeyed on and enjoyed you both
tremendously. I think the last three days in Auckland went better
than we dared hope when we first drove in in that teeming rain. It's
terribly sad it's over – but it'll be one of the memories for all time
and a marvellous bonus as you say for both of us.

We've just had a vast lunch preceded by champagne cocktails
renamed 'ladies-in-waiting neck' – the difference between
champagne and ginger ale. Reg, one of the footmen, is having a
dateline birthday so we were all decorated with paper caps and
blowers. It seems unbelievable that I shall be tucking Helen up in
bed in 24 hours time.

We land in Honolulu in 5 hours – consuming lobster thermidor
before – and everyone is sleeping and I must too. Darling darling girl
bless you both. You are wonders and the number of lumps I've had
in my throat at all the super things people have said (I mean real
people) of you both the whole way from Bluff to Auckland. They've
been said to all of us and Martin has been saying 'Never never has a
Governor-General and his lady been so loved . . .'

It took some time to return to normal life after that
extraordinary experience, but presently I was back to eating
frugally off a tray watching rather uninspiring programmes on
the television. There was much catching up with my three
children, millions of letters to answer, and the garden to catch up
with. At the airport, Robert announced, rather pink with
embarrassment, that he had been elected into 'Pop' at Eton,
whereupon the Queen Mother at once swept him up for
luncheon. I told David McMicking to teach him to bow, and
could hear him complaining vigorously: 'Don't be such a bloody
fool. I couldn't do that!'

10. Lt Colonel Frederick Burnaby-Atkins, Comptroller to the Governor-General's
Household, and a prisoner-of-war with Patrick.

TWENTY-TWO

Inverawe

AFTER MY return from the tour I was faced by a startling proposal from Bobby and Angela. For the past ten years the River Awe where Bobby owned one bank of salmon fishing, had been re-shaped by a hydro-electric scheme. This resulted in the flow of the river being emasculated. Bobby realised that he needed to purchase the opposite bank to his beat as otherwise the river was too narrow. The hydro-electric company had bought the Inverawe Estate which owned this bank, and when they had completed the scheme, they put the entire estate up for sale. The main house had been their headquarters and they had divided the living rooms into cubicles. Some of the upper floors had been divided into flats. The house smelt of stale cabbage and cigarette smoke.

Angela and Bobby bought the whole estate, and found the house a white elephant, so suggested that I sold Polfearn and bought it. Robert and I felt considerably daunted and doubted whether the sale of Polfearn would finance the restoration wanted. In the end Bobby gave me the house. It was hard to grasp the implications of being given a vast house, as this rarely happens. I knew it would be lovely even if a considerable undertaking. Despite myself I felt apprehensive, if excited. I was plunged into activity. The process of doing up the house caused something of a panic. It looked so like a barrack and every room needed to be done, with new carpets and curtains, and walls to be painted.

It was a house with a long history. Built in the eighteenth century by the Campbells of Inverawe, it had been a square two-storied house, which still remains its core. The house is connected to a famous ghost story which appears in the writings of Sir Walter Scott and Dean Swift. The Ticonderoga story is related by my son-in-law, Alastair Campbell, in his history of the Clan Campbell:

A Campbell of Inverawe, well known in Highland history, is Major Duncan Campbell of Inverawe, of the 42nd Highlanders, the Black Watch, of whom a famous story is told. One day he was in the hall at Inverawe when a man burst in and, touching the hearthstone, claimed sanctuary, explaining that he had killed a man and was on the run. Following the unwritten law of the Highlands, Inverawe duly hid the man. He was horrified to learn, when the pursuit arrived, that it was his foster-brother who was the victim, but he stuck to his oath and did not give the murderer away.

That night, as he tossed and turned, the ghost of his foster-brother appeared, pressing him to give up the killer, but Inverawe refused. After a second night, on which the ghost again appeared, he could stand having the murderer under the same roof no more and took the wretch to a safe cave on Cruachan, promising to bring him food the next day. When he did so, the cave was empty; the man had fled. That night the ghost appeared for the last time, saying to Duncan, 'Farewell, we meet again at Ticonderoga'.

The name meant nothing to Duncan and as the years passed it went out of his mind. He joined the army and rose to be second-in-command of the famous Black Watch, with whom he went to America to fight the French. The British Army advanced north from New York and finally came up against the enemy at Fort Carillon on Lake George in 1758. The night before the battle, his foster-brother's ghost once more appeared to Inverawe. Enquiry revealed that the Indian name for Fort Carillon was Ticonderoga and Inverawe knew that his fate was sealed.

So it proved; the French position was behind a strong palisade further protected by a tangle of trees felled deliberately to form a near-impenetrable obstacle. Successive British attacks foundered in a hail of fire; the Black Watch were in reserve and could only watch as their comrades were cut down. Eventually their turn came and unhesitatingly they charged forward only to meet the same fate. A few Highlanders got through and scaled the palisade but the French were waiting for them and they were bayoneted one by one. At last the British gave up and the remnants of the 42nd pulled back. Among the heavy casualties was Major Duncan Campbell; mortally wounded, he died ten days later.

In the Regency period the house was altered. It acquired a tower, a smart front staircase, drawing room, dining room and several extra bedrooms and it became three-storied. In the 1920s its new owner employed the famous architect, Lorimer, to convert the core of the house into an imposing high hall. This was what principally daunted me, as baronial had never been my natural habitat. At some point in this upgrading the ground in front of the house was built up to make a large level lawn before the ground sloped across fields to the river.

Angela's compelling interest was drawing meticulous plans. She could have been a professional architect. She loved restoring houses and set to work with a vengeance. From time to time she telephoned saying that it was snowing and there was nothing for Duncan, the gamekeeper, to do outside and so she had bought fourteen million gallons of white paint and thought she would start him painting. 'You can never go wrong with white,' she declared wisely.

Time was at a premium, and I felt disorganised. In fact I dashed about between my fortnights 'in-waiting', either in London, at Birkhall, or at the Castle of Mey. Life consisted of ceaseless activity and engagements. And when I was not 'in-waiting', there were schools, clothes, half terms, letters, bills, telephoning and the general impossibility of keeping ahead. But I was lucky to have such a full life and so many friends.

In the midst of preparing Helen's clothes for St Mary's, and all the Christmas shopping, I had to prepare the flat for the

Christmas let. I was 'in-waiting' that December, and on the evening that I finished the Queen Mother suddenly went into hospital, so I had to return to help with the deluge of letters, flowers and cards. Even when I officially went back to work there were still five hundred cards to answer.

Like all mothers with teenagers in the Sixties, I had to face up to the changes of this surprising new generation, as I explained to Laura:

The talk at Helen's schools, all sex and the facts of life, but mercifully not bottled up and certainly not worried about. It is surprising to us but I am sure one must play it their way, as I feel they are right and some other parent will simply understand better then one does oneself.

It's quite remarkable to go to the theatre in London and find the audience full of 16 or 15 year olds and stuff we'd never have seen till we were adult, and then wouldn't have enjoyed it if one had sat next to Daddy. Now everyone laughs quite easily together. It does mean a lot of humbug goes and one can and does talk much straighter to the young. The drugs thing is frightening. There's no doubt marijuana and hashish or something are passed round at most parties, and its said a conservative estimate is that 10% at Oxford are addicts, viz 800 out of 8,000, rather a lot. It's desperately hard to know how to cope. One feels the young ought to know exactly what is involved. On the other hand they say too much publicity makes them feel they must try just to see what it's like. It's said to be starting at Eton too. Sometimes one wonders if just an ordinary war wasn't much easier to cope with at 19!

I resigned from the County Council after an undistinguished stint of ten years, which had been an enjoyable experience for me. I acquired another interest. The Labour Government was reforming the juvenile Bench in Scotland, and brought in legislation for a Children's Panel. Each county was to have a panel of lay people and for each sitting three people from that group would sit and advise on cases of juvenile delinquency referred to them, through an appointed individual called the Reporter. Their decisions were mandatory, but each case had to be reviewed every six months. I applied to join and was appointed Chairman for Argyll and Bute. It was interesting to be involved in the groundwork for this reform, which since those days has become a sophisticated and established arm of the law.

We were not judges, since any violent case went to the Sheriff, and the family of the children who came before us had to admit guilt. Parents often brought their children voluntarily when they felt they were out of control. In theory we had authority to recommend any solution – but in practice it resolved itself in reference to the Social Services Department or a special school. We were cursorily trained amateurs, with no guidelines or precedents, and we knew nothing about child abuse in those days.

Robert was about to leave Eton and had decided to go and work in a leper colony in Zambia run by Anglican monks. He was to be away for about nine months to a year. He was as delighted as if he had been invited to an eternal party for Ascot.

Bernard and Laura continued their various duties in New Zealand. In December 1965 the New Zealand government hosted the Commonwealth Parliamentary Association. They attended the opening and the Reception:

> The poor Nigerian delegate woke up to read the headline to say that he had said he would hit Mr [Keith] Holyoake [the Prime Minister] on the nose the next time. We were quite intrigued as Andrew Parker Bowles found he was sitting between them at the opening ceremony. He can't move in his uniform so he wouldn't have been able to interfere. Eventually they came face to face with each other and Holyoake said laughingly 'Here's your chance.' They fell on each other's neck and decided the only person needing blipping was the reporter.

Laura and Bernard then flew to Melbourne, Australia, for an

official visit in July 1966.

A month later, they had a visit from some of the family but missed the young Prince of Wales, when he visited from Australia:

Since I last wrote we have had a tremendous family pie here, with Reg and Joyce – and Bill Blezard [her accompanist], and then overlapping them, Katie and Pat. It was the greatest fun. All were in great form. Joyce went over here in a big way, and had fantastic publicity before arriving.

Just before all this, we'd had quite a week with flying down to Dunedin to lay a stone for a University block – unfortunately the day Prince Charles touched down at Auckland for 40 mins on his way home. There had been a bit of correspondence about what to do with the 40 mins. I flew up to Auckland the following day and found everyone in a tremendous glow over his time there. He managed to shake lots of hands, to drift from one side to another of the passage way he walked along, talking easily and cheerfully and obviously gave that valuable impression of being delighted to be where he was and keen on meeting whoever it was he was talking to at any given moment. He really did go over big – in the shortest possible time too. Very impressive.

We had the Test Match with the Lions here, which was a rather tense affair as diplomatic relations with Britain were nearly broken off because somebody biffed someone else and a fight had started up in Auckland. Everyone was involved, and Bernard summoned the two Captains, who are incidentally quite charming, and said if foul play took place he'd had no alternative but to leave the ground as publicly as possible. Anyway in the end everyone played a gentlemanly game, the referee gave one doubtful decision which became a peaceful talking point, and honour was saved. So our reception here immediately afterwards wasn't as embarrassing as it might have been. The referee was quite charming to talk to.

Towards the end of their time in New Zealand, in October 1966, they received a visit from Lyndon Johnson, President of the

United States:

Life has taken on a distinctly Mad Hatter aspect since we heard LBJ was heading this way. Luckily there has only been a fortnight to make plans – anything longer would have driven everyone mad. Teams of men have flown out from America to check over security obviously – and the President's personal needs – some of them not so obvious. It gets complicated and hellish for Freddy [Burnaby-Atkins – the Comptroller] that it hasn't been hoisted in that this is a private house with a life to be lived in it that exists before and will exist after the visit, and the notion that we are hosts and he a guest hardly comes in to it.

Telephone lines are being installed everywhere, a complete internal hook up between rooms they will be using, and also I suppose the hot lines and direct lines to Washington. One in the porch, one in the hall on the round table all of eight yards away, and so on. Refrigerators, cooking rings, coffee, percolators, hamburgers, tins of soup, decaffeinated coffee, cocktail snacks without peanuts. Cutty Sark Whisky – so on and so on. On top of this comes a 7ft square bed, with every complication of the bedclothes being too small – no valance so that it looks horrid and no bed cover. It's not even an old friend, it's a brand new one from Chio and they are having trouble getting the parts to stay put. Thank goodness it's their headache to try and fix it, not ours. By the time he's eaten his hamburgers and drunk his whisky and coffee and had his soups. I don't suppose he minds much anyway.

The Press are a bally nuisance and don't reckon we exist. They suddenly turn up and demand to take photographs (we've firmly kept them from going upstairs) and won't take no for any answer and are sometimes quite unpleasant.

It's a great moment in history for N.Z. There is a vocal factor out here who are strongly anti the fighting in Vietnam, and they will make trouble.

The visit began with much formality at the airport, guards of honour to be expected, diplomatic and Cabinet husbands and wives to be presented, a speech from Bernard, incorporating a message from the Queen and a reply from the President. Laura was surprised to find that everything was different to what had gone before, particularly when LBJ broke from the planned schedule:

As everyone was prepared for him to get in the car and set off, he dived away across the tarmac to the crowd, and shook hands right left and centre, showering presents of ballpoint pens with his or her name on, as he went. Complete jostlement from his security guards, the press, and everyone else, including the poor Governor-General who found himself complete with spurs being jostled around, which is never his best state of enjoyment. All planned orderliness and dignity was gone, and the general impression was one of press fighting security men, and all of them fighting Bernard, more or less! All this took place in a biting southerly wind such as only Wellington really knows how to blow. The LBJ's had already had a cold and raining welcome at the RNZAF airport where their own huge plane touched down, so were already pretty chilled to the bone. She said she was cold and could she please get in the car, so she and I climbed into our car. (I afterwards discovered that the rug we had put in was removed by the security man as it was a security risk!) We just sat rather helplessly until LBJ decided O.K. for off.

The motorcade formed up with outriders, then the bullet proof car, with security men jammed on the front seat with their walkie talkies and black plastic macs. LBJ and Bernard on the back seat, and close behind an open tourer with about six or seven security chaps – each with walkie talkie and black plastic mac, who leap in and out without opening doors – exactly like the James Bond films. Off we set thankfully. With good crowds on both sides, a longish drive round Oriental Bay, as to come through the Victoria Tunnel was considered too bad a security risk – and about half hour to dinner. Suddenly the cortege stopped, the chaps in the security car in front of us hurled themselves out and all we could see was a meleé.

Of course I thought that was it. To my astonishment, I found that LBJ had leapt out of the car, and was shaking hands with anyone he could reach, and walking from one side of the road to the other. Of course people rushed to be there, and a complete scrum took place. Eventually he got back in, and this time seized a microphone and talked through a loudhailer system 'Glad to see yer' 'Thank yer for coming' 'Nice to know yer'. If he wanted to wave to the right he thrust a great huge fist right past Bernard's face – as far as he was concerned Bernard wasn't there.

Laura felt especially sorry for Lady Bird Johnson, who was cold, exhausted and longing to get home. She kept saying she was scared, but what really frightened her was that a child might be pushed under the wheel of the Presidential motorcade in the scrum. Meanwhile Bernard was worried about the schedule, particularly a dinner followed by a big reception. The Anti-Vietnam committee had created a bigger demonstration than anticipated, but thanks to the security team the cars were soon safely through the gates. Dinner was half an hour late.

With all the bally hoo that had been going on for days, such strange things were omitted from their list of needs. Robertson [Laura's lady's maid] had a field day when a cry went up for the bed in his dressing room (he had the Duke's suite – double room, dressing room and bathroom, and she was across the way in double room and bathroom) to be made up for his massage. The housemaids had had to go down to cope with dinner guests and reception, and Robertson was tickled pink at having to cope and finding herself walking along the passage with LBJ himself. Then a panic cry went up for face flannels, and she had to whip one of mine and some others for Mrs LBJ and the maid.

All of this was going on in an incredibly short time – so you can imagine the pressure. We collected them to go down to dinner, and had a five or ten minute wait until the last of the guests arrived, having done the most fantastic turns of speed to get dressed then through the crowds of G.H. I took a great liking to Mrs LBJ. She had read up quite a lot of stuff and was trying hard to react to being in New Zealand. He has a most disconcerting way of going through the mechanics of speaking, shaking hands etc. and just not being with one at all. He certainly had every reason to be tired after their long journey, but it wasn't just tiredness. He is known to be the biggest egotist out, and so far as we could see it takes this form, when he is involved he switches on. Otherwise he switches right off and can be and is rude to the people around him. She on the other hand turns on the charm – if you like – but she has to with TV cameras churning a way at her ear. She does listen – and she quite often prompts him to nudge him back to his surroundings. It's quite extraordinary to see. Everything about him is on a different scale to ordinary human beings. He's pretty ruthless, absolutely unthinking about the extra work and strain he is putting on everyone – most of all his wife and immediate staff, but also everyone like the men lining routes, servicemen in Guards of Honour, and the tremendously wide circle of people involved if his timetable gets out of gear. I don't believe he ever gives them a thought or would care if he did. Yet he's terribly sensitive to criticism and minds demonstrations deeply.

I sat between him and our PM at dinner which was one of the most nightmarish meals I've ever sat through. We were late starting, so had to bustle a bit, which isn't easy for a formal party of 26. He called for a second helping of potatoes (which got the pantry on the hop as the dishes were being swept straight from the dining room to various other meals going on in different rooms of the house simultaneously). He bullied the PM across me, and I think switched off so as not to bother to hear the answer, though he is deaf too. It all became a horrible scrum of trying to get the meal finished, urging him on to eat what he'd piled on his plate or restraining him from getting up before the toasts (Though when he came to the point he proposed the Queen without prompting, so knew perfectly well it was coming). He assumes the scene will be set for him as principal actor and makes it as difficult as he can for one to achieve it.

There was one delicious exchange of conversation. Mr Holyoake I think wanted to switch the conversation and cut across the rather petulant bullying and asked what cattle LBJ ran on his ranch. LBJ said Herefords and Angus. Mrs LBJ picked this up across the table and said she infinitely preferred the Herefords. The PM cut in with 'Oh, I'm an Angus man.' Mrs Holyoake, from Bernard's other side just heard this from him and chipped in with 'You're not, Keith, you're a Presbyterian.'

After dinner there was a reception in the ballroom, with beautiful flowers, though very hot due to a platform of television cameras and lights. Bernard and Laura stood with the Presidential couple for the National Anthems, and then divided into pairs to meet the guests. Evidently LBJ 'switched off' and was consequently rather rude to the guests lined up for him.

The press coverage of this trip was more extensive than anything the New Zealand Tourist Board could have dared hope. On the next day Mrs Johnson took her cine camera out to film flowers. Meanwhile the house was packed with people, Laura knowing very few of them:

Fired by the general scale of operations, a NZ TV man was stopped walking out of the house with a whole crate of champagne under his mackintosh. He said it was part of his equipment. Such was the general scrum that the crate was removed from him and he vanished from sight and nothing more could be done. I wonder what else went that we haven't yet noticed.

The President spent the morning at meetings and continued to bound out of his car, shaking hands and distributing ballpoint pens by the score. As a result he was an hour and a half late for the state luncheon for 200. At the end of it he delivered an eloquent speech, which impressed Laura for its statesmanship. They then flew to visit a farm and left New Zealand only half an hour late. It was all over, as Laura concluded:

We have had a Bank Holiday weekend to recover in, which has been very pleasant and today gloriously sunny. We took our books out and went up the hill at the back of the house where the broom is blooming quite beautifully, and read and snoozed in privacy and peace. Thank goodness we know how to do that!

I was dealing less dramatically with London life. During this phase, our mother's life went on with enormous activity. We complained, moaned and let off steam but in fact we all enjoyed it as she never failed to produce some surprising happening. I was frequently telephoned and ordered to drive her to Hampton Court where Lady Fisher, an admiral's widow, was in trouble, or asked to take my mother to early service in Camberwell where there was a young vicar in urgent need of discarded matchboxes, paper clips, safety pins and old stamp books, or to Holloway Prison where the Governor had become a new friend. It was often stimulating, and even more often funny:

Our darling Ma hasn't been utterly easy. Millicent [her then housekeeper] got really quite bad with asthma and looked ghastly. Ma packed Millicent off helter-skelter to the National Assistance, got in a frenzy when a cleaning woman asked 7/6 an hour, the London rate, imported the first, a raving loony, who I think I wrote to you about, followed by an old lady of 94 with pneumonia who nearly died on us. Ma spent three happy days searching London for an Eventide Home and got it. Finally she ended in chaos having interviewed one or two candidates, we believe saying 'I only charge £5-10-0 and you get three good meals and a nice room'. Finally I exploded.

In August 1967, Robert returned, quite grown up after his experiences in Africa, where he helped deliver babies, nursed lepers and coped with anti-white Africans, as well as organizing his monks.

The same August my sister-in-law Peg and her husband, Raymond Baring, were staying at Ardchattan and were due for dinner, when Peter Huntington arrived in the kitchen summoning me to the river, saying that Raymond had had a heart attack and that Peg thought he was dead. This proved to be true. I brought her back with me and was able to stay with her until after the funeral. Hardly was it over than Prince Charles came to stay:

On Monday Prince Charles arrived – a reel party that night, Oban ball on Tuesday with dinner here for 28 before bed at 5.15 a.m. and now its Thursday! The Prince Charles visit I think went well, he arrived alone with a detective but is a dedicated fisherman and he and Robert fished every waking hour. Our party were excellent and very merry. We'd kept it all so quiet the press never cottoned on till too late, so he was able and did go fishing entirely alone, getting up at 8 a.m. and wandering down entirely alone. Even at the end of the ball only about half the guests knew he was there. He danced all the time and finally he and I left early (at 4.30 a.m.!) and came back and sat on my kitchen table while he drank milk and ate chocolate biscuits and we talked of lots of things.

He's a specially charming boy, with loads of charm and real genuineness.

In the autumn of 1967 the Fergussons began organising their return, planning an exotic journey home via every imaginable country – as far as we could judge:

We are all really goggle eyed about your journey and wonder where the energy is coming from, after your marvellous but surely most exhausting departure from NZ. I am so glad it's so VIP and so exciting. What different lives you and I are led by fate to live and how satisfactory that they are so mutually satisfying to us.

Everything to me has rose-tinted glasses just now – back from Birkhall to a golden and marvellous autumn at Inverawe. It's funny but I now love Inverawe as I did Polfearn when Patrick was there,

only I think even more so. There's great pleasure in remembering
Patrick saying he'd buy Inverawe if he won the pools. A slight smug
feeling that perhaps he has goes about with me.

Laura and Bernard settled back at Auchairne in Ayrshire after
their return home. The telephone had come of age, so we rang
each other constantly, when not visiting. He became Chairman of
the British Council until 1976 and Colonel of the Black Watch,
and he was made a life peer in 1972 and a Knight of the Thistle
in 1974. They continued to travel extensively.

My mother moved flats again and became increasingly frail. She
celebrated her 80th birthday in 1966 with a party at Chewton,
where she clearly enjoyed everything. She still pursued her
mission to enlighten us about Chardin, but her journeys abroad
ceased. Instead she set out to found the Teilhard de Chardin
Association, eagerly addressing its constitution. Soon afterwards
her health deteriorated.

Laura found her a devoted companion/housekeeper as she
relapsed into mental illness. She had always dreaded that this
form of illness might hit her and, when it did, she told us she
wished to be put in a nunnery. She even had the name of one, but
never gave it to us. Before she got seriously ill, she took to making
several wills, and was apt to walk into a succession of
undertakers' establishments, asking each in turn to arrange her
funeral. After she died in 1972, this took some sorting out, and
we finally chose the most recently contacted undertaker from
several claimants.

Even after death, my mother made an impact. She left
instructions that she was to be buried at Betteshanger beside my
father. The service to be in the village church, but the music would
have taxed a cathedral choir – the village choir did their manifold
best. She had always disliked the tailcoats and funereal black
worn by undertakers so left rather ill-defined instructions that
they were to wear Gannex mackintoshes – the kind made famous
by Harold Wilson when he was Prime Minister. Her funeral was

on a lovely warm June day. The poor undertakers looked hot, conscientiously obeying what they interpreted as her last wishes.

The Bidding Prayer at my mother's funeral was written by Vera, her step-daughter, who gave thanks for:

Her integrity of character and her constant example, for her gifts of mind and intellect whereby many were inspired, challenged and directed. For her public spirited interest in many causes, especially her service to the YWCA. For her love of beauty in art, literature and music and all that is fair and honourable and of good report. For her intense love of family and home, for her unswerving loyalty to friends, and her gift of friendship. For her beauty and graciousness; her kindness, dignity and mercy, for her calm courage in adversity. Above all for her devotion and service to the church and the Christian faith . . .

Soon after Hilda died, Minnie died. After her retirement, she had lived in a bed-sitting room on the ground floor of a house in the King's Road, Chelsea. She loved watching the crowds go by, but was principally pleased that she had no need to turn her lights on as the street lights lit the room perfectly. She took to watching television, sceptically believing that it was all fantasy, and stoutly refused to believe that man had landed on the moon, maintaining if they did do such a thing 'they would run out of benzine'.

Minnie had devoted her whole life to our family. In a later age her talents for efficiency and loyalty would have received great recognition in many spheres. She had wanted to be a nurse and would have ended up as a matron. Besides being a perfect nanny, she was a gifted cook. Arthur, who was no mean gourmet, thought her one of the finest cooks he knew. It was all our gain, and we were devoted to her and thankful for her. She was wise and loving and funny. She was immensely thrifty, and left her money to Laura and me. My share bought the first tractor for the fish farm.

On his return from a year in Africa, Robert spent a short time in industry and three years later he and Rosalind Forrest married in Eton College Chapel, her father being Lower Master of Eton at the time. They decided to set up fish farming at Inverawe.

There came a day when thousands of fish had to be harvested and gutted for the market. We sat in the farm courtyard and gutted fish all day. I went to London on the night train and was 'in-waiting' at Clarence House the next day.

Sitting next to Sir Roy Strong at that day's luncheon party he kindly asked me where I came from. In a rush of unwise candour I told him that 24 hours earlier I was gutting thousands of fish. He looked horrified, turned his back on me and never addressed another word to me. He was probably right – I may still have smelt of fish.

TWENTY-THREE

Queen Elizabeth The Queen Mother

IT IS IMPOSSIBLE to define the Queen Mother's character. Although I was with her for nearly forty years, I still cannot claim to have ever really known her. The outlines were obvious – her enjoyment of people of all sorts, her sense of fun and funniness, her skill at communicating, all wrapped up in her overriding sense of duty and service to Great Britain. She had a firm will, but that could also be described as courage. She had faith – not only in the religious sense, although that was a major ingredient – but she had faith in people and the British people in particular.

She was not a starry-eyed optimist. There were other qualities, rather paradoxical in nature. She had dignity but never pomposity or pretentiousness. She could be forceful in mocking people who she suspected of this. She possessed great powers of intuition, reacting quickly to moods or atmosphere. Though she was not always punctual at arriving for an engagement, she was never late when it mattered. And engagements invariably ran late as she engaged more people for longer in conversation than had been reckoned.

The Queen Mother's year was always planned many months ahead. When in the country it was laid down that luncheon must be a 'picnic' out of the house, thought to save trouble for the servants. At Birkhall or Balmoral there were various picnic houses, old abandoned cottages tidied up to make a suitable room. A footman would be driven there to unlock the place and light a fire to warm us up. the Queen Mother liked to go ahead of the guests to lay out the luncheon, accompanied by the lady-in-waiting. She set off in a Landrover with the equipment, comprising at least four large and heavy picnic baskets, and a basket with the drinks. There were picnic tables and chairs.

On one table were laid the drinks and glasses, then other tables were put up as side tables for the food in dishes – three courses, with plates. The main course was usually cold meats, salad and baked potatoes (which travelled in their own hot bag). Everyone helped themselves and sat down to a neatly laid table with salt, pepper and mustard (this in tubes). For her 80th birthday the Queen Mother was given a Norwegian log hut beside her favourite fishing pool on the Dee. This revolutionised picnic life and eliminated the danger of a picnic outside, with everyone muffled to the mouth in anoraks, and on one occasion struggling to eat before the wind blew the food off the plate. There was once a picnic in a snowstorm in the porch outside the front door at Birkhall.

In May 1974, I described life at Birkhall to Laura:

It's being a nice time here, peaceful and relaxed. Rachel Bowes Lyon, Raymond Seymour (who has come and gone), Andrew Haig and John Griffin [the Queen Mother's Press Secretary and Equerry]. They fish from 9 a.m. to 10 p.m. and rarely catch anything. Andrew Haig radiates niceness and suddenly chuckles quite silently if you tell him what the joke is. QE herself is in good form and laughs convulsively quite often.

I must now go and enjoy my fuller life by joining Andrew Haig and others for luncheon. We shall discuss the height of the river, the rainfall last night, what the ghillie said, whether it is, in fact, hot or cold out. We shall decide this entirely by the evidence of our teeth. If they chatter too much to close on the lobster mousse, we shall decide on the whole it's a bit parky for the time of year. QE will preside dressed in four jerseys, two head scarves, and an enormous tent-like mac lined in camel hair, and all to be seen will be a tiny pair of blue hands and a few flashing diamonds. Rachel is entirely dressed in Marks and Sparks, Andrew is in a thing called a 'Parka', so I am told. It zips you up to your chin and tightens round your face. I just feel cold.

This is not an entirely fair description of the fishing holiday. The guest list often had distinguished visitors – including, most years, the Poet Laureate, Ted Hughes.

At the Castle of Mey neighbours' lodges or houses were borrowed, usually Ralph Anstruther's who had an estate in Caithness. Sunday luncheon was always indoors, with roast beef and apple tart. The Queen Mother was an animated hostess who liked her guests to be entertained and their interests cared for. Once we were waiting at the log cabin for some guests to arrive for luncheon. These were not well known to her but we knew they were always immaculately dressed and had elegant slim figures. Suddenly the Queen Mother asked if we had sherry on the drinks table. It was not the usual tipple, but I found it and asked why. 'Oh,' she said vaguely, 'thin people always drink it.' They did.

The log cabin turned itself into a place for night picnics. This was hard work for the footman who had to prepare and set it out rather more elaborately than a luncheon picnic, with proper silver, and candles. There was a Dutch oven fire which warmed the place up beautifully. The guests did not change, and the evening dinner by candlelight in the dark wood and the sound of the river flowing by was romantic. It usually ended with singing round the table. The Queen Mother had a rich repertoire of folk songs. One could feel transported to another world.

At Clarence House there were frequently large luncheon parties, sometimes a mixture of people which the Queen Mother described as 'a Macedoine of a party', sometimes carefully selected. At first it was scary to find yourself sitting next to someone notably famous and sophisticated. I drew Noël Coward at one and felt a bit daunted. But the talk flowed as we discussed what to say to a friend whose work it was impossible to appreciate. Sir Noël said his cliché was to grasp the actor's arm and say 'Darling – what a night!'

The choreographer, Sir Frederick Ashton, was another frequent visitor – and being no connoisseur of ballet, I was equally daunted in anticipation. He was a marvellous conversationalist, more than happy not to mention ballet. At one party we were talking away, when I became aware of a number of ladies longing to nobble him. Knowing that my role was not to 'hog' the conversation, but to please the guests, I said so. 'Don't move!' he said. 'I always choose my hogs.'

The Castle of Mey was the only place the Queen Mother owned in her own right. By castle standards it was cosy rather than grand, pretty rather than beautiful. Built to withstand fearsome elements, it was a nice if somewhat smug feeling to lie in bed in the lady-in-waiting's turret bedroom with its three outside walls, with the wind proverbially howling round it and to feel safe inside.

There were two visits, one in August and another at the end of September. When the weather was sunny and hot the sun came all round the castle and the views of the sea and Orkney stretched for miles. In gales, when the sea was rough, one felt anxious watching the ships going through the Pentland Firth, whilst the forlorn wails of the foghorns were rather haunting.

In the small village of Mey at the gates of the castle, the Queen Mother knew everyone. She always presided over the Mey Highland Games and the Castle always entered a team to compete in the tug-o-war. On her last visit to Mey in August 2001, when the weather was unspeakable, with howling rain and wind, the Queen Mother still insisted on attending – at the age of 101.

For the Queen Mother Mey also meant her farm and her Aberdeen Angus herd, and although her visits may have been few, her connection all through the year was constant – every doing on the farm was reported to her, with Martin Leslie, the factor, sometimes in daily touch.

At Birkhall and at Mey the after dinner game was almost

invariably racing demon. The Queen Mother was a fervent, even passionate player, competitive and skilful (the only person acknowledged to be better than her was Princess Margaret) although not past a bit of blatant cheating. She definitely enjoyed winning. Frequent cries of 'That's my Queen!' obviously made for hilarity. Occasionally guests would display their loyalty by being competitive too. This could mean a long night and people who had been out on the hill all day shooting, fishing or stalking might start watching the clock and wondering about bedtime.

To deal with this problem Martin briefed each incoming equerry who kept the score that after a certain moment on the clock the royal total should be helped on with a little flexible accounting. The Duke of Atholl, as Chairman of the Lifeboats (RNLI) was asked to stay the night at Mey when en route to the Orkneys. It was the first time he'd ever stayed. Iain was renowned for his bridge, an extremely adept card player with a sharp mathematical brain. He was just as avid a competitor as his hostess and could see no point in games if you didn't play to win. He was also ignorant of the rules as applied by the Household. At the magical hour the equerry did as ordered and the royal score mounted. It did not take Iain any time to soundly accuse the equerry of being unable to add up and so he kindly helped him to get the score right. Iain won and a discomfited Household shrank to bed, rather late. He was not invited again.

The Queen Mother loved having information from experts. The head of the Marine Laboratory at Aberdeen University was regularly invited to Birkhall to explain the latest research into fish stocks and habits. Once at the Castle of Mey she became keen to know about fossils and determined to try and find one herself. So the Castle was searched for suitable hammers to hit stones with. The best we could muster were two rather delicate silver headed gavels presented by some organization, and forth we sallied. The Queen Mother's country brogues had heels only marginally lower than her town shoes, and I found myself on the shore with a precariously balanced Queen Mother, both of us bashing stones, from which small chips flew, and I was torn between worrying she might break her ankle or lose an eye. I was thankful when this exercise proved fruitless.

Reminiscing was not encouraged by the Queen Mother – she was always engaging with the interests and influences of younger people. She didn't always agree or, like the rest of us, understand, but she rarely beat the drum with 'good old days' sticks. Only occasionally did she speak of the war.

She once told me of an audience she gave to Lady Reading at Buckingham Palace, when she was Chairman of the WVS. She remembered Lady Reading as a stern-faced lady with great energy and an indomitable character, and a reputation for making cabinet ministers go weak at the knees. They were sitting together in a window when an air raid started and crumps seemed to be getting a little close. The Queen Mother felt she would like to suggest they moved away from the window, but Lady Reading appeared totally undisturbed. As she told the tale the Queen Mother said she found herself saying to herself, 'Don't be silly. Do remember you are Queen of England and you can't suggest retreat.'

Nor did she encourage moaning about old age. Approaching my 80th birthday, I began to say that I thought it was time I resigned. Before I could say another word, she said: 'Congratulations! You feel marvellous after you're eighty!' The subject of my retiring was never mentioned again. She was 98 at the time.

The Queen Mother's easy way of making contact with people was partly because she enjoyed them so much. She had an expression she often used, referring either to a group of people, or to individuals. She called them 'real people'. During a tour of miners' clubs and institutions in Durham with her husband, she was constantly describing the miners and the families she met with fond satisfaction as 'real people'. (She later hated the confrontation of the miners' strike).

East Enders during the war were 'real people'. Once she was

explaining to Mrs Thatcher at a tea party at Birkhall how she had found Presidents Roosevelt and Kennedy to be 'real people'. I was sitting next to Denis Thatcher who turned to me in bewilderment bordering on indignation saying: 'But they were both Democrats!'

One of the arrangements she disliked on her engagements was any cordons or ropes used to restrain the people she had come to meet. She never seemed quite persuaded these were necessary for order. On leaving a Cup Final at Wembley, the police had cleared a large area at the exit, holding the crowd well back, as there was at the time a security risk and their intention was that the royal car would drive quickly away. As we started off, the Queen Mother ordered the chauffeur to slow down, saying she wanted to see some of the people. Part of the crowd managed to break out and several people wormed a cheerful weaving way over to the car. The Queen Mother wound down the window and proceeded to shake hands with them all. I saw the back of the necks of the detective and the chauffeur getting redder and redder. After a bit she relented and we spun off.

In 1995, after the celebrations to mark the 50th anniversary of the end of the war, the Royal Family appeared on the balcony of Buckingham Palace and was cheered by a big crowd. When the Queen Mother came to leave, remains of the crowd were still milling around in front of the Palace and the police told her she could not go directly down the Mall to Clarence House, but must go out from the bottom of the garden and so round Hyde Park Corner and down Piccadilly. She was indignant – it was absurd to think the crowd was hostile and she certainly would come to no harm.

The police were adamant – and so was she. The Master of the Household, Admiral Sir Peter Ashmore, was called for to arbitrate. The Queen Mother respected the Navy and was fond of Peter Ashmore so allowed herself to be persuaded. We took the police route back, which took considerably longer and the Queen Mother remained cross. When she got out of the car she turned to her hapless detective (it wasn't his fault – he was also under orders) and said slowly: 'That was very pusillanimous!'

When we got inside Clarence House she said triumphantly to me how she was glad she had got that word out.

On her 100th Birthday it was arranged that she should ride up the Mall from Clarence House to Buckingham Palace in a carriage with Prince Charles. All through the planning she demurred about this plan. She thought it pretentious, pompous and who would turn out to see it anyhow? She would look silly driving up an empty Mall. She was forced to comply. As she sat in the hall at Clarence House waiting to board the carriage, she still seemed reluctant to go. Finally Prince Charles gave her his arm saying: 'Come on Granny – remember Hitler said you were the most dangerous woman in Europe!' So, laughing, they set off up the Mall and she was cheered by thousands of people.

In the same year, the *Oldie* magazine voted the Queen Mother 'Oldie of the Century'. She sent me to the lunch to accept this prize on her behalf. The next day this extract appeared in the Diary of the *Evening Standard*:

Icy response
Royal retainers are under orders to be very, very careful what they say to the press.

When the Queen Mother, 100, was given the Oldie of the Century award at Simpson's-in-the-Strand yesterday the prize was presented by Terry Wogan to her Woman of the Bedchamber, Dame Frances Campbell-Preston, 81. 'She very much envied me coming here in her place', she told the guests of Oldie magazine and editor Richard Ingrams.

When I enquired about the Queen Mother's health Dame Frances replied: 'Did you ask whether I'd like any ice cream?'

The last time I was officially 'in-waiting' was the week before Christmas 2001. It was a week with several engagements and a heavy post of Christmas cards and letters. The Queen Mother was almost blind and these had to be read to her. She had a fall during the week but refused to admit it was painful. She carried out the engagements, including the last one, attending the staff Christmas party in St James's Palace. It was for the staff, their friends and relations and numbered about 200 people. She consented to be wheeled round in a chair, but whenever she stopped to speak to a group of people, she stood up out of the chair. She did this over twenty times.

On the next day she was flown by helicopter to Sandringham with Princess Margaret, who was then very frail. There she stayed after the Queen left in mid-February and might well have stayed throughout the spring. But, on 9 February, three days after the 50th anniversary of the King's death, Princess Margaret died in London.

The Queen Mother was flown to Royal Lodge by helicopter to attend Princess Margaret's private funeral at Windsor. A few weeks later, on 30 March 2002, she died peacefully at Royal Lodge.

I was in Scotland for Easter, but returned immediately to Clarence House. Although we had expected this event for some time, in a curious way we were surprised. I don't think we had ever lost faith in the Queen Mother's way of bouncing back. She invariably gave a party at Royal Lodge to celebrate the Royal Military Meeting at Sandown. In 2002 the Queen deputized for her. But just as it looked as if she would never rise again, had she not suddenly appeared to receive her guests? Had she not also hosted the traditional lunch for the Provost and Head Master of Eton on the occasion of the Eton Beagles Meet at Royal Lodge, discussing future dates and plans with them? Perhaps there might be another decade? Now we realised that this was final.

Before the pageantry of the funeral procession to Westminster Hall and the Service in Westminster Abbey, I found the most poignant moment was when the coffin arrived at the Queen's Chapel, at Marlborough House. There it was met by the Bishop of London, and there followed a short and intimate personal service, attended by the Household and staff from Clarence

House. It was a private time in which we could savour our personal reflections of one who had enhanced our lives, before the great military ceremonial took over and we witnessed the tremendous response from the British public.

As one of the Household I was among those waiting in Westminster Hall for the funeral procession to arrive. It was a moment to reflect how, since the trauma of the Abdication, the majority of the Queen Mother's compatriots felt that she had truly represented the British people.

Epilogue

1979 AND 1980 were both 'Anni Horribiles' for the family. Joyce had been ill for some time, losing the sight of one eye. Although an operation had been advised, she refused to have it, being a Christian Scientist. Finally the pain got too bad and in the autumn of 1979 she finally consented. When they operated they found cancer, but the doctor's prognosis was that she might live for up to two years. Reggie told no one, not even Joyce. Virginia Graham gave a Golden Wedding party for them, to which all the family came.

It was the last time we were altogether. Joyce died a fortnight later. She had been my first in-law, the first outsider to penetrate our close family circle and widen its circumference. My mother had consigned to her the role of dressing us since she clearly knew, liked and understood material and dressmakers. When we were young, she was the sophisticated one, respecting the imagination of children, and treating us as adults before we were fully grown-up. She brought fascination, surprise and a fresh world of romance and gaiety into our young lives.

She had given me face powder and Odo-ro-no and an early lipstick called Tangee, which for years I considered the last word in sophistication. Once when sitting nervously in a train thinking of all the pitfalls facing me at a terrifying weekend party, I heard the sound of feet running down the platform. It was my mother, who pressed a small parcel into my hand saying breathlessly: 'Joyce gave it to me. Use very little, and never tell your father.' It was a small tin of rouge.

She had influenced us not only in our way of dressing – 'Choose one colour as a foundation and then you can cut down on bags and hats and shoes' – and she advised on the decoration of our houses. She favoured a measure of simplicity, eschewed elaborate flower arrangements, controlled flounces and lit rooms by lamps, never with ceiling lights.

When she arrived in our family, the songs sung round the piano changed from 'The Lass of Richmond Hill' and 'Early One Morning' to the latest current popular successes. From these emerged the stories, the mimics and the characters that later delighted such a wide audience. Urged by the young in the family, Joyce would be pressed to develop a new character. I remember 'Shirl' and her boyfriend 'Norm' arriving early, soon followed by the nervous debutante making inane conversation. And there was the older character who used Joyce's special 'mouth' with the tongue folded over the lower teeth. During the war, Joyce used to relate her experiences through the medium of any number of her characters.

I won't deny that when she became famous we slightly resented these figures emerging from within our secret family world to the medium of the stage and wireless. We felt they belonged somehow to us. As so often in families, we found it hard to assimilate Joyce's growing fame.

When Joyce died, Reggie sent for Laura and me, and we came immediately to support him as best we could. Bernard had also been diagnosed with cancer, and was having treatment, so Laura had to return to him.

Ten days later further tragedy struck when Laura was killed by a falling tree in a storm at Auchairne. Laura's life and Joyce's had led them into such very different fields, and yet a closeness remained until the end. It was strangely natural and comforting to think of them journeying on together.

Laura's memorial service was at the Royal Hospital, Chelsea, where she had been christened. The New Zealand soprano, Dame Kiri Te Kanawa, who had sung as a girl at Laura's and Bernard's musical evenings in New Zealand, sang 'I know that my Redeemer liveth'. A year later Bernard died. It was an exceptionally horrible time.

Mercifully there was soon a celebration, when Geordie, Laura and Bernard's son, married Margaret Wookey, who had supported him through his dual bereavement.

Such events change the patterns of life. In 1981 my sister-in-law, Angela, died suddenly, leaving another big gap. Through everything she had been such a mainstay as a friend, with her capacity to see both sides to any problem, not something that before had come naturally either to Campbell-Prestons or Grenfells.

I was not enjoying living alone in the large house at Inverawe. Helen and Colin had both married, Helen marrying Timothy Raikes and moving to East Grinstead, where Tim was working. Colin had left Wye College with a horticultural degree, his childhood ambition since boyhood having been to design a garden in some form. He married Rosemary Swift and lived in London. They began to build up a business in landscape gardening, running Capital Gardens Centre.

I had begun to toy with the idea of getting a base in London. Joyce and Reggie had planned to go to Australia for the winter of 1979 and to lend me their flat in their absence. Joyce's sudden death changed that.

After Joyce's death Reggie suggested I should go and live with him. It was tempting, but at first I felt I could not entirely sever my life from Inverawe. But I consulted Mary, and got a characteristic four-page letter detailing all the reasons why it was entirely the right idea for Reggie and me to be together. After two years there was a switch round of houses at Inverawe, Robert and Rosie at last moving into the big house.

Mary Ann and Alastair needed a house in Argyll and they moved to the Barn. Reggie and I had lived together happily for two years and we decided it was time for me to disperse my belongings round my family, as I was to get the London flat and its contents for my life. So we enjoyed our companionship till Reggie died in his 90th year in 1993.

Like me, my elder sister, Katie Lort Phillips, also widowed in 1979, has survived into the twenty-first century. We never knew our great-grand parents who were born in the Napoleonic age, at the end of the eighteenth century, or in the first decade of the nineteenth, while in contrast, Katie and I now watch our grandchildren, and our great-grandchildren growing up around us.

I am now in my eighties, and spend part of the year in my flat in London, retreating to Inverawe for holidays at Easter and in the summer. I am always happy to escape the heat of the south for Scotland's simpler pleasures and traditionally cooler weather. Thanks to the generosity of Bobby and Angela in 1967, to my rashness in accepting Inverawe, as well as Robert and Rosie's entrepreneurial skills and the open-handedness with which they and Mary Ann and Alastair run the place, I can now watch three generations of my family enjoying themselves at Inverawe. As the Queen Mother once wisely predicted to me, 'You'll enjoy being eighty.'

It was at Inverawe that I celebrated my eightieth birthday in September 1998, and was honoured with a telegram from The Queen. In thanking her, I could not resist saying that the arrival of the telegram had caused great excitement, but that now everyone in the village was convinced that I was 100!

Index

London (1940), 117-9; &
again, 135-6; in Argyll
(1941), 144-9; serves as
Immobile Wren, 144-9; &
letters to Patrick, 153-4;
visited by mother, 159;
leaves Wrens, 172; in
London, 173-5; in Argyll,
175, 176-7; takes cottage
near Reading, 178-9; sends
news to Vera, 180-1; works
in Huntley & Palmer fact-
ory, 191-2; awaits return of
Patrick, 203, 206; & his
return, 207-10; in Argyll
with Patrick, 211-2; follows
Patrick to Greece, 213; &
journey home again, 213-6;
& Laura's dance, 217-9; in
Perth, 222-3; in Duisberg,
Germany, 224-30; in Berlin,
232-3; in Buxtehide, 235;
& Patrick's ill-health, 235-6,
237, 239-42; visits Kenya,
242-5; in Scotland, 245-8;
& birth of Helen (1955),
247; & Patrick's death,
248-50; Joins Argyll
County Council, 251;
moves to Flood Street, 255;
visits Laura in New Zea-
land, 261-2; visits Australia,
265; & death of Molly,
265-6; invited to be Queen
Mother's lady-in-waiting,
268-9; comforts Jean
Rankin, 269; & life as lady-
in-waiting, 269-73, 289,
301; on Martin Gilliat, 273-
4; & racing with Queen
Mother, 275; & Australia
& New Zealand royal tour
(1966), 275-85; takes on
Inverawe, 286-8; resigns
from County Council, 289;
becomes Chairman,
Children's Panel, Argyll &
Bute, 289-90; copes with
ailing mother, 297; & death
of Raymond Baring, 298;
& visit of Prince of Wales,

298; & mother's death,
299-300; & Minnie's death,
300; on Queen Mother's
character, 302-11; on
Queen Mother's entertain-
ing, 302-6; lunches at
Oldie, 309; & Queen
Mother's death, 310-1; &
death of Joyce Grenfell,
312-3; & death of Ballan-
traes, 313-4; & marriages
of children, 314; & Queen's
telegram (1998), 315
Campbell-Preston, Helen,
17, 247-9, 251, 285, 287-
8, 314
Campbell-Preston, Mary
(Molly) (neé Thorne), 77-
81, 93-95, 98, 101-2, 108-
12, 124, 134, 146-7, 153,
166, 173, 175-7, 181,
199, 202, 207, 246-7, 251,
264, 265-6
Campbell-Preston, Mary
Ann, 15, 97, 137 153,
159, 167-8, 172, 174,
178-9, 180, 192, 196,
203, 208-10, 229-30, 247-
9, 251, 314, 315
Campbell-Preston, Mrs
Colin (Rosemary), 314
Campbell-Preston, Mrs
Robert (Rosalind), 301, 315
Campbell-Preston, Patrick,
meets Frances, 66-8; 69;
engaged, 72-4; family
background, 76-82; meets
Frances's mother, 83;
marries, 84-5; rejoins Black
Watch, 86; & army life, 88-
9; in Plymouth, 91; leaves
for war, 93; writes home,
95, 101; on leave, 97, 99,
102; & fighting in France,
107; rumours of imprison-
ment, 107-8, 109-115; as
prisoner in Germany, 149-
53, 172-3, 181-2, 198-9; &
post-war plans, 153-4; &
possible return, 203; returns,
206-10; in Scotland, 209,

211; to Greece, 213; at Staff
College, Camberley, 222; in
Perth, 222-3; to Germany,
224-30, 232-3; commands
Black Watch, 233-6; ill
health, 235-6; discharged
from army (1952), 237; in
Edinburgh, 237, 239;
suffers heart attack, 239-40;
recuperation, 240-2; visits
Kenya, 242-5; joins Argyll
County Council, 246; at
Polfearn, 247; death, 248;
mentioned, 13, 27, 167,
181, 251, 273, 298-9
Campbell-Preston, Robert
(Bobby)(brother-in-law),
76-7, 81, 92-3, 101, 124-
5, 146, 153, 165-6, 176-7,
179, 181-2, 199, 202, 236,
240-2, 249-50, 286, 315
Campbell-Preston, Robert
(son), 17, 237, 247, 249,
251, 269, 285, 286, 290,
297, 298, 300-1, 315
Campbell-Preston, Thomas
(Tommy), 76-7, 94, 99,
107, 109-111, 165-6, 174,
176-9, 181-2, 199, 202,
207
Chamberlain, Rt Hon
Neville, 82, 89, 92
Chardin, Teilhard de, 27,
265, 266, 299
Chewton, Viscount James
(13th Earl Waldegrave), 157
Churchill, (Clementine)
Lady, 43, 163, 171-2, 201,
207n, 223
Churchill, Hon Randolph, 43
Churchill, Rt Hon Sir
Winston, 43, 55, 75, 100,
108, 171-3, 193-6, 201,
205, 212, 223, 265, 266
Clarke-Campbell-Preston,
Robert, 77
Clarke-Preston, Rt Rev
William, 77
Clayton, Rev P.T.B., 260 & n
Clegg, Howard, 162
Clydesdale, Marquess of